UTILITARIANISM AND
CO-OPERATION

UTILITARIANISM AND CO-OPERATION

DONALD REGAN

CLARENDON PRESS · OXFORD
1980

Oxford University Press, Walton Street, Oxford OX2 6DP

OXFORD LONDON GLASGOW
NEW YORK TORONTO MELBOURNE WELLINGTON
KUALA LUMPUR SINGAPORE JAKARTA HONG KONG TOKYO
DELHI BOMBAY CALCUTTA MADRAS KARACHI
NAIROBI DAR ES SALAAM CAPE TOWN

Published in the United States by
Oxford University Press, New York

British Library Cataloguing in Publication Data

Regan, Donald
    Utilitarianism and co-operation.
    1. Utilitarianism
    I. Title
    171'.5   B843   79-41314

    ISBN 0-19-824609-9
    ISBN 0-19-824636-6 Pbk

*Set in IBM Baskerville by Graphic Services, Oxford
Printed in Great Britain*

To my parents

PREFACE

Let me begin with a grandiose claim: In this essay I shall first analyse and then dissolve a contradiction which the existing literature suggests is inherent in utilitarian theory and which, if it were genuinely indissoluble, would weigh heavily against the acceptability of any form of utilitarianism.

Utilitarians are currently divided into two camps, those who believe the maximization decision should focus on the consequences of individual acts (act-utilitarians) and those who believe the maximization decision should focus on the consequences of classes of acts or patterns of behaviour (utilitarian generalizers and rule-utilitarians). The theoretical debate between these two camps is essentially in stalemate. Efforts have been made by writers on each side of the divide to capture the position of the other camp without giving up their own, but these efforts, as I shall show in detail later on, have been unsuccessful.

The fact is that there are two distinct and equally compelling particular intuitions subsumed under the general utilitarian intuition that moral agents should be required to maximize good consequences. According to one of these particular intuitions, each individual agent should be required to act in such a way that the consequences of his own behaviour are the best possible in the circumstances confronting him as an individual. According to the other of these particular intuitions, any group of agents should be required to act in such a way that the consequences of their collective behaviour are the best possible in the circumstances confronting the group as a whole.

The present state of the literature suggests that these two particular intuitions may be irreconcilably in conflict. But if they are, then the general utilitarian intuition is in serious trouble. If we cannot find an approach to maximization which will reconcile what is required of the individual and the group, then quite possibly we must give up the idea that maximizing good consequences is what morality is all about.

In the course of this essay, I shall show both that the problem I have just indicated is a real problem, and that there is a solution. In the first half of the essay, I shall demonstrate that the two particular intuitions I have identified (and which I shall describe in more detail in Chapter 1) can *not* be reconciled by any moral theory of the general sort which utilitarian theorists have proposed up to now. The appearance of uncompromisable conflict between the existing camps is not illusory. In the second half of the essay, however, I shall show that the two intuitions *can* be reconciled if we turn to a quite different sort of theory. I shall produce a theory which reconciles the particular intuitions and rescues the utilitarian project from internal contradiction.

I hope I have aroused the reader's interest. With the large claims out of the way for the time being, I have some prefatory remarks of a more mundane sort about the themes and organization of this study.

One of the themes is that we need a new conceptual framework for thinking about the merits and demerits of utilitarian theories. Useful work has been done on the structure of utilitarianism. There are insightful individual contributions. But on the whole the literature is disappointing. It tends to be repetitive and to get bogged down in consideration of minutiae. Too much time is spent arguing, often inconclusively, about what particular theories require in particular cases. Too little time is spent on more general questions. So far as I am aware, no one has tried to identify explicitly the general properties we would like a utilitarian theory to have. As a result, no one has attempted to produce a systematic analysis telling us which theories have which desirable properties, and considering whether various kinds of theories can have various desirable properties, singly or in combination.

I shall not argue further that we need a new conceptual scheme. Instead, I shall produce one, and I shall attempt to make a start on the general questions mentioned in the preceding paragraph. In Chapter 1, I shall define some properties which are to be desired in utilitarian theories. The rest of the essay will be largely devoted to discussing these properties in one way or another. I shall prove some claims about the logical relations between the properties themselves. I shall prove some claims about which well-known utilitarian theories have which properties. Eventually, after concluding that no traditional theory has all the properties we want, I shall produce a new theory which has, in my estimation, more desirable properties than any traditional theory has. In the end, the reader will have to decide for himself whether my new scheme is useful.

In Chapters 2–6 I use the analytical framework developed in Chapter 1 to investigate the traditional utilitarian theories. These chapters are *not* intended as a survey of the literature concerning the traditional theories. Rather they are intended as a systematic inquiry into some basic issues concerning the merits and demerits of traditional theories. Although I shall of necessity cover some familiar ground, I think I have a number of new things to say even on these issues. To mention just one example: A central theme of Chapters 2–4 is that in thinking about act-utilitarianism we should distinguish between two questions which are almost never carefully separated in the literature. The first question is whether everyone's successfully following act-utilitarianism *ensures* the production of best possible consequences by the group of agents involved. The second question is whether everyone's successfully following act-utilitarianism is always *compatible* with the production of best possible consequences by the group. It may not seem to the reader at this stage that these are different questions, but they are. A great deal of confusion would be avoided if everyone who wrote about act-utilitarianism kept the difference in mind.

Because I do not attempt to survey the literature, I probably fail to mention some writers who have anticipated some of my points, and I know I do not discuss every writer who has argued against my claims. As to the omission of some writers with whom I disagree, I can only say that I try to deal with every significant argument against my views, even though I do not explain how I would answer every specific formulation of these arguments. As to the omission of writers who have anticipated me, I cite everyone I am aware of, and to those I do not cite, I apologize.

Chapter 7 also deals with the traditional theories, but in a quite different way from Chapters 2–6. Chapter 7 isolates a property which all the traditional theories have in common and presents a general proof that no theory with this property can possibly have all the other properties we want in a utilitarian theory. In other words, Chapter 7 shows that every traditional utilitarian theory, and every theory 'like' the traditional theories in a way to be defined in Chapter 7, is doomed to inadequacy. The proof in Chapter 7 is an important proof, and I would point out at this stage that it is almost entirely independent of the more traditional arguments about the deficiencies of various theories which I make in Chapters 2–6. In fact, Chapter 7 renders much of the material in Chapters 2–6 otiose, logically speaking. On the other hand, there is much to be learned from Chapters 2–6 about just how traditional theories fail. Chapter 7 should be easier to understand and to accept because of the chapters that precede it.

In Chapters 8–12 I present my own theory, which I call 'co-operative utilitarianism'. Two chapters in this part of the essay, Chapters 9 and 10, are rather heavy going, and the reader is likely to feel at some point that co-operative utilitarianism is hard to understand and that it would be impossible to put into practice. I hope that a few words now may help to counteract that feeling.

The basic idea of co-operative utilitarianism is really very simple. The basic idea is that each agent should proceed in two steps: First he should identify the other agents who are willing and able to co-operate in the production of best possible consequences. Then he should do his part in the best plan of behaviour for the group consisting of himself and the others so identified, in view of the behaviour of non-members of that group. I think this idea or something very like it was suggested by Roy Harrod in a neglected passage of his famous article 'Utilitarianism Revised'. Everybody knows the passage where Harrod suggests his 'first refinement' to the 'crude utilitarian principle'. The first refinement is a sophisticated sort of utilitarian generalization. But Harrod also mentions a second refinement. Speaking of whether a utilitarian should

follow a practice, such as promise-keeping, the general following of which is desirable but which is not generally followed,
Harrod says:

I believe that, where the practice is not general, a second refining process
is required. Will the gain due to its application by all conscientious, *i.e.*,
moral, people *only* be sufficient to offset the loss which the crude utilitarian principle registers? It may be objected to this that there are no
moral people, but only more or less moral people. To meet this, for the
word moral in the second refining principle, say people sufficiently
moral to act disinterestedly in this kind of case.[1]

To restate Harrod's point: Before an individual does his part
in a co-operative undertaking, he ought to ascertain just who
else is willing to take part and he ought to be certain that the
undertaking is a useful one even though participation is limited
to the group he has identified.

Unfortunately, this simple idea, Harrod's and mine, is not
without its problems. Jonathan Harrison, one of the few
people to notice Harrod's second refinement, dismisses it as
either circular or self contradictory.[2] I believe that Harrison
is mistaken. Properly understood, the idea embodied in
Harrod's second refinement is neither circular nor contradictory. Furthermore, it can be developed into a theory which
comes as close to perfection, from the utilitarian's point of view,
as any theory can possibly come. It is no easy matter, however,
to prove all of this. Harrison was certainly right in thinking
that serious difficulties attend Harrod's suggestion.

Chapters 9 and 10 are given over to proving that the basic
idea I have described is logically innocent; and that it gives rise
to a theory which has desirable properties no traditional theory
has; and that the theory in question, though it has a defect,
is as good as any theory of any kind can possibly be. The
arguments in Chapters 9 and 10 are novel and sometimes difficult, and the difficulty is compounded by the novelty. The
reader will find himself traversing a landscape for which his
previous reading about utilitarianism has not prepared him,
with a guide who has only recently charted a few plausible-
looking routes. I have tried to make Chapters 9 and 10 as
readable as possible, and to that end I have removed the most
difficult arguments to an Appendix, but I have not succeeded

in making these chapters easy. I hope the reader will keep in
mind that even if co-operative utilitarianism is more complicated than traditional theories, it is still not as complicated as
some of the arguments I make about it.

It may seem to some readers that the 'basic idea' of co-
operative utilitarianism, as I have described it, does not belong
to a new theory at all, but is part of act-utilitarianism. In fact,
a number of writers on act-utilitarianism have made suggestions
about how act-utilitarians should behave which have much in
common with my views about what co-operative utilitarianism
requires. I have in mind especially J. J. C. Smart, J. L. Mackie,
and Jan Narveson. In my view, these writers make some suggestions (which I shall identify specifically in due course)
which are eminently sensible, but which are not really act-
utilitarian suggestions at all. They are co-operative utilitarian
suggestions, imperfectly understood.

This brings us to a more general observation. Although I
criticize all the traditional theories in Chapters 2–7, and
although my desire to cover a wide range of issues may lead
me to adopt a rather didactic tone, I do not mean to suggest
that there is nothing good to be said for the traditional theories.
Actually, as Chapter 1 should begin to make clear, I believe
there is something good to be said for all of them. I do not
expect to convert act-utilitarians or others merely by the force
of my arguments against their theories. Even if my arguments
are correct, that is not the way converts are won. Instead, I
hope that act-utilitarians, utilitarian generalizers, and perhaps
even a few rule-utilitarians, will recognize that co-operative
utilitarianism is the theory they have been looking for all
along. I have already mentioned that some act-utilitarians seem
to be moving toward co-operative utilitarianism without
realizing it. I shall argue in Chapters 11 and 12 that there are
also strong affinities between co-operative utilitarianism and
utilitarian generalization, although there remain significant
differences.

I indicated earlier that some readers will have doubts about
whether co-operative utilitarianism can be put into practice.
I shall discuss this matter in Chapters 10 and 11. The reader
may feel in Chapter 9 and in the beginning of Chapter 10 that

the discussion of how the theory is to be practised is a long time coming, but he should rest assured that we will get there.

Still, considering the length of this essay, I shall say relatively little about the practice of co-operative utilitarianism, and I would emphasize that my main concern is *not* with practice. It is with theory. The debate between act-utilitarians, rule-utilitarians, and utilitarian generalizers would have fizzled out years ago if practical differences were really the issue. The fact is that all of these theories, as expounded by their best-known proponents, tend to coalesce in practice. Act-utilitarians appeal to rules of thumb and the power of example. Rule-utilitarians make it clear that their ideal sets of rules must be tempered by consideration of how people in the real world actually behave. Utilitarian generalizers wriggle and squirm to avoid the more outlandish consequences of their stark theoretical claims. It is only by discussing artificial examples, or else superficially realistic examples hedged about by detailed stipulations concerning consequences, that utilitarians of various stripes are able to be certain they disagree on any question of practice.

I do not take this to mean that the debate among utilitarians is pointless. I *do* take it to mean that the debate is primarily about which theory is most satisfactory *as a theory*. The real bone of contention is how the fundamental intuition that we ought to produce good consequences should be understood. My central claim for co-operative utilitarianism is that it provides the most theoretically appealing way of understanding that fundamental intuition.

Finally, a word about the notes. In addition to citations to the literature and cross-references, there are many discursive notes which enlarge on the argument of the text. Indeed, there are a few notes on topics not even hinted at in the text. I have attempted to make the text more or less self-contained, so that the reader who wishes to ignore the notes can do so. I encourage the reader to ignore the notes, for the most part, during a first reading. But where the reader thinks I slight some point or neglect some issue, he should at least check to see whether there is not a note which attempts to supply the deficiency.

It is a pleasure to acknowledge friends and colleagues who have given me aid and comfort. Robert Adams, Richard Brandt, and William Frankena commented helpfully on early drafts of parts of this essay, which began as a dissertation submitted in partial fulfilment of the requirements for the Ph.D. in the University of Michigan. Holly Goldman, who made valuable suggestions on successive drafts over many years, also encouraged me more than she knew by taking an interest in some of my most tortuous arguments at a time when I wondered if I would ever get them worked out to even my own satisfaction. At a later stage, Philip Soper and Gregory Kavka persuaded me that I needed to discuss certain difficulties I had underestimated and planned to ignore. Finally, Derek Parfit, who read the manuscript for the Oxford University Press, gave me many pages of detailed and constructive criticism; every chapter of the final version reflects his suggestions. To all of the above, my sincere thanks.

D. R.

Ann Arbor, Michigan
March 1979

TABLE OF CONTENTS

1

INTRODUCTION

I have described my objectives in general terms in the Preface. This Introduction deals with some preliminaries of a more specific nature.

To begin with, there are two points to be made about the scope of the inquiry. The first point is that I shall not advance in these pages any particular view about what consequences are to be promoted and what to be avoided. The word 'utilitarianism' once referred to the view that pleasure was the only good and pain the only evil, as well as to the view that the rightness of acts was somehow related to their consequences. Utilitarianism can almost certainly be made more plausible, however, if one takes a broader view of what consequences are good and what bad. Most recent discussions of utilitarianism have ignored the question of what consequences are to be promoted and what to be avoided, and have focused solely on the question of how consequences determine rightness. That is the question I am concerned with also. For the sake of precision, it might be best to abandon the words 'utilitarianism', 'act-utilitarianism', and so on, in favour of 'consequentialism', 'act-consequentialism', and the like. For the sake of familiarity, I shall use the common terms, relying on this gloss to forestall misunderstanding.

The second point to be emphasized is that this study is concerned with the consequences of agents' *actually doing* what is required of them by whatever theory we are focusing on. It has been suggested that one should evaluate a consequentialist theory by reference to its consequences if agents *try* to follow it, or if agents merely *accept* it. None the less, this essay focuses on the consequences of agents' actually doing what various theories tell them to do. It will be convenient to have a single word to refer to an agent's actually doing what a theory requires. I shall use the word 'satisfies'.

Thus, an agent will be said to satisfy a moral theory (in a particular choice situation) if and only if he actually does what the theory requires of him (in that situation).

I concentrate on the consequences of satisfaction of theories for two reasons. First, it is possible to prove some interesting things about the consequences of satisfaction of various theories. So far as I can see, it is not possible to say very much at all about the consequences of agents' trying to satisfy, or accepting, various theories. Second, the consequences of agents' satisfying theories seem to me more significant for the choice between theories than the consequences of agents' accepting theories, or whatever. Admittedly, no theory will be satisfied by all agents all the time. Even so, it seems more appropriate to deal with difficulties of application by appealing to rules of thumb and such devices, than to deal with them by redesigning the theory so that the consequences of satisfaction, of the behaviour the theory actually requires, are lost sight of entirely.

There is a great deal more that could be said concerning whether we should worry about the consequences of satisfaction of theories or about the consequences of acceptance, or whatever. To discuss the issue fully would take us deep into metaethics—into questions about whether morality is something we discover or something we invent, and into questions about the relations between judgements concerning acts, motives, intentions, and so on. I have no space for such an inquiry in this essay. Just as most recent work on utilitarianism has focused on the relation of consequences to rightness (ignoring the question of just what consequences are good or bad), so most recent work has focused on the consequences of agents' satisfying various theories and not on the consequences of agents' merely accepting theories or attempting to satisfy them. My own view is that it is appropriate to focus primarily on the consequences of satisfaction. Whether this is correct or not, enough has been written on the assumption that it is the consequences of satisfaction that are important, and sufficiently little progress has been made in showing what can be established on this assumption, so that I feel justified in pursuing the investigation.

Turning now to the real matter of the essay: if one stands back from the debate between utilitarians of various persuasions and views it as a whole, it becomes clear that the participants are inspired in the main by two distinct but equally fundamental intuitions. On the one hand, there is the intuition that whatever the correct moral theory is, it ought to be a good theory for *individuals* to follow as individuals. It ought to be the case that when an individual satisfies the theory, he produces the best consequences he can produce in the circumstances in which he finds himself. This is the intuition that underlies act-utilitarianism. On the other hand, there is the intuition that whatever the correct moral theory is, it ought to be a good theory for *everyone* to follow. It ought to be the case that if all agents satisfy the theory, then the class of all agents produce the best consequences they can produce collectively by any pattern of behaviour. This intuition gives rise to the varieties of rule-utilitarianism and utilitarian generalization.

Obviously, the story is more complicated than the preceding paragraph suggests. One pervasive object of this essay is to consider these two fundamental intuitions more closely. I shall demonstrate that they are distinct; that neither entails the other; that they are none the less logically compatible; that no traditional theory manages to satisfy both intuitions, though certain variants of rule-utilitarianism and utilitarian generalization attempt to do so; and that no theory that shares a certain feature common to all traditional theories could possibly satisfy both intuitions.

In order to facilitate the discussion of these intuitions, I shall define three properties which consequentialist theories may possess. (These properties are not defined so as to be logically limited to consequentialist theories, but only a consequentialist theory is likely to possess any of them.) The first property I shall call 'PropAU'. PropAU is named after act-utilitarianism, because it is the property which the fundamental act-utilitarian intuition says a consequentialist theory should have. 'The theory T has PropAU' is defined to mean: 'For any agent, in any choice situation, if the agent satisfies T in that situation, he produces by his act the best consequences he can possibly produce in that situation.' In other words, a theory T has PropAU if and only if any agent who satisfies T in any choice situation is guaranteed to produce the best consequences he can produce in that situation. Note that the 'situation' of the agent includes all causally relevant features of the rest of the world. In particular, it includes the behaviour of other agents whose behaviour the agent in question is not able to influence, and it includes the facts about the way other agents whom the agent in question is able to influence would respond to various choices on his part. We can sum this up in a more convenient form, in phraseology which I shall use when I want to make the same point or an analogous point elsewhere in the essay, by saying that the agent's situation includes the behaviour of other agents whose behaviour he is not able to influence, and the dispositions to behave of other agents whom he is able to influence. Observe that when I refer to other agents' 'dispositions to behave', I am not speaking of their characters or habits, nor of probabilities, but of how they would be influenced by various acts of the agent (or, further on, of some group of agents) whose behaviour we are consider-ing the consequences of.

It should be clear that act-utilitarianism, as it is ordinarily understood, has PropAU, and that its having PropAU is the primary source of its appeal. The best argument for act-utili-tarianism has always been the rhetorical question 'Should not an agent always do the act which will have best consequences in the circumstances?' In other words, 'Should not an accept-able consequentialist theory always require an agent to do the act with best consequences among those open to him?' Or, 'Should not an acceptable consequentialist theory have PropAU?'

The second property I shall call 'PropCOP'. PropCOP is named after a theory, COP, which will be introduced in Chapter 5 as the pure embodiment of the second fundamental consequentialist intuition. (For the reader who is curious about the acronym, 'COP' stands for 'co-ordinated optimiza-tion principle'.) 'The theory T has PropCOP' is defined to mean: 'If all agents satisfy T in all choice situations, then the class of all agents produce by their acts taken together the best consequences that they can possibly produce by any pattern of behaviour.' In other words, a theory T has PropCOP if and only if universal satisfaction of T (satisfaction by all agents all the time) would guarantee the best consequences that any pattern of behaviour by the universe of agents could possibly produce.

The idea that an acceptable consequentialist theory ought to have PropCOP is an important source of the intuitive appeal of various forms of rule-utilitarianism and utilitarian generalization. What the various forms of rule-utilitarianism have in common is the notion that agents ought to follow a set of rules which it would be best for *everyone* to follow. Similarly, utilitarian generalizers hold that each agent ought to do whatever it would be best for *himself and everyone else similarly situated* to do. PropCOP does not, however, bear exactly the same relation to the common forms of rule-utilitarianism and utilitarian generalization that PropAU bears to act-utilitarianism. None of these theories actually has PropCOP, as we shall see later on. The main reason is that the common variants of rule-utilitarianism and utilitarian generalization move away from COP in an attempt to build in PropAU as well as PropCOP, and they give up PropCOP in the process. (This rough statement is more accurate with regard to rule-utilitarianism than with regard to utilitarian generalization, but it will do for both until I discuss these theories in detail in later chapters.) Still, the persistent appeal of rule-utilitarianism and utilitarian generalization depends to a considerable extent on the notion that a consequentialist theory ought to have PropCOP, and on the largely unexamined belief that rule-utilitarianism and utilitarian generalization are steps in that direction.[1]

At this point it may appear that PropAU and PropCOP, if they are not equivalent, are at least related by logical implication in one direction or the other. Specifically, it may seem that PropAU entails PropCOP. It does not. Act-utilitarianism, under the usual interpretation, has PropAU. I shall show in Chapter 2 that it does not have PropCOP. It is not the case that a universe of agents all of whom satisfy the act-utilitarian principle necessarily produce the best consequences possible as a group. It is probably clearer to most readers that PropCOP does not entail PropAU. I shall establish this non-entailment by producing in Chapter 5 a theory which has PropCOP but not PropAU. Since neither PropAU nor PropCOP entails the other, the intuition that a theory should have PropAU and the intuition that a theory should have PropCOP are distinct. The next question is whether they are compatible. They are. It is possible for a single theory to have both PropAU and PropCOP (although, as we shall see, a theory which has both must be rather different from any traditional theory). Indeed, it is possible for a theory to have another property of the same type which is stronger than the conjunction of PropAU and PropCOP. This property I shall call 'adaptability'.

'The theory T is adaptable' is defined to mean: 'In any situation involving choices by any number of agents, the agents who satisfy T in that situation produce by their acts taken together the best consequences that they can possibly produce by any pattern of behaviour, given the behaviour of agents who do not satisfy T.' In other words, a theory T is adaptable if and only if the agents who satisfy T, whoever and however numerous they may be, are guaranteed to produce the best consequences possible as a group, given the behaviour of everyone else.[2] Note that 'the behaviour' of agents who do not satisfy T refers to the actual behaviour of non-satisfying agents whom the satisfying agents are not able to influence, and to the dispositions to behave (as I have used that phrase previously) of non-satisfying agents whom the satisfying agents, individually or together, are able to influence.

Loosely speaking, the property of adaptability is a generalization of both PropAU and PropCOP. If a theory has PropAU, then any *individual* agent who satisfies the theory produces the best consequences possible in his circumstances, but we cannot say anything about the success of collections of agents who satisfy the theory. If a theory has PropCOP, then best consequences will be produced if *everyone* satisfies the theory, but we cannot say what will be accomplished by any individual or any group if one or more agents fail to satisfy the theory. If a theory is adaptable, then regardless of how many agents satisfy it, whether it be one agent, or all agents, or something in between, we know that the agents who satisfy it produce collectively the best consequences possible. Although adaptability is a generalization of PropAU and PropCOP, it is not simply the conjunction of PropAU and PropCOP. As we shall see in Chapter 7, adaptability entails both PropAU and PropCOP, but it is stonger than their conjunction.

There is one further point about all three of our definitions (of PropAU, PropCOP, and adaptability) which should be mentioned here, even though it will not make any difference to the argument for many chapters. In the statement of all three definitions, I assume implicitly that each agent whose behaviour is under consideration is presented (in effect) with a list of acts from which he must choose. If we are considering the act of an individual agent (in connection with the issue of whether a theory has PropAU), then each act from the list of possibilities is assumed to have specified consequences (the behaviour or dispositions to behave of other agents being taken as given). If we are considering collections of acts by groups of agents (in connection with the issue of whether a theory has PropCOP or is adaptable), then each possible pattern of behaviour is assumed to have specified consequences (the behaviour or dispositions to behave of any agents outside the relevant group being taken as given). Various moral theories, applied to the choice problems so specified, will direct various acts by the agents concerned. In deciding whether any particular theory has PropAU, or PropCOP, or adaptability, we consider only the specified consequences already referred to of the acts or patterns of behaviour directed by the theory. We do *not* consider any consequences which may flow from any agent's satisfying the theory *other than* the specified consequences of the act or acts chosen.

The reader may wonder just what it is that the last sentence of the previous paragraph is intended to exclude from consideration. What else might we be inclined to consider, in the context of this utilitarian investigation, besides the consequences of the act or acts chosen? What the sentence in question is intended to exclude from consideration is any consequences of the application of a required decision procedure for choosing among the acts available to an agent, if we should happen to be considering a theory which actually requires a particular decision procedure. (To be slightly more precise, what we are excluding from consideration is any consequences of the application of a required decision procedure *aside from* the consequences of the act or acts chosen by that procedure. Since the application of any required decision procedure will result in the choice of some act by each agent who applies it, the consequences of the act or acts chosen are themselves indirect consequences of the application of the decision procedure. It is any *other* consequences of the application of the required decision procedure which we are excluding from consideration.[3])

The limitation just described on the consequences which we consider for purposes of deciding whether a theory has PropAU, or PropCOP, or adaptability, is not really a limitation at all when we are discussing traditional theories like act-utilitarianism, rule-utilitarianism, and so on. These theories do not require any particular decision procedures,[4] and excluding from consideration the consequences of the application of any required decision procedure excludes nothing at all when we are discussing these traditional theories. We shall therefore have no occasion to discuss the limitation on relevant consequences in the part of the essay which deals with traditional theories (Chapters 2–7).

The limitation on the consequences of satisfaction which are relevant to possession of PropAU, PropCOP, and adaptability does become important in the second half of the essay. My own theory, co-operative utilitarianism, is adaptable, and achieves adaptability by requiring a particular decision procedure. Co-operative utilitarianism benefits, in a sense, from the exclusion of the consequences of the application of the decision procedure from the consequences which are considered in determining whether a theory has PropAU, or Prop-COP, or adaptability.

I shall argue in due course (in Chapter 10) that the case for co-operative utilitarianism is not undermined, and indeed is only slightly damaged, by the fact that the decision procedure required by co-operative utilitarianism may have consequences which are not taken into account by the definitions of our three properties. This is undeniably an imperfection in co-operative utilitarianism; but I shall show that it is the least imperfection any utilitarian theory can possibly have.

The discussion in the last few paragraphs about the exclusion of the consequences of any required decision procedure when we are considering whether a theory has PropAU, or PropCOP, or adaptability, may seem very mysterious. It could be made less mysterious by an example or two, but that would involve a considerable digression from what ought to be our present concerns. As I have noted, this matter of the possible consequences of a required decision procedure has no bearing at all on the discussion or conclusions of the first half of the essay. I have raised the matter now only because if I did not, it might seem to the reader when I eventually raised it that I had been concealing something which was important to the acceptability of my definitions and to the acceptability of co-operative utilitarianism. Having noted the relevant feature of the definitions, I shall postpone further discussion of its significance until what I regard as the appropriate time. I recommend that the reader put the matter entirely out of mind until we return to it in Chapter 10.

With the definitions of PropAU, PropCOP, and adaptability at hand, it is possible to sketch the argument of the essay in more detail than was possible in the Preface. Chapters 2–4 are about act-utilitarianism. In Chapter 2, I show that act-utilitarianism does not have PropCOP. Universal satisfaction of act-utilitarianism (satisfaction by all agents) does not guarantee the achievement of best possible consequences overall. Chapters 3 and 4 demonstrate that even though universal satisfaction of act-utilitarianism does not *guarantee* the achievement of best possible consequences, it is still always *compatible* with the achievement of best possible consequences. Just how it is that these claims can be true together will become clear as the argument progresses. Chapters 3 and 4 constitute a defence of act-utilitarianism against some well-known arguments to the effect that it is 'self-defeating'. Chapter 3 includes a refutation of the criticism of act-utilitarianism based on an analogy to 'Prisoners' Dilemma'; and Chapter 4 reveals the fallacy in Hodgson's treatment of act-utilitarian punishment, which has received much less attention than his discussion of promising and truth-telling. Chapters 3 and 4 are relevant to the broader purposes of the essay, not because they are a partial defence of act-utilitarianism, but because they pave the way for the proof in Chapter 7 that adaptability entails PropAU. Chapters 2–4 taken together establish the proposition that satisfaction of act-utilitarianism by all the members of any group of agents is a necessary but not a sufficient condition for the achievement of the best possible consequences by that group.

Chapter 5 is about rule-utilitarianism. I show that the standard forms of rule-utilitarianism, although obviously designed to have both PropCOP and PropAU, in fact have neither, because they attempt to combine the fundamental consequentialist intuitions in the wrong way.

In Chapter 6 I show that utilitarian generalization, as traditionally understood, has neither PropCOP nor PropAU. Both of these conclusions I would regard as obvious to the point of triviality were it not for David Lyons's argument that utilitarian generalization and act-utilitarianism are extensionally equivalent. I shall argue that in his approach to the specification of the agent's circumstances Lyons misconstrues traditional utilitarian generalization. I shall consider versions of utilitarian generalization which result from adopting Lyons's approach, and I shall demonstrate that none of these theories is acceptable. Finally, I shall point out the fundamental error in Lyons's argument for extensional equivalence. Although that argument has been refuted by others, most discussions either miss or obscure the central point.

Chapter 7 contains two important theorems about adaptability. The first theorem is that adaptability entails both PropAU and PropCOP. The second theorem is that no moral theory which is 'exclusively act-oriented' can be adaptable. I shall say more about what 'exclusive act-orientation' means in Chapter 7. Roughly, a theory is exclusively act-oriented if it can be stated in the form 'An agent should do that act which . . .'. The traditional consequentialist theories, as they are usually understood, are all exclusively act-oriented. This second theorem is important precisely because consequentialists have consistently defended exclusively act-oriented theories. They have not at the same time been self-consciously seeking an adaptable theory, but if my arguments concerning the relationship of PropAU, PropCOP, and adaptability are correct, they should have been. An adaptable theory would combine to a great extent the appeal of act-utilitarianism on the one hand and the appeal of rule-utilitarianism and utilitarian generalization on the other. It is therefore worth knowing that an adaptable theory will not be found if the search is conducted in traditional precincts.

Chapters 8 through 12 develop the theory I call 'co-operative utilitarianism'. The theory can be summed up in the statement that each agent ought to co-operate, with whoever else is co-operating, in the production of the best consequences possible given the behaviour of non-co-operators. Chapter 8 begins with an explication of the notion of co-operation which is embedded in co-operative utilitarianism. This explication makes it clear that co-operative utilitarianism is *not* exclusively act-oriented. I believe the notion of co-operation in question is the central 'ordinary language' notion of co-operation, but some readers may not agree. Chapter 8 also includes a tentative discussion of what is involved in an agent's co-operating 'with whoever else is co-operating', followed by an argument to the effect that co-operative utilitarianism is adaptable. This argument raises further questions about the meaning of co-operating 'with whoever else is co-operating', which are treated at length in Chapter 9 and an Appendix thereto.

Chapter 10 completes the exposition of the theory of co-operative utilitarianism and discusses a series of possible objections to the theory. It also says something about how the theory should be applied in practice. Chapter 11 discusses in greater depth some practical aspects of an important class of cases which serve as a vehicle for comparing co-operative utilitarianism, act-utilitarianism and utilitarian generalization.

In Chapter 12 I elaborate on the claim, discussed briefly in Chapter 8, that in addition to being adaptable co-operative utilitarianism reflects more faithfully than any other consequentialist theory the true nature of the moral enterprise.

THE INADEQUACY OF ACT-UTILITARIANISM

The primary object of this chapter is to demonstrate that act-utilitarianism, as it is commonly interpreted, does not have PropCOP—that is, to demonstrate that universal satisfaction of act-utilitarianism does not in all cases guarantee the achievement of the best consequences possible overall. The direct argument for this claim is fairly brief. The chapter is long because there are some possible objections to the argument which repay consideration beyond what is strictly necessary to rebut them for our present purposes.

We shall consider the following formulation of act-utilitarianism:

(AU) An act is right if and only if it has at least as good consequences under the circumstances as any other act open to the agent.

It would be possible to spend many words describing just how AU is to be interpreted. I believe there is a generally understood 'standard' interpretation, however, and for the most part I propose to rely on the general understanding. I shall point out a few issues on which the standard interpretation of AU may be unclear or on which my view may be nonstandard as they become relevant in this and later chapters. For now, let us note three points:

First, we are interested in AU as an *objective* theory. The agent's beliefs about his obligation or about the state of the world do not determine what he should do according to AU.

Second, at least so far as the physical world is concerned, we may construe 'circumstances' and 'consequences' as referring either to the actual state of the world and actual consequences or to objective probabilities concerning the state of the world and the (objective) expected value of the consequences. The discussion proceeds the same way on either approach, provided we are consistent. Note that when I refer to 'objective probabilities', I do *not* mean anything like 'what a rational agent ought to regard as the probabilities, given the information available to him'. 'Rationally justifiable subjective probabilities', as we might call the sort of thing I have just described, are in an obvious sense one step more objective than what are usually referred to as 'subjective probabilities', namely the agent's actual estimates of the probabilities. But 'rationally justifiable subjective probabilities' are still subjective for my purposes. They still depend not merely on the agent's circumstances but on his knowledge of his circumstances. What I mean by 'objective probabilities' are *true* probabilities, which (if they exist at all) exist whether anyone is aware of them or not and whether anyone ought to be aware of them or not. It is of course a controversial question whether such true probabilities exist. But I am not committed to their existence. I say only that if they exist, then we have a choice whether to state an objective AU in terms of the facts or in terms of the true probabilities. If such true probabilities do not exist, then the only way of stating a fully objective AU is in terms of the facts.[1]

Third, it has been suggested by Peter Singer and others that AU should be interpreted to consider what we might call 'contributory consequences' as opposed to 'marginal consequences'.[2] The distinction is illustrated in the following case. Suppose there are 100 agents, all symmetrically situated so far as the basic description of the problem is concerned. There is a possible benefit which can be secured by the participation of at least sixty agents. Any sixty will do, and the participation of more than sixty produces no extra benefit. Suppose eighty agents are in fact participating. The question is, for purposes of AU, how much credit does each individual agent get for the production of the benefit which results. The 'marginal consequences' approach says that each agent gets credit for nothing. The benefit would have been produced despite the non-participation of any individual agent, since seventy-nine others would still have been participating. For each agent, if the benefit would have been produced despite his non-participation, then his participation does no good.

The 'contributory consequences' approach says that each agent gets credit for one-eightieth of the benefit. The benefit is, after all, being produced, so somebody must get credit. The only plausible way to divide the credit is to divide it equally among the agents who participate, since there are no relevant distinctions between them with regard to the production of the benefit.

I believe the 'contributory consequences' approach is not part of the standard interpretation of AU (and the 'marginal consequences' approach is). None the less, the contributory consequences approach has enough currency so that it is worth pointing out a number of reasons why it should not be adopted. I shall begin by describing two cases in which the contributory consequences approach leads to conclusions about what an agent should do which anyone who claims to be an act-utilitarian ought to regard as highly counterintuitive:

Case 1: There are 100 agents. A benefit worth 110 units can be secured by the participation of at least sixty agents. Participation by more than sixty does not increase the benefit. The benefit which each agent can produce individually and independently of the 110-unit benefit if he does *not* participate is worth 1 unit. There are no other relevant costs or benefits. Now, if ninety-nine agents are participating in the production of the participatory benefit, what should the other agent, whom we shall call Jones, do, according to the contributory consequences approach? If he participates, he gets one-hundredth of the credit for the production of a benefit with a value of 110 units. He gets credit for slightly over 1 unit of value. If he does not participate, he will produce a benefit worth 1 unit. Therefore he should participate, forgoing the benefit he could produce if he did not participate, despite the fact that even without him there are thirty-nine more agents participating than are needed to produce the participatory benefit.

Case 2: There are 100 agents. A benefit worth 50 units can be secured by the participation of at least sixty agents. The benefit each agent can produce if he does not participate is worth one unit. If fifty-nine agents other than Jones are participating in an attempt to produce the participatory benefit and forty agents other than Jones are not participating, what should Jones do? According to the contributory consequences approach, if Jones participates, he gets one-sixtieth of the credit for a benefit valued at 50 units, or slightly less than 1 unit. If he does not participate, he will produce consequences worth 1 unit. Therefore, he should not participate, despite the fact that his participation is all that is needed to secure 50 units of benefit which his non-participation will leave unachieved. (Needless to say, it would be best if *no one* participated in the case just described, but we assume in both of our cases that Jones cannot alter the other agents' behaviour.)

We could multiply cases like these, and more complicated cases, almost without limit; but to do so would serve no purpose. The point of the cases is to make clear what an odd position the advocate of 'contributory consequences' is in for an act-utilitarian. We cannot do more by the method of producing examples. I do not claim that the advocate of contributory consequences necessarily commits any logical error; nor do I deny that with effort and imagination he might produce a more complicated theory which would avoid the counterintuitive consequences of his approach in at least the more straightforward cases. But he starts off with a heavy burden.

Not only does the advocate of contributory consequences start off with a heavy burden—it is a burden there is no reason to assume. It may seem that because AU requires each agent to do an act with best consequences, the act-utilitarian must deal somehow with the issue of how consequences like participatory benefits are to be allocated among agents. This is a red herring. We can state AU, or any other traditional consequentialist theory, without the use of the word 'consequences' and in a way which makes the allocation problem disappear. Consider AU. The common understanding is that an agent has a list of acts he might perform. All other causally relevant facts about the world are given. There corresponds to each act on the agent's list a future course of the world (perhaps probabilistically described) which will be realized if that act is chosen. Each possible future course of the world has a specified value (or expected value). What AU requires the agent to do is that act (or any act) which brings about a course of the world with (expected) value at least as great as the (expected) value of any other course of the world corresponding to an act on the agent's list. It is convenient to summarize this by saying that AU requires the agent to do the act with the best consequences, but the longer explanation avoids both the word 'consequences' *and* any difficulty comparable to the allocation difficulty. The question of allocation simply does not arise. To be sure, the longer explanation corresponds to the 'marginal consequences' approach to AU as it is usually stated, so the believer in contributory consequences may reject it; but it does show that we are not compelled to worry about allocation.

Singer suggests that if we adopt the marginal consequences approach and ignore the allocation problem with respect to a participatory benefit, we shall sometimes be left with 'a result which [is] unconnected with the actions of any of the [agents] '.[3] The short answer is that even if the result is in some sense unconnected with the action of any individual agent, it is not unconnected with the actions of all the agents taken together. There is thus no danger of the benefit not being explained by the way the agents behave. Indeed, the real problem is that the achievement of the benefit is over-explained. In our Case 1, the achievement of the benefit can be explained in as many ways as one can select sixty agents from a group of ninety-nine, even assuming Jones does not participate.

Two other possible reasons for believing that the contributory consequences approach is necessary to maintain the plausibility of AU are also illusory. First, it might be thought that adoption of the contributory consequences approach makes it the case that universal satisfaction of AU ensures the achievement of participatory benefits. That is, it might be thought that if we adopt the contributory consequences approach, then we can rest assured that groups of agents who satisfy AU will always achieve any worthwhile participatory benefits, and will necessarily have useful practices such as truth-telling and promise-keeping, and so on. This is not so, as we shall see near the end of this chapter.[4] Universal satisfaction of AU with the contributory consequences approach does not guarantee the achievement of participatory benefits or the existence of desirable practices. Alternatively, it might be thought that consideration of contributory consequences is necessary to *avoid* the conclusion that in some cases universal satisfaction of AU ensures the *non*-existence of desirable practices. That is, it might be thought that only with the contributory consequences approach is universal satisfaction of AU always *consistent* with the production of best possible consequences. This is not so either. The surprising truth is that universal satisfaction of AU is always consistent with the production of best possible consequences from group action *if and only if* we adopt the *marginal* consequences approach. This will be shown in the next chapter.[5]

For the benefit of the reader who thinks I have not given enough attention to the contributory consequences approach, let me emphasize that my claims in the preceding paragraph are not mere afterthoughts. They are important claims, and they undercut what I believe are the commonest reasons for adherence to the contributory consequences approach. The reader who did not notice this might do well to read the last paragraph once more. I prove the claims of the last paragraph at other points in this chapter and the next because that is the most convenient way to develop the arguments. The reader who is inclined to favour the contributory consequences approach should therefore take note that although the main points of my case against that approach are summarized here, the complete case includes a number of arguments which appear further on. My conclusion, for the reasons stated, is that there is much to be said against the contributory consequences approach and little if anything to be said in its favour that withstands analysis.[6] In the remainder of this essay, I adopt the marginal consequences approach, both to AU and (what could almost certainly go without saying) to PropAU as well.

It is clear that AU has PropAU. As we defined PropAU, the statement 'AU has PropAU' means: 'For any agent, in any choice situation, if the agent satisfies AU in that situation, he produces by his act the best consequences he can possibly produce in that situation.' An agent satisfies AU if and only if he does an act which is right, according to AU; in other words, if and only if he does an act which has at least as good consequences as any other available under the circumstances. Thus, an agent who satisfies AU in any situation produces the best consequences he can possibly produce in that situation. In short, AU has PropAU.

We turn now to the question of whether AU has PropCOP. The argument that it does not is based on the following example.[7] Suppose that there are only two agents in the moral universe, called Whiff and Poof. Each has a button in front of him which he can push or not. If both Whiff and Poof push their buttons, the consequences will be such that the overall state of the world has a value of ten units. If neither Whiff nor Poof pushes his button, the consequences will be such that the overall state of the world has a value of 6 units. Finally, if one and only one of the pair pushes his button (and it does not matter who pushes and who does not), the consequences will be such that the overall state of the world has a value of 0 (zero) units. Neither agent, we assume, is in a position to influence the other's choice. We can sum up the situation in a diagram of a familiar sort:

		Poof	
		Push	Not-push
	Push	10	0
Whiff			
	Not-push	0	6

Now, if we ask what AU directs Whiff to do, we find that we cannot say. If Poof pushes, then AU directs Whiff to push. If Poof does not push, then AU directs Whiff not to push. Until we specify how Poof behaves, AU gives Whiff no clear direction. The same is true, *mutatis mutandis,* of Poof.

If we shift our attention to patterns of behaviour for the pair, we can decide whether each agent satisfies AU in any specified pattern. Suppose, for example, Whiff and Poof both push their buttons. The total value thereby achieved is ten units. Does Whiff satisfy AU? Yes. The only other thing he might do is not push his button. But under the circumstances, which include the fact that Poof pushes his button, Whiff's not pushing would result in a total utility of zero. Therefore Whiff's pushing his button has at least as good consequences as any other act available to him under the circumstances. Therefore, it is right according to AU. We may conclude by an exactly parallel argument that Poof also satisfies AU. Thus, if both Whiff and Poof push, both satisfy AU.

Now suppose instead that neither Whiff nor Poof pushes his button. Does Whiff satisfy AU? Yes. Under the circumstances, that is, given Poof's failure to push his button, Whiff's pushing his own button would result in a total utility of zero. By failing to push his button, Whiff produces a total utility of six. Therefore not pushing the button has at least as good consequences as any other act under the circumstances. Therefore Whiff satisfies AU. By an exactly parallel argument, we can show that Poof satisfies AU. Therefore both satisfy AU.

We have just seen that if neither Whiff nor Poof pushes his button, *both* Whiff and Poof satisfy AU. The consequences produced, however, have a value of only 6 units, 4 units less than the best possible. Therefore, universal satisfaction of AU does not guarantee the production of the best consequences possible overall. AU does not have PropCOP. (Recall the definition of PropCOP. 'AU has PropCOP' means: 'If all agents satisfy AU in all choice situations, then the class of all agents produce by their acts taken together the best consequences that they can possibly produce by any pattern of behaviour.')

The direct argument for the claim that AU fails to have PropCOP is complete. Presently, we shall consider a series of counterarguments designed to show that in our example AU unequivocally directs each of Whiff and Poof to push. If this were true, it would of course mean that AU was universally satisfied only when both pushed, and the example would not show what I claim.

Before we turn to the counterarguments, however, I want to say a bit more about just what it is the example illustrates. Remember that there are two patterns of behaviour in which AU is universally satisfied. One of these patterns produces consequences valued at only 6 units, less than the best possible.

The other pattern, however, is the best possible. I shall argue in the next two chapters that universal satisfaction of AU is always *consistent* with the production of the best possible consequences. In other words, whatever example we consider, any best possible pattern of behaviour is always one in which AU is universally satisfied. But in some cases, like the one before us, there are other patterns of behaviour in which AU is universally satisfied and which produce inferior consequences.

I shall refer to the fact that, in some cases, AU can be universally satisfied by different patterns of behaviour which produce consequences of different value by saying that AU is 'indeterminate'. The word 'indeterminate' is chosen to remind us that in some cases we cannot infer from the bare proposition that AU is universally satisfied either the pattern of behaviour involved *or the value of the consequences achieved.* Observe that indeterminacy entails non-possession of PropCOP. A theory which is indeterminate can be universally satisfied (in some cases) by different patterns of behaviour producing consequences of different value. Some one of the patterns in question must therefore have consequences of less value than some other pattern. That means that some pattern in which the theory is universally satisfied produces less than the best possible consequences. In other words, the theory does not have PropCOP.

It should be emphasized that in commenting on the indeterminacy of AU I am not merely dressing up in fancy language a hoary objection to AU, to wit, that it is hard to apply. The point of that objection is presumably that if everyone tries to follow AU, they may fail. Our example shows that even if everyone *satisfies* AU, that is not enough to guarantee the achievement of the best possible consequences overall.[8]

It is because AU is indeterminate that it can be true *both* that universal satisfaction of AU does not always guarantee the achievement of best possible consequences (which we are in the process of proving in this chapter) *and* that universal satisfaction of AU is always consistent with the achievement of best possible consequences, or in other words that any best pattern of group behaviour is always a pattern in which AU is universally satisfied (which we shall prove in the next two chapters). *Universal satisfaction of AU is a necessary but not a sufficient condition for the achievement of the best consequences possible overall.*

The phenomenon of indeterminacy is of more than merely logical interest. Although we have presented only a single artificial example of the indeterminacy of AU, AU is not indeterminate only in rare or pathological cases. It is almost certainly indeterminate in many of the cases which have occupied disputing consequentialists for years. We shall discuss the familiar grass-walking case, and point out how it manifests the indeterminacy of AU, in Chapter 3. Preserving grass may not be among the highest functions of morality, but readers who are sceptical of button-pushing examples may yet agree that the grass-walking case is a revealing model of many very important cases involving taxpaying, conserving resources in time of shortage, voting (which does present somewhat special problems), and so on. Institutions such as keeping agreements and punishing also reveal the indeterminacy of AU, as we shall see near the end of this chapter and in Chapter 4. Not only is AU indeterminate in a wide range of cases, but a variety of other consequentialist theories are indeterminate as well, as we shall demonstrate in Chapters 5 and 6. Indeed, indeterminacy is the trap into which traditional theories that attempt to achieve PropAU almost inevitably fall.

We turn now to the arguments designed to show that AU unequivocally directs each of Whiff and Poof to push:

(1) The first argument is that if Whiff and Poof are both aware of the situation, and both know that both are aware, and so on, then it is simply obvious that both should push.

The trouble with this suggestion is that it is not an argument about what *AU* requires Whiff and Poof to do. No doubt it is obvious in some sense what they should do. But that is beside the point. It is not obvious by virtue of AU. Indeed, the trouble with AU is precisely that both satisfy it if they do what they 'obviously' should not, that is, if both not-push.

The argument would look somewhat more act-utilitarian if it began with the claim that Whiff should figure out that it must be obvious to Poof that he (Poof) should push, and if it continued with the assertion that Whiff is required by AU to

push in response to this choice by Poof. This is no real improvement. If for some reason Poof does *not* find it obvious that
he should push, and if he in fact not-pushes, then AU requires
Whiff to not-push. It is no answer to say Whiff can reasonably
expect Poof to find it obvious he (Poof) should push. What
Whiff can reasonably expect is not relevant to what an *objective* AU requires of him in this example. Poof may not-push.
If Poof not-pushes, for whatever reason, AU requires Whiff to
not-push. By extension, if Whiff and Poof both not-push, for
whatever reasons, both satisfy AU.

   J. L. Mackie, defending act-utilitarianism, advances what is
essentially the 'obviousness' argument in connection with a
similar example of his own. I quote, altering the dramatis
personae:

Assuming simple rationality, goodwill, and knowledge both of the causal
connections between action-combinations and utility and of each other's
rationality, goodwill, and knowledge [Whiff and Poof] will each so act
that their combined action will maximize utility. The situation is radi-
cally different from those commonly discussed in games theory where
the players are playing *against* each other . . . Here the two players are
on the same side, and knowing this, they will rationally choose actions
that will lead to a utility peak. They will act, even independently, as if
their choices were concerted.[9]

Observe that in this passage, which is the core of Mackie's
argument that act-utilitarians would achieve the best possible
results in the general sort of situation we are discussing, there
is no mention at all of the act-utilitarian principle. Mackie is
right to emphasize the absence of conflict, as we shall see in
Chapter 3.[10] But pointing to the absence of conflict is not
the same as explaining why universal satisfaction of a particular theory guarantees best possible results. Mackie may have
been encouraged to overlook the problem of explaining just
how act-utilitarianism leads to co-ordination by the fact that
he does not notice the special difficulty raised by the existence
of a sub-optimal pattern of behaviour (such as both not-pushing
in our example) in which each individual agent's behaviour is
the best possible given the behaviour of the other.

   There is a strain of reliance on the obviousness argument in
much recent writing on act-utilitarianism.[11] I think a number
of defenders of act-utilitarianism are led to rely on arguments

which are not successful by the feeling that act-utilitarians can surely be counted on to accomplish whatever ordinary people ordinarily accomplish by the application of common sense. I was an act-utilitarian when I embarked on this study, and I understand the feeling that act-utilitarianism is thoroughly commonsensical. Still, the act-utilitarian principle and common sense are not self-evidently the same thing. They are loudly claimed not to be the same thing by proponents of other versions of utilitarianism. It may be that the defender of act-utilitarianism can prove that his principle and common sense are one and the same (though I do not now believe this). But he cannot prove it just by asserting it. Nor can he supply the deficiency in any other argument he may offer by assuming it.

I suggested in the Preface that certain act-utilitarians seem to be moving in the direction of co-operative utilitarianism without realizing it. It is pre-eminently act-utilitarians with a penchant for the obviousness argument that I have in mind. I hope the discussion of co-operative utilitarianism, when we get to it, will make it clear why this is so.

(2) The next argument is related to the obviousness argument, but is perhaps a slight improvement. It relies explicitly on the symmetry of the situation, thus: 'Whiff and Poof are symmetrically situated in all respects. Whatever AU requires Whiff to do, it must require Poof to do. It must require both to do the same thing. But if it requires them to do the same thing, then it is obvious what it must require them to do. That is to push.'

As stated, this argument shares the defect of the obviousness argument. It is not an act-utilitarian argument at all. It substitutes hand-waving for analysis of AU at the crucial step, and it ignores the fact that AU prescribes for each individual on the basis of what it would be best for *him* to do, and not on the basis of what it would be best for some larger group to do.[12]

Despite what we have said, it may seem that some act-utilitarian argument from symmetry can be patched together. To show that this is not possible, we consider a new example, which we present simply by means of the following array:

Poof

		Push	Not-push
	Push	3	4
Whiff			
	Not-push	4	0

I take it the argument from symmetry in this situation must lead to the conclusion that Whiff and Poof should both push. That is certainly the best thing for them to do if they are required to do the same thing. And yet if both push it is not the case either that they produce the best possible results as a group or that they universally satisfy AU. They will universally satisfy AU in this example only if one of them pushes and the other does not. In fact, this is a case where universal satisfaction of AU would guarantee the achievement of the best possible results. But universal satisfaction of AU would require the symmetrically situated parties to behave differently.

Note the universal satisfaction of AU would not merely require the agents to behave differently in the sense that one would have to push and the other to not-push. It might plausibly be claimed that the descriptions of Whiff's and Poof's acts as 'pushing' and 'not-pushing' are irrelevant to the essential structure of the problem. The essential structure, I take it, is that each agent has one choice consistent with outcomes having values of 3 units and 4 units (a '3–4 strategy') and another choice consistent with outcomes having values of 4 units and 0 units (a '4–0 strategy') and that the outcome depends in a specified way on how many agents choose each strategy but not on who chooses which. Even in these terms, AU is universally satisfied only if Whiff and Poof choose differently. AU and the argument from symmetry do not go together.[13]

J. J. C. Smart has suggested, in connection with an example like our latest example, that AU requires each agent to select the randomized strategy which it would be best for all to select.[14] This is an attractive suggestion. It is not really an act-utilitarian suggestion, as we shall demonstrate when we discuss the use of randomization in cases like this in Chapter 11.[15] For the moment, it should suffice to point out that if both parties adopt any randomized strategy, the expected return to the pattern of behaviour will be less than 4 units. Therefore even if Smart's suggestion were accepted as act-utilitarian, it would not establish that universal satisfaction of AU guaranteed the best possible consequences. It would leave intact the basic claim of this chapter. (Let me emphasize that although I dismiss Smart's suggestion, which has been echoed by Narveson[16] rather shortly in the present context, I discuss it in some detail in Chapter 11. The reader who is interested in what I have to say in general about act-utilitarianism should not overlook the later discussion.)

(3) The next argument begins by suggesting that Whiff should reason as follows: 'I have no information about what Poof is going to do. Therefore the only reasonable course is to assume that he is just as likely to do one thing as another, to push his button as not. On that assumption, the expected utility if I push my button is $\frac{1}{2} (10) + \frac{1}{2} (0) = 5$. The expected utility if I do not push is $\frac{1}{2} (0) + \frac{1}{2} (6) = 3$. Obviously, I should push my button.' The argument continues by pointing out that Poof should reason the same way, and by concluding that if both reason this way, then both will push their buttons and best results will in fact be achieved.

This argument is rather loosely stated, and there are three ways it might be interpreted, but it fails on any interpretation. First, the argument might be taken to assume that Whiff actually believes that Poof is equally likely to push or not-push, and to endorse Whiff's acting on that belief. This will not do, for two reasons. First, the description of the example said nothing about Whiff's beliefs. Second, Whiff's beliefs are irrelevant to what Whiff is required to do by the *objective* formulation of AU we are interested in.

Next, the argument might be taken to assert that Whiff ought to behave *as if* Poof were equally likely to push or not to push, whatever Whiff's actual beliefs. This has a more objective sound, but it still will not do. It is clear that no one would seriously suggest AU requires Whiff to choose *in every case* as if Poof were equally likely to elect any of the alternatives open to him. We are tempted to recommend this approach to Whiff only if we assume some degree of ignorance on Whiff's part about Poof's behaviour. But then it turns out that this approach is not part of an objective version of AU, since whether it is to be adopted depends on the state of Whiff's knowledge.

Finally, the argument under consideration might be taken to assume that the objective probabilities really are that Poof (and similarly Whiff) is equally likely to push or not. Once again, the obvious difficulty is that no such assumption was included in the description of the example.

There is a further reason why the 'probabilistic' argument cannot do what it is supposed to, however it is interpreted. The object of the argument is to show that if both Whiff and Poof satisfy AU then best possible results will be achieved. But it is a mere accident that in our example the 'natural' assignment of equal probabilities to each choice by each agent leads, in the course of the argument, to the pattern of behaviour in which both push their buttons. Consider a slightly different example:

		Poof	
		Push	Not-push
	Push	10	5
Whiff			
	Not-push	0	6

In this situation, if each agent maximizes the expected return on the assumption that the other is equally likely to push or not (whether because that is what each believes, or because that is what each hypothesizes in the absence of any information, or because that is what the objective probabilities really are), Whiff will push, but Poof will not. The result achieved will have a value of 5 units, considerably less than the best possible.[17]

(4) The next argument designed to show that AU requires each of Whiff and Poof to push (in our original example, again) is a bit more complicated than the previous arguments. To some readers it may sound implausible from the start. But it raises some interesting issues, and our response to it will shed some light on what precisely we are investigating when we investigate the consequences of universal satisfaction of AU.

We shall have occasion to refer back to the conclusion of this section in the course of discussing a seemingly unrelated defence of AU at the end of the chapter.

The argument runs: 'Whiff, being an act-utilitarian and knowing that Poof is an act-utilitarian, should reason thus: "If I push my button, then the act-utilitarian thing for Poof to do will be to push his button. Since Poof is an act-utilitarian, that is what he will do. Therefore if I push my button Poof will push his button, and the total value achieved will be 10 units. On the other hand, if I do not push my button, then the act-utilitarian thing for Poof to do will be not to push his button. Since Poof is an act-utilitarian, that is what he will do. Therefore if I do not push my button, Poof will not push his button, and the total value achieved will be 6 units. Since the total utility achieved if I push my button is 10, and the total utility achieved if I do not push my button is 6, AU plainly dictates that I should push my button." By this reasoning Whiff could decide, solely by appeal to AU and the knowledge that Poof is following AU, to push his button. Poof could do likewise. Therefore by applying AU the pair would in fact arrive at the best result.'

Before we explain the error in this argument, one point should be made about the statement of the argument. The argument is stated, and the response will be stated, in terms of Whiff's *knowing* that Poof is an act-utilitarian, and so on. This is an expository convenience only. The argument presents itself most naturally in terms of proposed reasoning by Whiff. However, it is not Whiff's knowledge that is really important. Since we are dealing with an objective AU, the relevance of the fact that Poof is an act-utilitarian, and any facts that follow therefrom, would be the same even if Whiff were unaware of them. The entire discussion of this argument could be recast, without affecting either argument or response, in such a way as to make no reference to Whiff's mental state.

The natural response to the current argument, I think, is to point out that Whiff assumes Poof will satisfy AU *whatever* he (Whiff) does, and to claim that under the circumstances that amounts to an assumption on Whiff's part that he can cause Poof's behaviour, an assumption which was explicitly excluded in the description of the example. This response seems intuitively correct. Unfortunately, I do not know how to prove that Whiff's assumption 'amounts to' an assumption that he can cause Poof's act. Accordingly, I shall offer a more formal argument, which makes a substantially similar point in slightly more general terms.

We begin by considering the status in Whiff's reasoning of the conditionals he derives to the effect that 'If I push, then Poof will push' and 'If I do not push, then Poof will not push'. These cannot be merely material conditionals if Whiff's argument is to work. The conjunction of these propositions, if each is interpreted as a material conditional, is logically consistent with the proposition 'Poof will not push regardless of what I do'. But the proposition 'Poof will not push regardless of what I do', which is of course a more-than-material conditional of some sort, logically entails, in the context of this example, 'I should not push (according to AU)'. Now, if one proposition is logically consistent with a second, and the second logically entails a third, then the first must be logically consistent with the third. Since the conjunction of 'If I push, then Poof will push' and 'If I do not push, then Poof will not push' (both interpreted as material conditionals) is consistent with 'Poof will not push regardless of what I do', and since this in turn entails 'I should not push (according to AU)', the original conjunction must be consistent with the proposition 'I should not push (according to AU)'. Therefore, the original conjuncts (interpreted as merely material conditionals) cannot justify the conclusion that Whiff is required by AU to push.

We have established that the conditionals which relate Poof's behaviour to Whiff's must be in some more-than-material mode. Are they? They are derived in the course of Whiff's reasoning from the proposition that Poof is an act-utilitarian. The proposition that Poof is an act-utilitarian can be interpreted in such a way as to justify the inference to the conclusion (in a more-than-material mode) that Poof will do whatever Whiff does. But not just any interpretation of the claim that Poof is an act-utilitarian will suffice. It will not suffice, for example, that we interpet 'Poof is an act-utilitarian' to mean 'Poof is doing his best to do what AU requires of him'. Poof's best might not be good enough in the case at hand. More importantly, it will not suffice that we interpret 'Poof is an act-utilitarian' to mean 'Poof satisfies AU, under the circumstances'. If we take this last proposition as being in the material mode, which is how it is intended, then it is consistent with the proposition 'Poof does not push and would not push regardless of how Whiff behaved'. If the circumstances are that Whiff does not push and Poof cannot alter Whiff's behaviour, then Poof satisfies AU under those circumstances by not-pushing regardless of what he would do if Whiff behaved otherwise. But if 'Poof satisfies AU, under the circumstances' is consistent with 'Poof does not push and would not push regardless of how Whiff behaved', then plainly 'Poof satisfies AU, under the circumstances' cannot entail a more-than-material claim that Poof will do whatever Whiff does.

The interpretation of 'Poof is an act-utilitarian' that is needed if the proposed reasoning by Whiff is to be acceptable is 'Poof will satisfy AU whatever Whiff does', construed as a more-than-material claim. Nothing less will suffice.

It is established that Whiff needs to assume 'Poof will satisfy AU whatever I do' in some more-than-material mode. The remaining question is whether this assumption is justified. Certainly no explicit assumption to this effect was included in the description of the case. The only possible justification is that we have been making this assumption implicitly by focusing, as we are focusing in this chapter, on the consequences of universal satisfaction of AU. Indeed, it may seem paradoxical to deny the availability of the assumption that Poof will satisfy AU regardless, in the context of this chapter. There is no paradox, however, so long as we keep our modalities straight.

We are interested, to be sure, in cases of universal satisfaction. We are interested first in *identifying* cases of universal satisfaction, and then in using the knowledge about what are cases of universal satisfaction to decide what follows from the assumption that universal satisfaction occurs. Thus— Question: 'Does it follow from the fact that AU is universally satisfied that the best possible results are produced?' Answer: 'No, because (assuming the overall argument of this chapter is correct) there is a case in which AU is universally satisfied and inferior results are produced.'

Now, what patterns of behaviour by various agents constitute universal satisfaction of AU depends on the facts of each case. Included in the relevant facts of *some* cases are more-than-material propositions specifying how the behaviour of one agent varies with the behaviour of another. Thus, if it is a fact of some case that Poof will satisfy AU whatever Whiff does, that fact is relevant to what Whiff ought to do and therefore relevant to what constitutes universal satisfaction of AU. On the other hand, if it is not given that Poof will satisfy AU whatever Whiff does, we still have a case in which some patterns of behaviour do, and some do not, constitute universal satisfaction of AU; and we can intelligibly ask what constitutes universal satisfaction of AU in that case without committing ourselves to the assumption that Poof will satisfy AU whatever Whiff does. Indeed, to make that assumption would be to change the case.

To put the matter briefly, there is a vast difference between assuming every agent satisfies AU and assuming every agent would satisfy AU whatever every other agent did. We are in a sense assuming the former for most of this chapter, since we are concerned with the consequences of universal satisfaction. But we never assume the latter. The counterargument under consideration fails because it requires Whiff to rely on a premise which simply is not given in the description of the case.

Of course, even if it is granted that we have not made the assumption that each agent will satisfy AU regardless of what the other does, either explicitly or implicitly, the question might still be raised whether we *should* make such an assumption. Perhaps we should be inquiring into the consequences of universal satisfaction of AU in a world of 'perfect act-utilitarians'—that is to say, in a world of agents each of whom is guaranteed to satisfy AU whatever the others do. I disagree, for two reasons.

First, there never has been and never will be even one perfect act-utilitarian in this sense, much less a world of them. Human being are fallible, and no human agent can be guaranteed to satisfy AU whatever the circumstances. This does not mean that we should not interest ourselves in the consequences of universal satisfaction of AU. Universal satisfaction of whatever moral theory is put before us remains in some sense the 'ideal' implied by that moral theory, and theories should be judged at least in part by the acceptability of the ideals they imply. But surely the ideal implied by AU is just the situation in which everyone *does* satisfy AU. It is not the situation in which everyone does what he would be required by AU to do if it were true that everyone *would* satisfy AU whatever anyone else did.

Second, I think we are now justified in repeating the suggestion made earlier in this section, that intuitively the assumption that Poof is a perfect act-utilitarian seems to amount to an assumption that Whiff can cause Poof's behaviour. The claim that Poof is a perfect act-utilitarian is a more-than-material claim of some sort. If it is not a claim that Whiff can cause Poof's behaviour, it is difficult to see what else it might be. However, if the claim that Poof is a perfect act-utilitarian means that Whiff can cause Poof's behaviour, then the claim that Whiff is a perfect act-utilitarian means that Poof can cause Whiff's behaviour. Saying that Whiff and Poof are *both* perfect act-utilitarians would then amount to saying that each could cause the other's behaviour. Since we are dealing with a case in which each agent makes only one choice, between pushing or not, the claim that each can cause the other's behaviour amounts to a claim that Whiff's act of pushing or not will both cause and be caused by Poof's act of pushing or not. This is very paradoxical.

Even if the claim that Poof is a perfect act-utilitarian does not amount to a claim that Whiff can cause Poof's behaviour, it seems to amount to a claim that Whiff's choice somehow determines Poof's. But then the claim that both are perfect act-utilitarians would mean that the act of one both determines and is determined by the act of the other. All of this suggests that we should avoid assuming the existence of a multiplicity of perfect act-utilitarians.[18] (This discussion of perfect act-utilitarians is recalled and developed slightly in the last part of this chapter.)

(5) We turn now to a new objection to the claim that universal satisfaction of AU does not guarantee the best possible results. The new objection is that we have ignored the possibility of Whiff and Poof getting together and *agreeing* that both will push their buttons.

The obvious response to this objection is that it may not be possible for Whiff and Poof to get together and agree. They may have no way of communicating before the time when the decisions about the buttons must be made. This is a problem in the real world, and not merely in our example. AU is almost certainly indeterminate in most of the standard cases involving interaction effects from grass-walking to voting, and it can hardly be suggested that the act-utilitarian solution to all these problems is for everyone concerned to get together and make an agreement.

Not only is there often no opportunity to make an agreement, but in some cases in which there is the possibility of making an agreement, it will not be worth the trouble to make one. If the potential gains from co-ordination are not great, it is quite possible that on balance AU would forbid one to go to the trouble of creating an explicit agreement about how to behave, even where the opportunity for making such an agreement was at hand.[19]

We might reasonably terminate the discussion of agreements at this point. Nevertheless, in view of the attention which has been devoted recently to the issue of whether act-utilitarians can make use of agreements, I think a rather substantial digression is justified. In the remainder of this section, I shall explain why even costless opportunities to make explicit agreements would not necessarily rescue AU from indeterminacy.

Suppose that in our standard example Whiff and Poof are allowed an opportunity to discuss what they should do. They agree to push their buttons. Each sits down in front of his own button. When the moment for acting comes, what should they do? Of course we will get nowhere by considering what AU requires apart from the agreement, but it is natural to suppose the agreement will help. Alas, it does not. If Poof keeps the agreement, then Whiff should keep it. But if Poof violates it, Whiff should violate it also. If Whiff keeps it, then

Poof should keep it, but if Whiff violates it, Poof should follow suit. It turns out that AU is universally satisfied if both keep the agreement, *or* if both violate it. Even with the agreement, the indeterminacy remains.[20]

There are two basic lines of argument the defender of AU might rely on in attempting to refute the argument I have just made. One line depends on considerations related to a practice of agreement-keeping. The other does not. I shall consider first the line which does not depend on any assumption about the existence of a practice, and I shall then consider whether the possibility of a practice makes a difference.

The defender of AU might say I have overlooked the following fact: the existence of the agreement between Whiff and Poof gives each a reason to expect that the other will push and therefore gives each a reason to push that he did not have before. Plausible as it sounds, this suggestion is beside the point. In order to see why, we must distinguish two ways in which expectations can be relevant to questions about act-utilitarian obligation. On the one hand, each agent's expectations are part of his beliefs about his circumstances and therefore help to determine his *subjective* act-utilitarian obligations. On the other hand, expectations sometimes affect the consequences of behaviour (as where some agent will be pleased to see his predictions fulfilled) or themselves constitute valuable consequences (for example, pleasurable anticipation). Only if they affect consequences or themselves constitute significant consequences do expectations affect *objective* act-utilitarian obligations.

In the Whiff and Poof example, we have stipulated the values of the consequences of various patterns of behaviour without reference to expectations. We have assumed implicitly that the parties' expectations do not affect the consequences of various patterns of behaviour. There is no reason why this should not be true, even if there is an agreement. One does not necessarily feel disappointment just because an agreement to which one is a party has been violated. Because the consequences of various patterns of behaviour do not depend in our example on the parties' expectations, expectations are not relevant to the parties' objective obligations, which are all we are concerned with. Whatever the agreement may do to the parties' expectations, it does not change the fact that if both not-push, each does what is objectively required of him by AU.

The defender of AU, who may suspect me of being wilfully obtuse, would presumably respond as follows: If the agreement makes Poof expect Whiff to push, then it will alter the *objective* probabilities about how Poof will behave. It will make Poof objectively more likely to push. That in turn will affect Whiff's *objective* obligation under AU. The same argument, with the parties reversed, shows that the agreement will alter Poof's objective obligation. AU will in fact objectively require both parties to push, and all will be well.[21]

The trouble with this argument is that we have as yet been given no reason to think the agreement will have any effect at all on Whiff's and Poof's expectations. This was a point I was prepared to overlook in the first stage of my response to this general line of argument, when I assumed the defender of AU was discussing subjective obligations. But I have not conceded that the agreement must have any effect on expectations, and I do not concede it, now that it seems to be the crucial issue.

It may seem odd to suggest that the agreement between Whiff and Poof might have no effect on their expectations. Why else did they make the agreement? Is it not part of the concept of an agreement that it affects expectations? It may well be part of the concept of an agreement that it affects expectations, but if that is so, then what I am suggesting is that the act-utilitarian Whiff and Poof, presented with an opportunity to make an agreement, may simply not be able to manage it. Whether we call the result of their abortive attempts an agreement which does not affect their expectations or a non-agreement, the point is the same. Mutual reformulation of expectations may be beyond their power.

Arguments designed to show that act-utilitarians must be able to affect each other's expectations have been made by Peter Singer[22] and J. L. Mackie[23] in response to D. H. Hodgson.[24] Singer and Mackie both argue that if one party can produce even the slightest effect on the other's expectations, then the spiral of expectations which Hodgson sees as whirling off into nothingness will instead amplify that initial effect into adequate reasons for both parties to keep the agreement. But Singer and Mackie produce no sufficient ground for thinking there will be even the slightest initial effect. The basic problem is this: They consistently assume that the behaviour of one agent which is supposed to constitute assent to the agreement will be taken by the other agent who perceives it to have *some* communicative impact. But there is no reason to assume there will be any communicative impact at all.

Singer says: '[E]ven if there is no good reason for *B* to believe that *A* will tell him the truth, there is also no good reason for him to believe that *A* will tell him a lie, and so there is an even chance that *B* will take the information *A* gives him to be true.'[25] Developing his argument from this point, Singer completely ignores the possibility that *B* will pay no attention whatsoever to what *A* says. (I treat arguments about truth-telling as effectively arguments about agreement-keeping. It seems to be generally recognized that the two problems are essentially the same.) Later on, in the process of explaining why he would believe a recommendation of a movie volunteered by *A*, despite the Hodgsonian suggestion that *A* might be speaking a falsehood with the hope and expectation of being disbelieved, Singer says: 'Why would *A* have bothered to speak at all, since I am just as likely to take his remark to be true as to be false?'[26] Singer goes on to argue that it is a little easier to take the volunteered remark as true than to take it as false, and that therefore he is, and is known to *A* to be, 'just a fraction more likely to take it at face value'.[27] But the easiest thing of all is to avoid the question of how to take *A*'s remark, by ignoring it entirely.

Singer assumes that an utterance will be taken by the hearer to have some communicative value, but there is no reason given why this must be true. There is no reason given why all utterances should not be simply ignored.

There is an obvious move with which Singer might attempt to fill in the gap in his argument. Mackie makes the move explicitly. Discussing the matter of how act-utilitarians would

manage not to collide head on as they approached each other
on a street, Mackie writes: 'Why could I not, when about to
run into a fellow English speaker on the pavement, call out,
say, "Go to your left!"'? Knowing that my sole object in the
situation is to get past him safely, and that this agrees with
his own sole object of getting safely past me, he will obey
my instruction with mutually satisfactory results . . .'[28] The
idea is that if Mackie has no object but to walk on without
a collision, then there is no way for his hearer to account for
his exclamation except by assuming that it is intended to have
some communicative value. But why could not Mackie be
making a vocal noise just to enjoy the sensations in his throat?

I admit that if I met Mackie on the street and we were
about to collide and he called out 'Go to your left!', I would
not take him to be merely exercising his larynx. That is because
Mackie and I live in a world in which verbal communication
is well established. But we might, as a matter of logical possibility, live in a world in which verbal communication was not
established. In such a world I would not only be unable to
interpret 'Go to your left!' as a direction to go to my left;
I would have better reason to think Mackie's utterance was
a pure vocal exercise than to think it was an attempt at communication. If verbal communication were not established,
people would not make vocal noises with the intent to communicate, and the only vocal noises I would hear would in
fact flow from other motives.[29]

At this point Mackie might suggest that in a society of
act-utilitarians people would do whatever was necessary to
bring it about that verbal communication became established.
This suggestion brings us to the threshold of the second line
of argument in defence of act-utilitarian agreement-keeping,
the line involving practice-related considerations. I shall
therefore abandon Singer and Mackie and discuss the issue in
the simpler world of Whiff and Poof.[30]

Actually, before going on I want to clarify the relation
between my position and Hodgson's. I have been explaining
why certain arguments made in response to Hodgson do not
refute me. I do not deny that the arguments in question
refute Hodgson. I think they do. But there is an extremely

important difference between Hodgson's position and mine. Hodgson claims that act-utilitarians *cannot possibly* make use of agreements. All I claim is that it *may be* the case that a collection of act-utilitarians are not in a position to benefit from opportunites to make agreements. To put my point the other way around, all I claim is that it does not follow from the fact that certain parties are act-utilitarians that an 'agreement' between them will have any effect on their expectations or behaviour. Whether an agreement is effective or not depends on facts about the parties other than the fact that they are act-utilitarians.

The difference between Hodgson's position and mine should not be difficult to grasp, but it is easy to forget in the thick of battle. Some critics of Hodgson have been admirably precise and have made it clear that their arguments against Hodgson establish only the *possibility* of act-utilitarian agreements.[31] With such critics of Hodgson I have no quarrel at all. But others, like Singer and Mackie, have sometimes appeared to claim more. They have appeared to claim that act-utilitarians could *certainly* make use of agreements. It may be that they never meant to claim more than was necessary to refute Hodgson. Only if they did mean to claim more do I have any quarrel with them.

We turn now to the second line of argument against my assertion that even an explicit agreement does not necessarily avoid the indeterminacy of AU. We have supposed that Whiff and Poof have an agreement to push their buttons. I have argued that the agreement does not solve the problem because the facts about the parties' expectations may be such that either agent should violate the agreement if the other does, from which it follows that AU is universally satisfied if both violate the agreement. The defender of AU will respond at this point that Whiff should keep the agreement even if Poof violates it. There will be a loss of utility from the resulting pattern of behaviour in this one situation, since Whiff will push while Poof not-pushes, but that loss will be outweighed by the gain from the reinforcement of a general expectation that agreements will be kept.

To begin with, we note an implicit assumption that there

are a series of cases in which agreements are made and that whether Whiff keeps the agreement in this case will be known to at least some agents involved in other cases. Let us accept this assumption and look more closely at the series of cases which are assumed to exist.

If agreements are generally kept, then it may be that every individual instance of keeping an agreement contributes to a general expectation that agreements will be kept. It may be that Whiff (or Poof) should therefore keep the agreement to push even if Poof (or Whiff) violates it, and that AU is universally satisfied in our example only if both keep the agreement and push. But what if agreements are *not* generally kept? If agreements are generally ignored, then it seems unlikely that a single instance of agreement-keeping would have any significant influence on general expectations about whether agreements will be kept. But that means that if agreements are not generally kept, then even though Whiff and Poof have an agreement, if Poof violates the agreement, AU requires Whiff to violate it also. Whiff's keeping the agreement would produce no good consequences to outweigh the loss of utility from not co-ordinating in this case. By the same token, if Whiff violates the agreement (still against a background where agreements are generally ignored), then AU requires Poof to violate. In sum, AU is universally satisfied if both violate. It turns out that whether AU requires individual agreements to be kept depends on whether agreements are generally kept or not.[32]

The argument of the preceding paragraph might elicit the following objection: Even if it is granted that Whiff and Poof both satisfy AU if they both violate their agreement against a background where agreements are generally ignored, this is still not a case in which AU is universally satisfied. AU has not been satisfied by all those other agents whose nonchalance about their agreements is responsible for putting Whiff and Poof into a context where their keeping their agreement would do no good. This objection is mistaken. If agreements are generally ignored, then *everyone* who is faced with the decision whether to keep an agreement is equally in a context where agreements are generally ignored. So we cannot accuse *anyone* of failing to satisfy AU just on the ground that he violated an agreement, any more than we can accuse Whiff and Poof on that ground.

Another possible objection to my argument is the claim that if Whiff keeps the agreement, his example will stimulate others to keep agreements also. Whiff's behaviour will therefore cause, not the negligible increase in expectations of agreement-keeping which would follow a single occurrence, but rather the significant increase in expectations of agreement-keeping which will follow all the occurrences of agreement-keeping Whiff's example will stimulate. The short answer to this objection is that there is no reason to assume Whiff's example will stimulate anyone else to keep an agreement. If Whiff's behaviour is not justified by AU aside from its power as an example, then it seems most reasonable to assume that other act-utilitarians will not regard it as an example to be followed. They will regard it as an aberration. (If this treatment of the power of examples seems too curt, we will consider the matter further when we get to the 'snowball argument' in the next section.)

Our conclusion thus far is that whether Whiff should keep his agreement depends on whether there is a practice of agreement-keeping in existence. There is a passage in which Peter Singer might be taken to argue that if AU is universally satisfied, a practice of agreement-keeping will necessarily be built up.[33] Singer's argument depends on the contributory consequences approach, but even with the contributory consequences approach universal satisfaction of AU does not guarantee that a practice of agreement-keeping will appear. If agreements are generally ignored, and if no one but Whiff makes any effort to get a practice of agreement-keeping established, then an individual act of agreement-keeping by Whiff would not have any good consequences of its own (any good 'marginal' consequences) in terms of establishing a practice, and furthermore there would not be any general benefit in the form of the establishment of a practice for Whiff to get credit for a share of. Therefore, if there is no practice and no one does anything to start one, no one violates AU even on the contributory consequences approach.[34]

Another suggestion about building up a practice has been

made by Norbert Hoerster.[35] If we consider that Whiff has many opportunites to keep agreements, should we not inquire into the consequences of his keeping all of them, not just keeping any one of them? Might not Whiff's keeping all of his agreements have sufficient good consequences so that AU requires him to do so? There are two difficulties with this argument, both of which Hoerster is aware of.

First, if Whiff keeps all of his agreements against a background where others generally ignore their agreements, he may be able to affect the behaviour of his intimates, but he can hardly affect the behaviour of persons with whom he deals only occasionally. This suggests that if everyone keeps all of his agreements with intimates but none of his agreements with non-intimates, no one can be accused of failing to make a required contribution to the practice of agreement-keeping among non-intimates, because no single individual's attempt to establish that practice would have any positive effect. The most Hoerster's argument can prove, as Hoerster explicitly notes, is that universal satisfaction of AU guarantees the establishment of agreement-keeping among intimates.

Second, it is not clear that AU can be regarded as prescribing that Whiff keep all of his agreements, even with intimates. The effect of Whiff's keeping any one agreement depends on whether he keeps the others. If Whiff generally does not keep his agreements, then AU would arguably not require him to keep any single agreement considered by itself. The same sort of co-ordination problem which arises between Whiff and Poof arises also between time-slices of Whiff.

The question we are now faced with is whether AU is to be construed as addressed to agents-continuing-through-time or to time-slices of agents. Hoerster explicitly adopts the former construction, as he must to support his conclusion. I am not convinced the former construction should be preferred. Hoerster suggests that the successive acts are, after all, the acts of the same agent. This seems to beg the question. Whiff-at-t_1 may have special knowledge of the likely behaviour of Whiff-at-t_2, and he may have special ability to influence the behaviour of Whiff-at-t_2, but he cannot make Whiff-at-t_2's decision for him. Therefore it is not clear that Whiff-at-t_1 should be faulted for ignoring the best pattern of behaviour for all the time-slices if he knows that Whiff-at-t_2 is not going to do his part. Indeed, if Whiff-at-t_1 can do nothing to alter Whiff-at-t_2's behaviour, it seems that Whiff-at-t_1 *ought* to ignore the best pattern, assuming that is what is necessary to make the best of the situation created by Whiff-at-t_2's defection.

We cannot discuss this issue fully, but what we have said suggests one further comment. It may seem hard to swallow the general claim of this chapter, that AU sometimes provides no ground for criticizing either Whiff or Poof when they fail to co-ordinate on the best possible result. If so, it probably seems outrageous to suggest a view of AU on which it would sometimes provide no ground for criticizing any time-slice of Whiff, and therefore no ground for criticizing Whiff, when 'he' failed to 'co-ordinate' with 'himself'. This objection would dissolve if we could find an adaptable theory to rely on in place of AU. Since any group of agents who all satisfy an adaptable theory produce the best results possible (by the definition of adaptability),[36] any group of agents who fail to produce the best results possible would have to include at least one agent who failed to satisfy our adaptable theory (if we had one). Therefore an adaptable theory would always provide a ground for criticizing at least one time-slice of an agent-continuing-through-time whose time-slices failed to co-ordinate. I do not mention this as a great virtue of adaptable theories, but rather as a point to remember in connection with the general issue of which sort of agents moral theories are addressed to.[37]

The attempt to show that universal satisfaction of AU would necessarily lead to a general practice of agreement-keeping fails, and we are left with our conclusion of a few pages ago, that whether AU requires individual agreements to be kept depends on whether agreements are generally kept or not.[38] If the defender of AU proposes to rely on agreements as even a partial solution to the problem of the indeterminacy of AU, he must assume as an empirical matter that agreements are generally kept. Universal satisfaction of AU does not guarantee this.

The defender of AU may ask why the need for this assumption is supposed to trouble him. After all, if we look around we will see that agreements *are* generally kept. What can be the harm in making an empirical assumption that is patently true? To answer this question, we must remember the nature of our project. We are not primarily interested in whether AU gives the right directions in actual cases involving agreements. We are interested in whether AU is an adequate consequentialist theory. If agreements are useful, as the defender of AU concedes, then an adequate consequentialist theory ought not only to *permit* the existence of a practice of agreement-keeping, it ought to *ensure* it. It ought not to depend for its success on the existence of a pattern of behaviour which it must regard in effect as a happy accident.

At this point the defender of AU might retrench just a little. He might suggest that AU can be turned into an adequate theory if it is supplemented with further principles, including but not limited to a principle requiring agreement-keeping. He could suggest that the indeterminacy of AU leaves room for supplementation by principles which encourage the achievement of superior patterns of universal satisfaction of AU (as opposed to inferior patterns of universal satisfaction) without ever requiring behaviour inconsistent with AU.[39] Certainly this suggestion reflects considerable insight into what is wrong with AU. I cannot deal fully with this suggestion without anticipating Chapters 7 and 8. Let me summarize now what those chapters will reveal. First, if the supplementary principles are themselves 'exclusively act-oriented' (which I shall define in Chapter 7), as all traditional utilitarian theories have been, then no amount of supplementation will transform AU into an adequate theory. Second, if the supplementation is to be in fact a more radical transformation into a non-exclusively-act-oriented theory, then the suggestion leads in the direction of my own theory, co-operative utilitarianism. I shall note in Chapter 8 passages in others' work that might be seen as anticipating co-operative utilitarianism. But so far as I am aware no one (with the possible exception of Harrod)[40] has understood what is the crucial feature of co-operative utilitarianism, and no one (with the possible exception of Harrison)[41] has seen the difficulties that must be overcome.

Here ends the digression on agreements. Without meaning

to denigrate my arguments on this topic, I should like to remind the reader that my general criticism of AU does not stand or fall on this issue. We want a moral theory to require the best possible behaviour by groups even in cases where there is no opportunity to make an agreement. The arguments elsewhere in this chapter show that AU does not do that.

(6) We shall consider one more argument designed to show that universal satisfaction of AU guarantees the achievement of best possible results from group behviour. That is the argument I have already referred to as the 'snowball argument'. The central difficulty in discussing the snowball argument is that it does not really exist. That is to say, no one has produced a formulation of the snowball argument sufficiently precise so that we can simply attack that formulation. A number of writers, however, suggest in one way or another that certain difficulties with AU will dissolve if we keep in mind that individual acts can stimulate other acts by the power of example.[42] That is the basic idea of the snowball argument. One individual act of participation in a desirable practice will stimulate a second; together they will stimulate a third and a fourth; together these will stimulate some further number; and so on, until the desired general behaviour is an established fact.

Our Whiff and Poof example is obviously not well suited to discussion of the snowball argument. Let us therefore consider a case which was suggested by Gerald Barnes[43] (who is not a snowball theorist) and taken up by Jan Narveson[44] (who is). I shall make more precise assumptions about the case than either Barnes or Narveson does: There is a society which is in the grip of an efficient and tyrannical dictator. There are 1,000 persons in this society, not counting the dictator and his henchmen. If 500 persons rise up in insurrection, the dictator will topple, which would be a good thing by utilitarian standards. On the other hand, any attempt at insurrection which involves fewer than 500 persons will fail, and the unsuccessful insurrectionists will be executed, producing a net loss of utility as compared to the situation in which no insurrection is attempted. Furthermore, any attempt to organize an insurrection will be nipped in the bud by the dictator's secret police and the would-be organizers will be executed.

In effect, only a spontaneous uprising involving at least 500 persons will produce any good results.

Barnes's point about this example, with which I agree, is that if no one does anything towards overthrowing the dictator, then everyone (except the dictator and his henchmen, whom we leave out of account) satisfies AU. No individual could bring about a successful insurrection all by himself. Therefore if no one does anything, every individual behaves in the way which has best consequences given the behaviour of everyone else.

Narveson's response to Barnes is that what is required is for some would-be insurrectionist to 'start the ball rolling by dashing through the city streets with gun in hand'.[45] Narveson does point out that it would be better to have a prearranged signal for concerted action if advance planning were possible, but dashing-through-the-streets is his recommended course of action when no plan can be made. On its face Narveson's suggestion is remarkably implausible. One cannot help but wonder if *he* would begin dashing through the streets. We shall see, however, that there is more to Narveson's argument than meets the eye.

The first point to be established is that Narveson needs some assumptions which are not mentioned in the example as I have described it. Let me begin by suggesting an extra assumption of my own. Suppose we assume that all 1,000 people in the society are selfish and risk-averse, and that no one of them could be moved to take part in an insurrection by any action of any single other person. This assumption is perfectly consistent with our previous assumptions, including the assumption that it would be a good thing on balance if a successful insurrection occurred. But this assumption entails that nothing any single individual can do, not even dashing through the streets with a gun, will bring about an insurrection. With this new assumption, Barnes's conclusion is clearly correct. Any individual who attempted by himself to start an insurrection would be wasting his time, and his life. If no one does anything to start an insurrection, everyone satisfies AU.

Narveson's response must be that we cannot assume everyone is selfish and risk-averse. Instead, we should assume that everyone is motivated by a desire to satisfy AU. Narveson is not *obviously* right about this. It makes perfectly good sense to inquire into the consequences of universal satisfaction of AU under circumstances where we do *not* assume that people are motivated to try to satisfy AU.[46] AU itself makes no reference to any assumption about motivation. Still, Narveson has a point. If we are trying to evaluate AU as a moral theory, and if it makes a difference to the consequences of universal satisfaction of AU whether we assume that people are generally motivated to satisfy AU, then perhaps we should be willing to assume that they generally are so motivated.[47]

Even this assumption is not enough for Narveson's purposes, however. Suppose that everyone in the society is motivated to try to satisfy AU, but that everyone believes that everyone else is selfish and risk-averse and that a few others are stupid to boot. Now, I submit that if no one does anything to start an insurrection under these circumstances, everyone satisfies AU. Even if some individual did attempt to start an insurrection by, say, dashing through the streets, no one else would respond. Each viewer of the behaviour, motivated as he is by utilitarian considerations, would like to take part in a broadly based uprising. But each viewer of the behaviour, thinking that everyone else is selfish and risk-averse, is convinced that an insurrection is impossible. He would not be shaken in his belief that everyone else was selfish by the spectacle of the lone instigator. He could explain that away as a case of stupidity. If Narveson is to avoid the force of this argument, then in addition to assuming everyone is motivated to satisfy AU, he must also assume that everyone knows this about everyone else.[48]

Even the assumption of general knowledge of general act-utilitarian motivation is not enough for Narveson's purposes. To see why, suppose that everyone is motivated to satisfy AU, and that everyone knows that everyone is motivated to satisfy AU, but suppose also that everyone believes (erroneously) that the cost of even a successful insurrection would exceed the benefits. This situation is perfectly possible. General motivation to satisfy AU and general knowledge of that motivation do not guarantee that anyone knows what the true consequences of various patterns of behaviour would be. Under these circumstances, if no one does anything to start an insurrection, everyone satisfies AU. Even if one person went dashing through the streets, no one else would join him, since everyone believes that even a successful insurrection would be counterproductive. We see that if Narveson is to avoid Barnes's conclusion, he must assume, in addition to general act-utilitarian motivation and general knowledge of that general act-utilitarian motivation, general knowledge of the consequences of various possible patterns of behaviour.

We could go on. We could show, by arguments like those just presented, that in addition to assuming that everyone is motivated to satisfy AU, and that everyone knows that everyone is motivated to satisfy AU, and that everyone understands the consequences of various patterns of behaviour, Narveson must also assume that everyone knows that everyone understands the consequences of various patterns of behaviour, and that everyone knows that everyone knows that everyone is motivated to satisfy AU, and so on without limit. Actually, Narveson does not need to make all these assumptions about 'everyone'. But he does need to make them about a group large enough to carry out a successful insurrection, 500 people in our example.

At some point we must wonder whether Narveson is entitled to all the assumptions he needs. Defenders of AU have got into the habit of making these assumptions, often implicitly, because Hodgson flung out such an extreme challenge. Hodgson said that even with all these assumptions AU was self-defeating. Given Hodgson's claim, it is perfectly appropriate to make all these assumptions in trying to refute Hodgson. But it does not follow that it is appropriate to make them in defending AU against all comers, or against, say, Barnes.

For myself, I think Narveson assumes too much for us to regard him as simply defending AU. It is easy to let assumptions such as Narveson implicitly relies on slip by. It is easy to accept unquestioningly the notion that what we are interested in is not just the consequences of universal satisfaction of AU, but rather the consequences of universal satisfaction of AU in a world of act-utilitarians, or some such. But when the idea of a 'world of act-utilitarians' is spelled out to mean a world in which all of the infinite list of assumptions we have described are satisfied, then I think it becomes clear that that is not what we are interested in either.[49]

We are not done with Narveson. We have established that he needs all the assumptions we have mentioned, by showing that if any of these assumptions is omitted Barnes may be right after all. But we have not established that all these assumptions taken together are enough for Narveson to carry his point. Perhaps we should pause to make certain it is clear how we have shown Narveson needs these assumptions without showing they are sufficient to support his conclusion that universal satisfaction of AU guarantees best possible results. We started with a basic description of the example. We then pointed out that there was a new assumption which Barnes could add, which was perfectly consistent with the example as so far described, but under which it would be clear beyond doubt that Barnes's conclusion (that universal satisfaction of AU did *not* guarantee best possible results) was correct. We concluded that Narveson needed to add to his description of the example the opposite of the new assumption Barnes suggested.[50] After each addition of an assumption by Narveson, we repeated the process, with a new assumption by Barnes (still one consistent with the description of the example as supplemented by Narveson's answering assumptions to date), followed by a new assumption by Narveson. And so on. All we have at the end is a set of 'defensive' assumptions by Narveson. We have no argument that all of these assumptions taken together establish that universal satisfaction of AU guarantees that the insurrection will occur. In fact, they do not, as we shall now demonstrate.

Let us suppose that everyone in our hypothetical society (still excluding the dictator and his henchmen) is an act-utilitarian, that everyone knows this, that everyone understands the consequences of various patterns of behaviour, that everyone knows that everyone understands the consequences of various patterns of behaviour, and so on. Let us suppose further that no one does anything about starting an insurrection. We know that any individual's effort to start an insurrection would have bad consequences on balance unless it was enough to stimulate a total of 500 people to revolt. Therefore, when nobody does anything about starting an insurrection, everyone does the right thing, according to AU, unless one person's example would move 499 others to take up arms. It seems most implausible to suppose that one person's example would have that effect. It seems therefore that Barnes is still right.

Narveson might respond that one example would make it somewhat more likely that a *second* example would bring the rebels out in the required numbers. Indeed, this may be true. But to say that one example would make it somewhat more likely that a second example would have the desired effect is not to say that one example would make it the case that a second example *would* have the desired effect. Therefore we cannot argue that one example would so change the circumstances that exemplary behaviour by a *second* individual would be required by AU. We just don't know. Everything depends on facts about how people will respond to examples which cannot be deduced from the assumptions we have already conceded about everyone's utilitarian motivation and general knowledge.

Narveson plainly envisages that a single example will cause everyone to fall into line and exhibit the desired group behaviour. But there is no reason to think one example will cause everyone to fall into line. Indeed, the presence or absence of a single example seems likely to be insignificant. It seems no more plausible to suppose that everyone will fall into line if given one example than to suppose that everyone will fall into line automatically without the need for any example at all. In fact, I suspect Narveson thinks everyone *would* just fall into line without any example. I suspect he thinks it is obvious.[51] And there is the rub. What we are really dealing with is a new variant of the obviousness argument. The reference to the power of example is mere window-dressing. But the obviousness argument, as I have said before, is no argument at all.

I think we have now dealt with everything Narveson says.

Let me suggest a new argument which he might find congenial. The new argument runs as follows: 'Suppose that exactly 499 people attempted an insurrection. This attempt would fail, but it could be pushed over the edge to success by the participation of one more person. Therefore if 499 people participated, any non-participant would be required by AU to participate, thereby making up the full complement. We can put the matter briefly by saying that the 500th act of insurrection is required by AU. Furthermore, if the 500th act of insurrection is required by AU, we can be certain, in view of our assumptions about everyone's act-utilitarian motivation and general knowledge, that if 499 persons revolt, the 500th will appear. But now suppose that 498 persons arise. We know that if a 499th person arose, the 500th would arise also, and the insurrection would succeed. Therefore the 499th act of insurrection is required by AU. But then given all our assumptions we can be certain that if 498 persons revolt, the 499th person will appear. His appearance will produce the 500th, and the insurrection will succeed. Now if we suppose that 497 persons arise, we can show that the 498th act of insurrection is required by AU. And so on. By this process we can obviously argue right back to the proposition that the first act of insurrection is required by AU. But if the first act of insurrection is required by AU, then it is *not* true that if no one does anything AU is universally satisfied. QED.'

The main point to notice about this argument is that it depends on an assumption over and above the assumptions we have already shown that Narveson needs. The latest argument depends on the assumption that each individual will respond in the manner required by AU to other individuals' actual behaviour. Thus, it is assumed that if 499 acts of insurrection occur, the 500th will occur as well, because it will be required by AU. But at this stage in the argument, the obligatoriness of the 500th act depends on the occurrence of the first 499. So what is being assumed is that the agent of the 500th act will do whatever is required by AU given the actual behaviour of the other 499 agents. A similar assumption is relied on with regard to the agent of the 499th act, since his participation will be required by AU if 498 others engage in acts of insurrection. And so on. Every agent is assumed to be certain to do the AU thing given the behaviour of everyone else.

This assumption, that everyone will do the AU thing given the behaviour of everyone else is a new assumption. We have allowed Narveson for purposes of argument the assumptions that everyone is motivated to satisfy AU, that everyone knows everyone is motivated to satisfy AU, that everyone understands the consequences of various patterns of behaviour, that everyone knows everyone understands the consequences of various patterns of behaviour, and so on. But these assumptions do not entail that any individual will know how other individuals behave. Therefore these assumptions do not entail that any individual will actually satisfy AU, given the way others behave.

It may seem that I have erred at the point in the preceding paragraph where I said 'these assumptions do not entail that any individual will know how other individuals behave'. Sometimes, of course, knowing that some individual is motivated to follow AU and understands the consequences of various patterns of behaviour *is* enough to allow us to deduce how he will behave. That will be so when AU requires a particular act from him regardless of how anyone else behaves.[52] But if what AU requires of him depends on how others behave, then knowing that he is well motivated and that he understands the consequences of various patterns of behaviour is not enough to deduce what he will do without some assumption about what others do, and about his knowledge of what others do.[53]

We see that the latest version of the snowball argument depends on the new assumption that every agent will satisfy AU given the way everyone else behaves. In effect, this version assumes that everyone is what we have referred to previously as a 'perfect act-utilitarian'. We have already mentioned two considerations which weigh against assuming that everyone is a perfect act-utilitarian. The first consideration was just that such creatures do not exist, even in the ideal world AU most naturally implies. The second consideration was that, intuitively, assuming a multiplicity of perfect act-utilitarians seems to amount to assuming that different agents can, while acting without communication, cause each others' behaviour. This second consideration is illustrated in an interesting way by the latest version of the snowball argument. The argument purports to provide an explanation why each of 500 agents is required by AU to take part in an insurrection. The explanation given depends logically on the possibility of identifying one of the agents as doing the 500th act, another as doing the 499th and so on. In the real world, however, if the insurrection takes place, there will be no question of numbering the acts in this way. Many or all of the acts will be simultaneous. The argument under consideration conceals the assumption of reciprocal causation (intuitively speaking) among these 500 acts by inventing an ordering of the acts which has no basis at all outside the argument.[54]

If we are prepared to countenance the existence of a multiplicity of perfect act-utilitarians, then we can reformulate the snowball argument in a way which brings out with new clarity just what it involves. For purposes of the argument I am about to state, I shall grant the snowball theorist three assumptions: (1) All agents are perfect act-utilitarians. (2) Any pattern of behaviour in which exactly 500 agents join to topple the dictator is *a* pattern of universal satisfaction of AU. (3) No other pattern of behaviour is a pattern of universal satisfaction of AU, except possibly the pattern of universal quietism, in which no one does anything towards starting an insurrection.

The final version of the snowball argument runs as follows: 'If everyone is a perfect act-utilitarian, then it is certain that some pattern of universal satisfaction of AU will be achieved. Now, suppose that no one does anything towards starting an insurrection, and consider an arbitrarily chosen agent, whom we shall call Spartacus. If Spartacus did an act of insurrection, he would bring it about that the pattern of behaviour involving universal quietism was not achieved. Since some pattern of universal satisfaction of AU must be achieved, one of the patterns involving a successful insurrection would have to occur. But that means that if no one does anything, then Spartacus, by acting, could guarantee the occurrence of a successful insurrection. If no one does anything, Spartacus violates AU. Therefore, the pattern of universal quietism is not a pattern of universal satisfaction of AU. The only patterns of universal satisfaction of AU are patterns involving an insurrection. QED.'

It would be possible to object to certain features of this argument, but I should say that once we have conceded the possibility of a multiplicity of perfect act-utilitarians, we can fairly be taken to have waived all the objections. I shall therefore admit that this argument is good, as an argument. Still, putting the snowball argument into this form makes it clear just what extraordinary causal or quasi-causal assumptions are involved. It is assumed that an act of insurrection by any arbitrarily chosen individual will determine the acts of 499 others. No explanation of this remarkable phenomenon is offered beyond the logic of the assumption that the agents involved are perfect act-utilitarians. I think this latest version is what the snowball argument finally comes to, and I find it hard to believe that anyone would wish to defend AU on this ground. If someone does, then I invite the reader to consider whether what is offered counts as a defence of AU at all.

There has been a good deal of writing about act-utilitarianism in recent years, by critics and by defenders. It seems to me that each side has got hold of an important part of the truth. The critics believe, correctly, that universal satisfaction of AU does not guarantee the production of the best results possible from group behaviour. The defenders believe, correctly, that universal satisfaction of AU is always consistent with the production of best possible results. (I have not yet proved this, but I shall in Chapters 3 and 4.) Unfortunately, the critics seem to think their arguments show that universal satisfaction of AU sometimes makes the achievement of best overall results impossible (which is false). The defenders seem to think their arguments show that universal satisfaction of AU guarantees best possible results (which is also false).

Each side has overestimated the force of its own arguments because hardly anyone has noticed the difference between the question whether universal satisfaction of AU *guarantees* the achievement of best possible results and the question whether universal satisfaction of AU is always *consistent* with the achievement of best possible results. I could write an essay the length of the present one documenting the claim that inattention to this distinction has been the source of immense confusion. I shall forbear. I hope I have said enough so that the reader could document the claim for himself if he were inclined to go through the literature with that in mind.

A PARTIAL DEFENCE OF ACT-UTILITARIANISM

In this chapter and the next I shall establish that universal satisfaction of AU, even if it does not guarantee best possible consequences, is not in any case inconsistent with the production of best possible consequences. I shall establish, in other words, the following claim: that for any group of agents in any situation, any pattern of behaviour by that group which produces the best consequences possible is a pattern in which the members of the group all satisfy AU. I shall call this claim the 'consistency claim', since what it says is that in any situation, satisfaction of AU by all the members of any group of agents is consistent with the production by that group of the best consequences possible. It may seem odd to bother with this claim, since we have already decided that AU is not a completely adequate consequentialist theory. By proving this claim we will establish a lemma which constitutes most of the proof that adaptability entails PropAU. (The proof is completed in Chapter 7.) Since we shall need to rely on the claim eventually, it seems best to prove it now, collecting the material on AU in contiguous chapters.

The direct argument for the consistency claim is straightforward. Consider a group of agents who are behaving in such a way as to produce the best consequences possible given the state of the physical world, the behaviour of agents outside the group whose behaviour members of the group are not able to influence, and the dispositions to behave of agents outside the group whose behaviour members of the group are able to influence. Suppose that some member of the group is not satisfying AU . Call that member Smith. To say Smith is not satisfying AU is to say there is something he could do which would have better consequences in the circumstances than what he is doing. In other words, by altering only his behaviour (and whatever else the change in his behaviour would cause to change), we could improve the overall consequences produced. But that means that from the point of view of the group, the consequences of their behaviour as a group could be improved by altering Smith's behaviour in the same way. That contradicts our original assumption. We conclude that a group which is producing the best consequences possible cannot include any agent who is not satisfying AU. Any best pattern of behaviour for any group is always a pattern of 'universal' satisfaction of AU by the group's members.

One doubt about the argument just given might be suggested by the reference to changing Smith's behaviour 'and whatever else the change in his behavior would cause to change'. Might not changing his behaviour cause a change in the behaviour of some other member of the group? It might, but that possibility does not affect the argument. The change in the other agent's behaviour was taken into account in deciding that changing Smith's behaviour would improve the consequences. The claim is not that if Smith is not satisfying AU then changing his behaviour will produce a better pattern for the group which differs from the old one only with respect to his behaviour. The claim is merely that changing his behaviour will produce a better pattern.

There are three further points to be made about this argument. First, note that the argument depends on the marginal consequences approach to AU. It is only because changing Smith's behaviour is assumed to make an improvement at the margin that we can assert that changing his behaviour improves the consequences produced by the group. If we were using the contributory consequences approach, then the 'improvement' in Smith's behaviour might come entirely at the expense of the good consequences previously attributed to the other members of the group. It is not the case that any best pattern of behaviour for the group must be one in which AU is universally satisfied under the contributory consequences interpretation. (An example is discussed in the notes.[1])

Second, the argument shows that there always exists at least one pattern in which AU is universally satisfied, at least if there always exists at least one (not necessarily unique) best pattern of behaviour for the group. It is not obvious that there always exists at least one best pattern of behaviour for the group, and I shall not discuss what sort of assumptions we would have to make to prove it.[2] I think the existence of at least one best pattern of behaviour is generally assumed by consequentialists. If that is the case, then our argument at least shows that AU could not be successfully attacked by a proponent of some other consequentialist theory on the ground that the interdependence of all the parties' behaviour and obligations makes universal satisfaction of AU impossible in some cases. I am not aware that this argument has ever been advanced against AU, but it would be a telling argument if it were available, and I am not aware that its unavailability has been previously demonstrated.[3]

Third, an argument precisely parallel to the one under consideration could be used to establish a slightly more general conclusion, which we will require in later chapters. That conclusion is: if we consider any group of agents who are behaving in such a way as to produce the best possible consequences, then any subgroup of that group must also be producing best possible consequences (taking as given all the circumstances we took as given from the point of view of the original group *and in addition* the behaviour or causally relevant dispositions to behave of the members of the group who are not members of the subgroup). I shall not state the argument for this conclusion. We have only to replace Smith in the original argument with the subgroup, and the conclusion falls out.

The affirmative case for the consistency claim is complete. In the remainder of this chapter I shall consider a common argument against the consistency claim, which I shall call the 'Prisoners' Dilemma' argument. Chapter 4 deals with some arguments of D. H. Hodgson which are also arguments against the consistency claim, in effect.

The Prisoners' Dilemma argument can be made, and has been made, in a great variety of contexts. For purposes of illustration, I shall consider the problem of walking on the grass. The argument goes as follows: Suppose there is a patch of grass which no one walks on and which constitutes a significant aesthetic amenity. No single act of walking across this grass would cause any damage. Every agent could produce some good consequences (usually a saving of time or energy) by walking across the grass. (Agents who have no reason at all to cross the grass we simply exclude from the class of agents under discussion.) In these circumstances, AU requires each agent to walk across the grass. But if everyone walked across the grass, the grass would be so damaged that the aesthetic amenity would be destroyed. This loss, it is assumed, would outweigh the gain from everyone's crossing the grass. Therefore, in this case everyone's doing what AU requires would be inconsistent with the production of best possible results.

Note that the argument just stated is intended to justify the conclusion that universal *satisfaction* of AU must produce bad results. The grass-walking situation is also frequently cited as showing that everyone's *trying* to follow AU would produce bad results. I think that even the argument that everyone's trying to follow AU would produce bad results is mistaken, resting on a misunderstanding of the subjective obligations AU gives rise to,[4] but that is not presently relevant. It is clear that the Prisoners' Dilemma argument is sometimes offered to demonstrate the bad consequences of everyone's satisfying AU. That is the matter we are now dealing with.

The Prisoners' Dilemma argument involves two fallacies, which are related but distinct. The first fallacy intrudes in the following manner. Early in the argument it is established that if no one walks on the grass, then AU requires each individual to walk on the grass. Later in the argument, the state-description 'everyone's walking on the grass' is equated with the state-description 'everyone's doing what AU requires'. Presumably the equivalence of these descriptions is supposed to follow from the fact that when no one crosses the grass each agent is required to do so by AU. But what is supposed to follow does not. What AU requires of any individual depends on what other individuals are doing. To say that AU requires Jones to walk on the grass if no one else is walking does not entail that AU requires Jones to walk on the grass even though everyone else is walking. The fact that AU *would* require any individual to cross the grass *if* no one else were doing so tells us nothing at all about whether anyone would be satisfying AU if he walked across the grass along with everyone else. In other words: if AU requires each individual to walk on the grass so long as no one else does so, then the state of affairs referred to by 'everyone's walking on the grass' is the same as the state of affairs referred to by 'everyone's doing what AU would require of him if no one else were walking on the grass'. But the latter phrase does not necessarily refer to a state of affairs in which everyone is doing what AU requires. That is the first fallacy.

The second fallacy, which tends in the argument given to mask the presence of the first, consists essentially in ignoring the indeterminacy of AU. Even if it were the case that when everyone crossed the grass everyone would be satisfying AU, it would not follow that the state-descriptions 'everyone's crossing the grass' and 'everyone's satisfying AU' were equivalent. The reason is that while 'everyone's crossing the grass' refers uniquely to one pattern of behaviour, 'everyone's satisfying AU' may not, just because AU may be indeterminate in this case. Therefore, even if it is true that when everyone crosses the grass, everyone satisfies AU, it does not follow that everyone's satisfying AU entails everyone's crossing the grass and the inferior consequences of that pattern of behaviour. That, accounts for the second fallacy.

At the beginning of the preceding paragraph I suggested that the presence of the second fallacy tended to mask the presence of the first. What I had in mind is the following. Although we cannot infer from the assumptions of the argument as given that everyone satisfies AU if everyone crosses the grass (the attempt to infer that involves the first fallacy), it is none the less highly realistic to suppose that if everyone crosses the grass then everyone satisfies AU. The reason is just that we may suppose the potential for damage to the grass is exhausted by a number of crossings smaller than the number which occur if everyone crosses; and if that is so, then whenever everyone but Jones is crossing, AU requires Jones to cross as well. So on this supposition, it is the case that when everyone crosses, everyone satisfies AU. Still, we cannot infer that everyone's satisfying AU necessarily produces bad consequences, without committing the second fallacy. As a matter of fact, we know that whatever the best pattern of behaviour is, it too involves everyone's satisfying AU. That is what we proved earlier in the chapter.

We have not made nearly enough assumptions so that we can say just what the best pattern of behaviour is. We know that the best pattern is *neither* the pattern in which everyone crosses, *nor* the pattern in which no one crosses, since the first of these is (by hypothesis) inferior to the second, and the second is (by hypothesis) inferior to any pattern in which exactly one person crosses. The best pattern will therefore require some people to cross and others not to. Roughly, we can say that however many people are required to cross in the best pattern, the particular people who are required to cross in the best pattern will be those who gain (or confer on others) the greatest benefit from crossing; and we can say that the total number of people required to cross will be chosen so as to maximize the difference between the total gain in convenience from crossing and the total loss from damage to the grass. More we cannot say, except to note that there is likely to be no unique best pattern at all, but rather a number of best patterns.

The proponent of the Prisoners' Dilemma argument might object that we have misconstrued one of his assumptions. He might say he did not intend to assume merely that an individual act of grass-crossing would have no bad effect when everyone else stayed off the grass. He intended to assume that an individual crossing never has any bad effect, regardless of how many other people cross. From this it follows that AU unequivocally requires each agent to cross, regardless of what others are doing. From this it follows that there is a unique pattern in which AU is universally satisfied, and that is the undesirable pattern in which everyone crosses the grass.

The proponent of this objection, however, is committed to logically inconsistent assumptions. On the one hand, he is committed to the assumption that a single crossing never makes a difference to the state of the grass. From this it follows that there is no difference (as far as the state of the grass is concerned) between the consequences of no one's crossing and one person's crossing. It also follows that there is no difference (as to the grass) between the consequences of one person's crossing and two persons' crossing; or between the consequences of two persons' crossing and three persons' crossing; and so on. Since the relation of 'there being no difference between the consequences of . . .' is transitive, we can conclude that there is no difference (as far as the grass is concerned) between the consequences of no one's crossing and the consequences of everyone's crossing. But this is inconsistent with another premiss of the argument, the premiss that the overall consequences of everyone's crossing are much worse than the overall consequences of everyone's walking around.

One cannot consistently hold both that an individual crossing never makes a difference under any circumstances and that a large number of crossings do make a difference. (This does not mean the marginal consequences approach to AU is inconsistent. The marginalist who says no individual makes a difference when eighty agents participate to produce a benefit achievable by sixty is saying nothing about what difference an individual would make under other circumstances.) If this seems startling, I think it is because the assertion that an individual crossing never makes a difference is usually intended to mean something weaker.

Sometimes this claim means that if any agent in the real world were setting out to discover the overall best pattern of behaviour, it would not be worth the trouble for him to try to specify the best pattern to within an error as small as one crossing. This may well be true, but it is irrelevant to the question of what pattern(s) of grass-crossing actually constitute universal satisfaction of AU.

Sometimes the assertion that an individual crossing never makes a difference seems to mean that an individual crossing never makes any *perceptible* difference. This suggestion does pose a problem for the defender of AU. On the one hand, the claim that no single crossing ever makes a perceptible difference sounds very plausible. On the other hand, it seems that only perceptible differences can affect obligations, given the value schemes that utilitarians are wont to adopt. Still, the claim of 'no perceptible difference' creates a problem for the proponent of the Prisoners' Dilemma argument as well. The proponent of that argument is still committed to the premise that a large number of crossings make a significant difference. It seems to me he ought still to be embarrassed by the question how a series of changes (from no one's crossing to one person's crossing, and from one person's crossing to two persons' crossing, and so on), no one of which makes any difference that affects obligations, together make a difference that does affect obligations. If the relation of 'there being no difference that affects obligations between the consequences of . . .' is transitive, then there is the same logical inconsistency as before. And this relation should be transitive, it seems.

I am tempted to leave the matter there. The problem of how imperceptible differences add up to perceptible differences is a certified stumper. The wisest course may be to argue that the problem is my opponent's, not mine, and to move on. But I will make a further suggestion. It seems to me that to say a single crossing of the grass never makes a perceptible difference must mean no more than that a single crossing never makes a difference that observers can reliably recognize. But as we move in a thought-experiment from the state where no one crosses the grass to the state where everyone crosses, changing the acts one by one, there must be some point at which changing a single act either produces a recognizable change in the grass or else at least alters the objective probability distribution of the values of perception-reactions of viewers of the grass. (By a 'perception-reaction' I mean a perception plus the associated aesthetic pleasure or displeasure.) If this were not so, then the whole string of changes together could make no difference. If this is so, then the crossing which makes a difference in the way just mentioned makes a difference which we can argue is relevant to AU, since it affects the objective expected value of the state of the world.[5]

If the proponent of the Prisoners' Dilemma argument now concedes that there must be some circumstances under which an individual crossing would make a relevant difference to the grass, he might still retreat to the claim that an individual crossing never makes enough difference to outweigh the good consequences achieved by the crossing. This would suffice for his purposes. However, the same thought-experiment we have already described can be used to show that there must be at least one point along the way from general avoidance to general crossing at which the marginal damage to the grass (or more precisely the marginal loss in the expected value from people's viewing the grass) does outweigh the marginal gain from crossing it. If this were not so, the total damage could not outweigh the total gain. Because it is so, the Prisoners' Dilemma argument collapses.

The proponent of the Prisoners' Dilemma argument has been misled by a specious analogy. Let us see why the grass case does not and cannot involve a genuine prisoner's dilemma. A genuine prisoner's dilemma involves parties who have different maximands. It is a situation in which each party has a strategy (called a 'dominant strategy') which produces at least as good results from his point of view as any other strategy regardless of what the other party does, and in which both parties' choosing their dominant strategies produces results which are inferior from both parties' points of view to the results achievable by some other pattern of choice.[6] (An n-person prisoner's dilemma may be defined analogously.) Such a situation is impossible if the parties have the same maximand, as in effect they do in a context where the question is what AU requires of them, since they are both required by AU to maximize the value of the same overall consequences, whatever the scheme for valuing consequences may be.

We can show the impossibility of what we might call the 'act-utilitarian prisoner's dilemma' by a simple *reductio*. Suppose we are confronted with what purports to be such a situation, involving any number of agents. Each party is supposed to have a dominant act-utilitarian strategy (a choice which satisfies AU regardless of others' behaviour), and the pattern in which everyone chooses his dominant strategy is supposed to have less good consequences than some second pattern of choice. Starting (in a thought-experiment) from the second pattern, we consider the agents in succession, changing the behaviour of each agent who is not choosing his dominant strategy so that he does choose his dominant strategy. Each such change must either leave the overall consequences unchanged or improve them. Eventually, we arrive at the pattern in which everyone chooses his dominant strategy, and the overall consequences must be at least as good as the consequences of the pattern from which we started. This is a contradiction. We conclude that what we have called an 'act-utilitarian prisoner's dilemma' cannot exist.[7]

In the course of this chapter I have relied on a number of thought-experiments and on claims about the results of those experiments. In particular, I have relied on the claims (1) that if all the marginal changes in the value of the consequences are zero, then the total change must be zero, (2) that if the consequences are divisible into 'gains' and 'losses', and if the total loss exceeds the total gain, then at some point the marginal loss must exceed the marginal gain, and (3) that if all the marginal increments are non-negative, then the total change must be non-negative as well. These claims are all entailed by a general claim that in one of these thought-experiments, the sum of the marginal changes in the value of the consequences as we move step by step from one pattern of behaviour to another must equal the total difference between the values of the consequences of the two patterns. I shall conclude the chapter by proving this general claim, both because proving it may help settle any doubts about the weaker claims I have used and because understanding the basis for all these claims is important to understanding consequentialism.

Consider a two-person grass case involving Charlotte and Emily:

		Charlotte	
		Not-Cross	Cross
	Not-Cross	10	11
Emily			
	Cross	11	8

This array represents a situation in which there is a plot of grass worth 10 units in its pristine state. A single crossing does three units worth of damage to the grass. Two crossings destroy the value of the grass entirely. The independent benefit achievable by any single crossing is 4 units.[8]

In this example, the consequences of general avoidance of

the grass are valued at +10 units. If we alter Charlotte's act, the consequences of the resulting pattern of behaviour are valued at +11, and the incremental change is +1 unit (analysable, if we are interested, into 3 units loss from damage to the grass and 4 units gain from Charlotte's crossing). If, *starting from the pattern produced by altering Charlotte's act,* we now alter Emily's act, the consequences of the resulting pattern of behaviour are valued at +8 and the incremental change is −3 (analysable as 7 units loss from further damage to the grass and 4 units gain from Emily's crossing). The sum of the incremental changes is (+1) + (−3), or (−2) units. This is indeed equal to the total change produced by moving from the original pattern of general avoidance of the grass to the new pattern of general crossing.

We see that the claim that the incremental changes add up to the total change is not a metaphysical claim. It is a claim about arithmetic. It is the claim that for any real numbers a, b, and c, $(b-a) + (c-b) = (c-a)$, which is obviously true. (In our example, $a = 10$, $b = 11$, and $c = 8$.) Nothing depends on either the symmetry or the simplicity of the example. Because our example is symmetric, we would get the same succession of marginal changes in the value of the consequences if we moved from the pattern of general avoidance to the pattern of general crossing by the other path (that is, by changing Emily's act and then Charlotte's). But the marginal differences would add up to the total difference even if the example were asymmetric and the entry in the lower-left corner were 12 or 9 (or anything else) instead of 11.

The same mode of proof would establish the claim for any number of agents with any number of acts open to them. If we change the acts of the agents one by one, as necessary, to get from one pattern of behaviour of the group to another pattern, the simplest laws of arithmetic guarantee that the marginal differences along any possible path of changes will add up to the total change. (Note again that this claim is perfectly compatible with the marginal consequences approach to AU. The marginalist who says that no individual agent makes a difference when eighty agents participate to produce a benefit achievable by sixty is saying that no agent makes a difference *at the margin at which his act occurs.* In our thought-experiments, we alter one act at a time in succession, and the margin at which the marginal consequences of each successive alteration are evaluated changes as we go along.) The possibility of causal connections among the agents' acts complicates matters slightly, but it does not affect the basic claim, as I show in a note.[9]

There is, of course, a metaphysical and moral assumption underlying the claim that the marginal changes always add up to the total change, even if the basic argument turns on the truths of arithmetic. The metaphysical and moral assumption is that we can associate with each pattern of behaviour of the group a real number representing either the actual value of the state of the world produced by that pattern of behaviour or the objective expected value of the state of the world produced by that pattern of behaviour (depending on how we resolve an issue about the interpretation of AU already noted). That is a large assumption. On the other hand, it is an assumption common to almost all consequentialist thinking. The time may come when we cannot improve our understanding of consequentialism without improving consequentialists' metaphysics; but I think that time has not yet arrived.[10]

HODGSON, EXPECTATIONS, AND ACT-UTILITARIAN PUNISHMENT

D. H. Hodgson has argued that truth-telling, promising, and punishment are useful institutions which cannot be justified consistently with AU. In effect, Hodgson denies the consistency claim of Chapter 3. It is tempting to say that by proving the consistency claim in Chapter 3, I have already shown Hodgson wrong. But that would be much too short a way with an important problem. Hodgson's arguments all involve the idea that act-utilitarians cannot produce certain kinds of *expectations,* and Hodgson is not alone in thinking that act-utilitarians face special difficulties in this area.[1] Although I think the proof in Chapter 3 is quite general, it does not address the problem of expectations directly. It will be worth our while to consider what Hodgson has to say.

I shall focus on the problem of punishment (although I shall consider in that context some arguments Hodgson raises in connection with analogous problems involving threats). Hodgson's arguments about punishment have received much less attention than his arguments about promising and truth-telling. And yet, the problem of punishment is more fundamental. Most of the responses to Hodgson have concentrated on explaining how promising and truth-telling may promote co-ordination between act-utilitarians. But this is the easiest of the problems Hodgson raises for the defender of AU, precisely because all the parties are assumed to have a common goal and to be disposed to co-ordinate if they can manage it. The harder issues are whether act-utilitarians can convince distrustful adherents of 'commonsense morality' that they (the act-utilitarians) can be counted on to keep faith; and whether act-utilitarians can convince criminals who are outside any moral community that they (the criminals) will be punished for wrongdoing. Solving the problem of co-ordination between act-utilitarians does not obviously solve these other problems. But if it were clear that act-utilitarians could establish an institution of punishment, we would have no doubt that they could similarly establish their credibility with commonsense moralists and between themselves.

Let me emphasize that I shall be concerned only to refute Hodgson. My goal is to show that it is *possible* for act-utilitarians to maintain an institution of punishment, not to show that they will necessarily do so. I shall note at the end of the chapter that AU is almost certainly indeterminate with respect to the punishment problem. The distinction between what AU permits and what it requires is as important here as it was in the last two chapters.

Let me also note that I shall rely on the consistency claim of Chapter 3 *to this extent*: With regard to any category of behaviour justified by its effect on expectations, such as punishment, I shall take it as established by Chapter 3 that in any optimal pattern of expectation-producing behaviour, it must be the case that each individual act has best consequences (including its consequences regarding expectations) at the margin. In other words, I shall assume that the argument 'Act-utilitarians cannot punish because no single act of punishment could have enough influence on expectations to outweigh the suffering imposed' has been adequately dealt with in Chapter 3. There is nothing in this argument that depends on expectations' being special.

The issue, then, is not whether any individual act can have *enough* influence on expectations to justify it. The issue is whether Hodgson shows that act-utilitarians are incapable *in principle* of influencing expectations by their behaviour.

The reader may have an obscure sense of dissatisfaction at this point. He may have a feeling that it is not just *behaviour* that influences expectations but also what is known about how agents *choose* their behaviour. He may have a feeling that this creates a difficulty for act-utilitarians. And he may have a feeling that whatever the difficulty is, it falls between the argument I have rejected as being dealt with by Chapter 3 and the claim that act-utilitarians are incapable in principle of influencing expectations. For the benefit of any reader who has these feelings, I note that in the course of answering

Hodgson I shall show that it is not a special source of difficulty for act-utilitarians to have their views known.

Turning to the matter of punishment, it might seem that the need for punishment could not possibly pose a problem for the consistency claim because the consistency claim concerns universal satisfaction of AU, and if AU were universally satisfied, then arguably no one would ever do any act which it would be desirable to punish. But the consistency claim is broader than this remark suggests. The consistency claim says that for *any group* of agents in any situation, any pattern of behaviour *by that group* which produces best consequences is one in which every member of the group satisfies AU.[2] Therefore we cannot assume there are no agents in the world who will engage in behaviour that ought to be punished. We need to show that if there are criminals, terrorists, or whatever, the remaining agents can punish them consistently with AU, at least if a general practice of punishment is assumed to be a good thing.

Let us be clear about the precise problem to be discussed. We shall ignore all possible utilitarian reasons for punishment except 'deterrence'. We shall ignore the fact that some punishment might be justified on utilitarian grounds because of the possibility of reforming the criminal, or because of the need to prevent repeated offences by incarcerating an offender, or because there is utility in satisfying public desires for vengeance, and so on. We shall also ignore the fact that some degree of deterrence of potential offenders would be secured by the known likelihood of punishment to the extent it would be justified on these other grounds. We are concerned with the problem of whether an act-utilitarian legal system could include an institution of punishment justified solely by the argument that a credible threat of punishment deters offences and that punishment in individual cases is justified to make the threat of punishment credible. In other words, the question is whether an act-utilitarian legal system can justify punishment because of the effect of individual instances of punishment on potential offenders' expectations of punishment in later instances. The question is of interest whether or not we think deterrence is a significant justification for punishment in the real world. The problem of punishment, in the form in which we discuss it, is representative of a family of real-world problems.

We have spoken in the previous paragraph of an 'act-utilitarian legal system'. Actually, we shall discuss the question of whether an act-utilitarian dictator, whom we shall call Rex, could punish, consistently with his act-utilitarian views. This saves worrying about the nature of legal justification, and so on. The problem of achieving co-ordination among the individual judges who direct the application of punishment in most actual legal systems may be greater than the problem of achieving co-ordination among time-slices of Rex, but we are concerned only with the consistency claim. If an act-utilitarian Rex could punish consistently with AU, then the group of judges could also punish consistently with AU to just the extent Rex could.

There is one way in which it might be thought Rex would have an advantage over the group of judges—it might seem that Rex would have an easier time keeping his own counsel and thus dissimulating his act-utilitarian views if that were necessary. Judges would have to communicate among themselves and are also called upon for public justification of their behaviour, so it might be thought that attempts to dissimulate on their part would be less effective and more costly. In fact, we shall discuss the question of whether a Rex who is *known* to be an act-utilitarian can punish, and we shall see that he can, at least if the circumstances are such that punishment can have good consequences. There is no need for an act-utilitarian dictator or judge to try to deceive potential offenders about his views. We shall refer to an act-utilitarian whose views are generally known as a 'known act-utilitarian'.

Hodgson's argument that the known act-utilitarian dictator Rex cannot usefully make threats of punishment proceeds by considering two cases. In the first case, there are a finite number of possible occasions for potential offenders to offend. In the second case, there are an infinite number of possible occasions. In both cases it is assumed that all parties, Rex as well as all potential offenders, are rational; that each party knows the others are rational; that all know whatever facts are assumed about the number of occasions for punishment; and that potential offenders know that Rex is an act-utilitarian who will apply his moral views accurately on all occasions.

First, we consider the finite case. Suppose there are exactly n possible occasions for potential offenders to offend. These occasions we will refer to as $O_1 \ldots O_n$. Now any potential offender can reason as follows: 'When O_n finally arrives, if the offence occurs, it will not have best consequences for Rex to punish the offender. Punishment has some bad consequences by definition, and punishment for an offence at O_n could not have any good consequences as a deterrent, since there would not be any potential offences left to deter. Therefore, Rex will not punish an offence at O_n. I know this, and he knows this, and every other potential offender who might offend at any O_i knows this. Now it occurs to me that when O_{n-1} arrives, if the offence occurs, it will not have best consequences for Rex to punish the offender. Punishment has bad consequences, and therefore punishment for an offence at O_{n-1} could be justified only if it would operate as a deterrent, that is, only if it would tend to make potential offenders expect to be punished for a later offence. But there is only one possible occasion for a later offence, namely O_n, and we have already decided that everybody knows that punishment will not follow an offence at O_n. Therefore punishment at O_{n-1} could not have any deterrent effect. Therefore Rex will not punish any offence at O_{n-1}. By this process, I can obviously work right back to the conclusion that Rex won't punish an offence any time. So I can do as I please.' In sum, the known act-utilitarian dictator who confronts rational potential offenders and a finite number of possible occasions for offences cannot deter offences by the threat of punishment.[3]

Hodgson observes that *if* Rex somehow managed to punish an offender at O_j—in a fit of forgetfulness perhaps—this might arouse expectations of future punishment, and might therefore have better consequences than not punishing the offender at O_j. But, he says, since we have shown that AU does not allow punishment at any time (if we retain our assumptions about knowledge and rationality), the punishment at O_j could arouse expectations of later punishment, and have best consequences, only by demonstrating that Rex did not in fact always behave as an act-utilitarian.[4] This is a very paradoxical assertion on Hodgson's part--that an act which has best consequences in the circumstances might be evidence that the agent was not behaving as an act-utilitarian. Hodgson does not seem much troubled by this paradox. There is no question that sometimes one just has to learn to live with apparently paradoxical consequences of valid arguments; but I shall suggest further on that this particular paradox can be dissolved once the real nature of Hodgson's argument is understood.

Obviously, the argument just given for the finite case will not work if there are an infinite number of possible occasions for offence, which we refer to as O_1, O_2 . . . I do not find Hodgson's discussion of the infinite case as clear as his discussion of the finite case, but I believe the following argument captures the core of what he has to say about the infinite case.[5]

The argument is a *reductio*. We shall assume that AU requires Rex to punish offenders at O_1, O_2 . . . and we shall demonstrate that this assumption leads to a contradiction. Now if (as we assume) Rex should punish offenders at O_1 and O_2 and . . . it follows that he should punish offenders at O_2 and O_3 and . . . Since Rex is known by all potential offenders to be an act-utilitarian, all potential offenders will know that he should and will punish offenders at O_2 and O_3 and . . . But since all potential offenders know that Rex should and will punish offences at O_2 and O_3 and . . . Rex's punishing an offender at O_1 cannot have any beneficial consequences by arousing expectations of punishment. The expectations are there in any case. Therefore Rex should not punish an offender at O_1. Since we started with the assumption that Rex should punish offenders at O_1 and O_2 and . . . and we have deduced the conclusion that Rex should not punish an offender at O_1, we have got a contradiction, and our starting assumption must have been false. Therefore it is not the case that an act-utilitarian dictator confronted with rational potential offenders and an infinite number of possible occasions for offending should punish on all occasions. Obviously, the same argument could be used to show that the assumption

Rex should punish on *any* specified set of occasions is self-contradictory, and thus to show that Rex should not punish at all.

Before we attempt to identify the central difficulty of these arguments, we note that the argument in the infinite case depends on an inference of doubtful validity. That is the inference from 'AU requires Rex to punish at $O_1, O_2 \ldots$' to 'AU requires Rex to punish at $O_2, O_3 \ldots$'. The problem with the inference would be clearer if we were talking about different judges confronted with the problem of whether to punish at O_1 and O_2 and $\ldots$ Since what AU requires of each judge may depend on what the others do, we cannot simply detach one piece (O_1) of the overall pattern. Indeed, it is doubtful that AU strictly speaking 'requires' any overall pattern of behaviour at the successive opportunities for punishment. AU speaks to the opportunities one at a time. But we could not even infer from 'AU is universally satisfied if judges punish at $O_1, O_2 \ldots$' that 'AU is satisfied at $O_2, O_3 \ldots$ if judges punish on those occasions'. What happens at O_1 may be crucial to what AU requires on later occasions. The same problem may arise with Rex, as we have noted in Chapter 2 in connection with Hoerster's answer to Hodgson on promising.[6] If AU is regarded as addressed to separate time-slices of Rex, then we cannot drop off any part of the pattern 'required' of all the time-slices and be certain that the remaining part of the pattern represents what AU 'requires' on the occasions left. Although reliance on the inference we have just oppugned is a genuine weakness of the argument concerning the infinite case,[7] it is not the gravest weakness. We shall concede this inference and move on to the central problem.

The most important thing to note about Hodgson's arguments, in both the finite and the infinite case, is that they depend on an unstated assumption that how Rex behaves has no effect at all on how he is expected to behave. In the finite case, this assumption is required at the point(s) where it is decided that punishment at O_{i-1} (for any i) could not have any good consequences because everyone already knows that punishment will not be justified and therefore will not occur at O_i. It is crucial here that the expectation about what will happen at O_i is taken to be completely unaffected by what happens at O_{i-1}. If it were admitted that punishment at O_{i-1} might raise some expectation of punishment at O_i, then the whole argument would collapse. But that possibility is not admitted, and on that ground the argument goes through. The same is true of the argument in the infinite case. It is assumed that punishment at O_1 could not raise any expectation of punishment on later occasions because that expectation would be present in any case. In other words, it is assumed that *failure* to punish at O_1 would not diminish in the slightest the expectation of punishment at O_2, and O_3, and so on. In both cases, then, it is assumed at some point that potential offenders' beliefs about Rex's act-utilitarianism and what that entails are totally unaffected by Rex's punishment-related behaviour. I shall refer to this circumstance by saying the potential offenders 'unalterably believe' Rex will follow a certain pattern of punishment-related behaviour, or by saying they have 'unalterable expectations'.

Reliance on the assumption of unalterable expectations undermines Hodgson's case against AU in two ways. First, Hodgson's general objection to AU is that known act-utilitarians cannot influence expectations by their behaviour. But in the arguments at hand, he does not prove that claim. He assumes it. Second, what Hodgson actually proves by his arguments about punishment is that if potential offenders' expectations are unalterable, then AU requires non-punishment. But that is not a defect of AU. It is a virtue. If expectations are unalterable, then punishment cannot influence expectations, and therefore cannot have any good consequences, and therefore should be eschewed.

Note that the desirability of non-punishment in the face of unalterable expectations does not depend on Rex's being unalterably believed to be an act-utilitarian. It is enough that he is unalterably believed to follow *any* principle which dictates a specific pattern of behaviour on possible occasions for punishment. Suppose, for example, Rex is unalterably believed to follow a rule requiring punishment of every offence. In the face of this belief it is obvious that it has best consequences for Rex not to punish. The only good consequences of punishment (for purposes of this chapter) are consequences which flow from deterrence. If the belief that Rex follows a rule requiring punishment is unalterable, then it will persist at full strength even if Rex does not punish. In such a situation Rex's actually punishing does not contribute anything to deterrence. His punishing would have some bad consequences (by definition) and no good consequences, and therefore it would have best consequences for him not to punish. In short, in the presence of *any* unalterable expectations (and not merely unalterable expectations of act-utilitarian behaviour), it is no criticism of a theory to observe that it does not require punishment. Punishment would be pointless.

Hodgson's argument that AU cannot require punishment has something in common with the argument involved in the well-known 'surprise quiz' paradox. That argument purports to show that a statement by a teacher to a class of students that they will have a quiz some day in the following week but will not know before the day of the quiz when it will occur involves a contradiction. (The parallel with Hodgson's argument is most obvious in the finite case.) Quine argues that the description of the surprise quiz is not self-contradictory.[8] He claims, in effect, that what is self-contradictory is the conjunction of the propositions (a) that the quiz will be given, satisfying the description, and (b) that the class know this fact with certainty at all relevant times. My response to Hodgson is analogous. There is no contradiction in supposing that AU requires punishment of offences. The contradiction is in the conjunction of this proposition and the proposition that offenders unalterably expect Rex to follow the pattern of punishment which they believe AU requires. This need not trouble act-utilitarians, since, more generally, there is a contradiction in the conjunction of the propositions (1) that *any* specific pattern of punishment-behaviour by Rex is unalterably expected, and (2) that punishment has good consequences.

We are now in a position to dissolve another paradox as well—the paradox in Hodgson's suggestion that if Rex somehow managed to punish on some occasion his doing so might have best consequences, but only by proving that he was not satisfying AU. The fact is that Rex's punishing could not possibly have best consequences unless expectations are *alterable*, and if expectations are alterable, then we have been given no reason to think AU requires Rex not to punish.

We have shown that the assumption of unalterable expectations is essential to Hodgson's argument against AU, and we have noted that the assumption undermines Hodgson's overall case against AU. Hodgson does not make the assumption explicitly, and we should note how it creeps in. What Hodgson explicitly assumes is that Rex is *known* to satisfy AU. This is the assumption that is transformed into the assumption of unalterable expectations. But knowledge and unalterable expectations are not the same thing. Indeed, if knowledge is something like justified true belief (or perhaps justified true belief which satisfies certain conditions on the etiology of the justifying evidence), then it might plausibly be suggested that knowledge and unalterable expectations are inconsistent. In most circumstances, being 'justified' in holding a belief would seem to require an openness to conviction by opposing evidence which unalterability of the belief precludes. The assumption of unalterable expectations bears somewhat the same relation to the assumption of knowledge that the assumption 'Poof will satisfy AU regardless' bore to our general assumption that Poof satisfied AU in Chapter 2.[9] In each case the stronger assumption seems not much different from the weaker, but it actually represents a radical change in the circumstances for purposes of applying AU.

We have agreed with Hodgson that if expectations about how Rex will behave are unalterable, then AU requires Rex not to punish. We have observed that this is a point in AU's favour, not a point against it. No bad consequences have been shown to follow from Rex's being an act-utilitarian. That is not to say, however, that there might not be bad consequences attached to Rex's being *unalterably believed* to be an act-utilitarian.

Let us assume that if Rex is unalterably believed to be an act-utilitarian, then Rex is unalterably expected never to punish. There is a bit of a jump here, at least in the infinite case, since all we have really proved about that case is that there is no specific pattern other than consistent non-punishment such that that pattern can be unalterably expected and can be permitted by AU. However, if potential offenders can unalterably believe Rex to be an act-utilitarian without having any unalterable belief about what specific pattern of punishment behaviour Rex will follow, then it is not clear that they ought to have any unalterable belief about what specific pattern he will follow, because it may not be clear just on the basis that Rex is unalterably believed to be an act-utilitarian what AU requires. The reason is that AU may be indeterminate in the infinite case. We will make the jump, however, and assume that if Rex is unalterably believed to be an act-utilitarian, then he is unalterably expected not to punish. If Rex is unalterably expected not to punish, then potential offenders are not deterred and cannot be deterred by any threat of punishment. This could have very bad consequences. In short, it might be a very bad thing for Rex to be *unalterably believed* to be an act-utilitarian.

Does this bolster Hodgson's case against AU? It does not. Once we have admitted that it might be bad for Rex to be unalterably believed to be an act-utilitarian, it is tempting to suggest that it might be worse for Rex to be-and-be-unalterably-believed-to-be an act-utilitarian than for him to be-and-be-unalterably-believed-to-be a follower of a rule requiring punishment of all offences (hereafter a 'rule-punisher'). After all, the good consequences of Rex's *being* an act-utilitarian (and not punishing in the face of unalterable expectations of any sort about his behaviour) might be outweighed by the bad consequences of his being *unalterably believed* to be one. The trouble is that the suggested comparison (between Rex's being-and-being-unalterably-believed-to-be an act-utilitarian and his being-and-being-unalterably-believed-to-be a rule-punisher) is totally irrelevant to the question of what moral theory Rex ought to adopt and follow.

The comparison would be relevant if Rex, by being a rule-punisher, could make it more likely that he was unalterably believed to be a rule-punisher, or if, by being an act-utilitarian, he would make it more likely that he was unalterably believed to be an act-utilitarian. But neither of these connections can exist. It is true that in general we would expect Rex's adopting and following one theory or the other to make it more likely that he was believed to hold that theory. We would expect this precisely because, in general, beliefs are alterable. It is sensible to assume that Rex's behaviour will affect beliefs about Rex's theory (and future behaviour) if beliefs about Rex are alterable; but not otherwise. It makes no sense at all to suppose that by adopting a particular theory Rex can increase the chance that potential offenders' *unalterable* beliefs about what theory he holds are the unalterable beliefs he would like them to have. Therefore we cannot sensibly argue that Rex should be a rule-punisher because that is what it would be best for him to be unalterably believed to be.[10]

We have conceded that it might be a bad thing for Rex to be unalterably believed to follow AU. Since unalterable belief is not the same as knowledge, our concession does not amount to a concession that it would be bad for Rex to be *known* to follow AU. We have seen no argument which proves anything about the consequences of Rex's being known to follow AU (without being unalterably believed to do so). Still, it might seem that what we have conceded can be reworked into an argument against AU, in either of two ways. First, it might seem that an assumption of very firm belief would be sufficiently 'close' to an assumption of unalterable belief so that we could show that a Rex who was firmly believed to follow AU could not consistently with AU punish as much as would be desirable. Second, it might seem that if AU requires punishment only because of a difference between knowledge and unalterable belief, then AU's requiring punishment depends on the existence of doubt about whether Rex is an act-utilitarian. This in turn sounds rather like the proposition that Rex would be required to engage in deception about his views, which might be a bad thing.

To answer these suggestions fully, it would be necessary to treat the finite and the infinite case separately. The treatment of the finite case, in which the suggestions have more force, would take considerably longer than the treatment of the infinite case. I think the suggestions can be dealt with adequately even in the finite case, but the discussion would not justify the necessary space. It is, after all, the infinite case that is most realistic. In the real world, potential offenders cannot identify any occasion for possible punishment as one in which AU unequivocally requires non-punishment because it is logically impossible that punishment should have any good consequences. It is the ability of potential offenders to do this which is the critical feature of the finite case. Accordingly, we limit our consideration of these suggestions to the infinite case.

As to the first suggestion, that firm belief is 'close' to unalterable belief—this may be true if the act-utilitarian Rex has only a small number of opportunities to affect the relevant belief. But if he has many opportunities, as many as he has in the infinite case or even as many as he would have in a sufficiently 'long' finite case, then any initial belief, of whatever firmness, could be altered. So it could well be consistent with AU to punish regularly even in the face of a firm initial belief that punishment would not occur. Furthermore, once we realize this, we see that a firm initial belief that punishment would not occur would not be justified by the firm initial belief that Rex was an act-utilitarian. The objection to AU dissolves completely.

As to the suggestion that Rex must deceive potential offenders about his view, that simply is not true. Rex could publish the following statement: 'I am an act-utilitarian. You, potential offenders, know that I am an act-utilitarian. None the less, you do not believe unalterably that I will satisfy AU. You do not believe unalterably that I will always try to follow AU, though I will and you know it. You do not believe unalterably that I will always succeed in satisfying AU if I try, though I will and you know it. Because you do not believe unalterably that I will satisfy AU, you do not believe unalterably that I will follow any specific pattern of punishment-related behaviour. In fact, so long as your expectations about my behaviour are alterable, logic alone does not allow you even to deduce what AU requires. In view of the fact that your expectations are alterable, AU will, as an empirical matter, require me to punish you for offences, thereby producing and maintaining the expectation on your part that I will punish. Because I am an act-utilitarian, I shall do what AU requires. I shall punish you if you offend. Be warned.'[11] In the statement just outlined, Rex describes what he is going to do, and he points out exactly why he will be justified by AU in doing it. Where is the deception there? (Near the end of the chapter I will suggest that Rex might want to engage in a bit of deception about some minor details of his punishment programme if the very best possible results are to be achieved, but the point remains that no *pervasive* deception about Rex's view is called for.)

We have now disposed of what I take to be Hodgson's principal argument against the possibility of punishment by a known act-utilitarian Rex. Hodgson suggests at various points a more general argument designed to show that no behaviour of any kind by a known act-utilitarian could ever be justified simply by a tendency to raise expectations of similar behaviour in the future. With respect to most agents, of course, instances of behaviour of any kind do tend to raise *some* expectation of similar behaviour in the future, just because of what we know about the way human beings operate. But Hodgson suggests that no behaviour by a known act-utilitarian could produce expectations in this way.[12]

The general argument, as it applies to the punishment context, runs thus: 'Consider an act of punishing by a known act-utilitarian Rex at O_1. This act of punishing can raise expectations of punishment at O_2 (or any later O_i) if and only if it changes the expectations of potential offenders about the consequences of punishment at O_2 (or the later O_i). But the only possible good consequences of punishment at O_2 are increased expectations of punishment at O_3 (or some later O_j). And so on. We cannot accept the proposition that punishment at O_1 raises expectations of later punishment without (a) accepting an infinite regress in the explanation of how punishment at O_1 produces this effect, and (b) producing some further explanation of how it is that punishment at O_1 *increases* the capacity of punishment at O_2 to produce expectations of punishment at O_3. It is only if punishment at O_1 increases the capacity of punishment at O_2 to produce expectations of punishment at O_3 that punishment at O_1 improves the consequences of punishment at O_2 and thus legitimately increases the expectation of punishment at O_2.'

This argument, like those previously considered, depends on an implicit assumption of unalterable expectations. It assumes that even if Rex does something (punishes at O_1) which, if the argument is correct, cannot be explained by the hypothesis that Rex is an act-utilitarian, potential offenders will continue to expect various later actions by Rex only to the extent that those actions would be justified by AU. It assumes that even if Rex punishes at O_1, potential offenders will not have *any* tendency to expect punishment at O_2 just on the ground that human beings tend to repeat themselves. On the contrary, potential offenders are unalterably committed to their beliefs about Rex's reasons for action and will expect only behaviour which they believe is required by the reasons they believe Rex to have, even if their beliefs do not (according to the argument in question) allow them to account for the behaviour they have already observed.

I have explained already why an argument which assumes unalterable expectations does Hodgson no good. First, because the inability of act-utilitarians to alter expectations is what he is trying to prove. Second, because if expectations are unalterable, a theory which forbids attempts to alter expectations is obviously in that respect correct.

I think I have now refuted Hodgson's arguments. But it might be said I have not shown him wrong in his conclusion. Hodgson does not prove that act-utilitarians cannot influence expectations. But have I shown they can? In truth, no. I am content to offer as my positive argument, 'Why not?' People in general can influence expectations about their behaviour by the way they behave. Why not act-utilitarians? I shall believe they can until I discover some convincing argument to the contrary.

There is a final obvious question about utilitarian punishment which I shall not try to answer. The question is, what is the best pattern of punishment? In responding to Hodgson's arguments, I have generally spoken as if the only relevant patterns of punishment were consistent non-punishment or consistent punishment. These are certainly not the only possible patterns, and indeed it seems likely that neither of these is the best pattern, just as neither general crossing of the grass nor general avoidance is the best pattern in the grass case.[13] The best pattern will probably involve some non-punishment. A few instances of non-punishment would probably cause less bad consequences in the form of erosion of expectations than good consequences in the form of suffering avoided. Whatever the best pattern is, we have seen that Hodgson gives us no reason to doubt that it involves only acts which are consistent with AU even for a known act-utilitarian Rex. Rex can announce what he will do, in general, and he can then, consistently with AU, do what he has announced in order to confirm the expectation that he will do what he has announced. He can even afford to have it known that sometimes he does not punish, though of course he cannot identify in advance particular potential offences which he would not punish if they were committed. It might possibly be best for him to engage in a little deception, if he can get away with it, on the question of just how often he fails to punish, but that is beside the point. The basis of Hodgson's argument against AU is that wholesale deception would be indispensable. That is not true.

In the last paragraph but one, we noted one parallel between the punishment case and the grass case. There is another significant parallel. It seems likely that the pattern in which Rex never punishes (or some pattern in which he punishes at a very low rate) is a pattern in which Rex, viewed as a succession of time-slices, universally satisfies AU. A few isolated instances of punishment would probably do so little to raise a general expectation of punishment that each instance of non-punishment would be justified against the general background of non-punishment. If there is some pattern involving very little punishment in which AU is universally satisfied, and if the best pattern involves fairly regular punishment (as seems likely), then AU is indeterminate in the punishment case just as it was in the grass case.

As it happens, there are two passages in which Hodgson's argument brings him to the verge of recognizing that AU is indeterminate in the punishment case, but he refuses to accept this implication of his own logic, and he avoids it by a rather artificial suggestion about how Rex should wring out of AU a specific direction not to punish that is not really justified by AU at all.[14] Hodgson is correct, both with regard to punishment and with regard to promising and truth-telling, to the extent that he argues universal satisfaction of AU does not guarantee the existence of these practices. He is wrong in supposing that universal satisfaction of AU makes these practices impossible.

RULE-UTILITARIANISM

In this chapter I shall consider whether some seemingly plausible variants of rule-utilitarianism have PropCOP and PropAU. In terms of particular conclusions, this chapter probably adds less to the literature than any other in the essay. But the chapter is short, and I think there are rewards to be had from surveying familiar ground from a new point of view.

As I noted in the Introduction, rule-utilitarianism can be rendered loosely as the theory that agents ought to follow whatever set of rules it would have best consequences for everyone to follow. I suggested that one source of the intuitive appeal of both rule-utilitarianism and utilitarian generalization is the idea that moral theories ought to guarantee the production of the best possible consequences if they are universally satisfied—in short, the idea that moral theories should have PropCOP. As it turns out, it is not difficult to state a rule-utilitarian theory that has PropCOP. But the most natural theory that has PropCOP fails to have PropAU. It is also not difficult to come up with a plausible modification of the theory, designed to endow rule-utilitarianism with PropAU. But the modification robs the original theory of PropCOP and does not in any event produce a theory with PropAU. Indeed, the modification produces a remarkable series of tangles.

My general object in this chapter is to make it seem plausible that all attempts to describe a rule-utilitarianism which has both PropCOP and PropAU are doomed to failure. I shall prove this rigorously in Chapter 7, and I do not prove it rigorously in this chapter. But I think this chapter is still useful heuristic preparation.

There are two preliminary points about the nature of the theories we shall consider. First, we shall interpret rule-utilitarianism as directing each agent to satisfy the set of rules it would be best for everyone to satisfy, as opposed to the set of rules it would be best for everyone to accept, or to try to satisfy, or whatever. Strictly speaking, we are not committed to this choice by the fact that we are interested in the consequences of satisfaction of theories. We could intelligibly ask about the consequences of universal satisfaction of a theory which directed each agent to satisfy the set of rules it would be best for everyone to accept, or to try to satisfy. However, if there is a difference between the set of rules it would be best for everyone to accept, or to try to satisfy, and the set of rules it would best for everyone actually to satisfy (as proponents of theories couched in terms of acceptance or trying presumably believe there is), then it is unlikely that anyone would claim that a theory which required each agent to satisfy the best rules for general acceptance or general trying-to-follow had either PropAU or PropCOP. Accordingly, we shall consider the sort of rule-utilitarianism which might be thought to have PropAU or PropCOP, namely, the sort which directs each agent to satisfy the set of rules it would be best for everyone to satisfy.

Second, we shall allow rules of any degree of complexity. We shall emphasize this by referring for the most part not to sets of rules, but to 'universal prescriptions for action', which are in effect detailed sets of instructions for all agents in the moral universe. To forestall objection to the decision to allow rules, or universal prescriptions for action, of any degree of complexity, I would point out that it is not an essential prop for the central conclusions of this chapter. At various points I shall assert that certain variants of rule-utilitarianism have PropCOP, or have it in a wide range of cases, and these claims *do* depend on the permissibility of rules of any degree of complexity. But the central conclusions of this chapter concern the *failure* of various versions of rule-utilitarianism. Such conclusions are obviously made harder to prove, not easier, by expanding the class of eligible sets of rules. In fact, the failures are demonstrated in the context of our original Whiff and Poof example, where the issue of the permissible complexity of the rules can hardly be said to arise.

Consider the following principle:

(COP) An act is right if and only if it is prescribed (for the agent whose act is in question) by that universal prescription for action, the universal satisfaction of which would produce the best possible consequences.

A 'universal prescription for action' (hereafter 'UPA') may be thought of as a list. On the list appear the names of all the agents in the moral universe. Beside the name of each agent appears a prescription for that agent. The individual prescriptions in the UPA's are assumed to be *unconditional*. Whatever Jones is directed to do, he is directed to do it regardless of Smith's behaviour.[1] An agent 'satisfies' a UPA when he does the act that UPA prescribes for him. (We assume in this discussion that each agent has only one decision to make.) A UPA is 'universally satisfied' when all agents satisfy it.

The name 'COP' is an acronym for 'co-ordinated optimization principle'. In effect, COP directs each agent to do his part in the best possible pattern of behaviour for the universe of agents, and to ignore the matter of whether other agents are doing their part. COP is the pure embodiment of the idea that a moral theory should have best possible consequences if everyone satisfies it.

The brief description of COP just given brings up one difficulty. The statement of COP implicitly assumes that there is a unique best pattern of behaviour. Only if there is a unique best pattern of behaviour is there a unique best UPA. A slightly complicated revised COP which is able to deal with multiple best patterns of behaviour is described in a note.[2] For the rest of this chapter, we shall consider only cases in which there is a unique best pattern of behaviour. Variants of rule-utilitarianism will be shown to have problems enough even with this simplifying assumption.

Let us see how COP works in an example which is already familiar:

		Poof	
		Push	Not-Push
	Push	10	0
Whiff			
	Not-Push	0	6

In this example, there are four possible UPA's. One says beside Whiff's name 'Push the button', and beside Poof's name also 'Push the button'. Another says beside Whiff's name 'Don't push the button', and beside Poof's name 'Push the button'. And so on. It is obvious which is the UPA, universal satisfaction of which has best consequences. It is the UPA which says to both Whiff and Poof 'Push the button'. Therefore the right act for Whiff, according to COP, is to push the button. The right act for Poof is also to push the button. Universal satisfaction of COP brings about the best possible results.

It should be obvious that universal satisfaction of COP brings about the best possible results in any situation. Any agent who satisfies COP does what is required of him by the UPA which has best consequences if universally satisfied (the 'best' UPA). If everyone satisfies COP, everyone satisfies the best UPA. If everyone satisfies the best UPA, the best possible consequences are achieved. In short, COP has PropCOP (so long as we consider only cases with unique best patterns of behaviour).

It should also be obvious that COP does not have PropAU. In the Whiff and Poof example, if Poof does not push his button, that will not affect what COP requires of Whiff. COP will require Whiff to push regardless. But if Whiff pushes while Poof does not, Whiff does not produce the best consequences possible in the circumstances in which he finds himself. So Whiff can satisfy COP without producing the best consequences possible in the circumstances. In short, COP does not have PropAU.

Because COP has been shown to have PropCOP only in cases involving a unique best pattern of behaviour, COP itself is not a genuine example of a theory which has PropCOP but not PropAU. The theory discussed in note 2 to this chapter is such a theory. For readers who do not wish to worry about the more complicated theory, COP will suffice to make it intuitively clear that a theory can have PropCOP without having PropAU. Since AU was shown in Chapter 2 to have PropAU but not PropCOP, we have now established that neither of these properties entails the other.

It may well seem that the source of COP's principal defect

(its failure to have PropAU) is its reliance on *unconditional* prescriptions. We would expect bad results from a theory which forbids each agent to pay any attention at all to what other agents are doing. Let us see what happens if the individual prescriptions which make up a universal prescription for action are allowed to condition the behaviour required of each agent on the behaviour of the others. We shall call a universal prescription for action which involves *conditional* individual prescriptions a UPA-C (for 'conditional UPA'). The theory which results from interpreting the phrase 'universal prescription for action' in the statement of COP as referring to UPA-C's (and not just UPA's) we shall call COP-C. This is the theory we consider next.

COP-C instructs each agent to do the act prescribed for him by that UPA-C, universal satisfaction of which would have the best possible consequences. There are two logical difficulties with COP-C. First, in order to identify the UPA-C, universal satisfaction of which would have best consequences, we must be able to figure out what the consequences of universal satisfaction of each possible UPA-C would be. But that is something we cannot do. Consider the following UPA-C, designed for our current Whiff and Poof example:

	Whiff	Poof
(UPA-C#1)	If Poof pushes, push.	If Whiff pushes, push.
	If Poof does not push, don't push.	If Whiff does not push, don't push.

UPA-C#1 is universally satisfied if Whiff and Poof both push. It is also universally satisfied if Whiff and Poof both not-push. These two patterns of universal satisfaction of UPA-C#1 produce consequences of different value. In effect, UPA-C#1 is indeterminate. That is not surprising, if we remark that UPA-C#1 is just AU put into the appropriate form. It does, however, represent a problem with COP-C. The consequences of universal satisfaction of some UPA-C's are not well defined.

We might be justified in terminating our consideration of COP-C—and generally of rule-utilitarian theories which rely on UPA-C's—at this point. It is clear that in this example the only UPA-C which can fully serve the purpose the UPA-C's were introduced for, that of allowing each agent to make the best of things if the other deviates from the best overall pattern of behaviour, is UPA-C#1. And yet, because of its indeterminacy, UPA-C#1 cannot even be evaluated by a criterion which focuses on the consequences of universal satisfaction of UPA-C's. Plainly, the same problem will also arise in connection with UPA-C's in more complicated cases involving any number of agents. Still, to stop at this point might seem to be giving very short shrift to a type of theory which has attracted considerable interest. If we press on, we shall discover that UPA-C's bring with them problems beyond the one already identified.

The second difficulty with COP-C is that even if we limit the field of eligible UPA-C's to those which are determinate (that is, to those the consequences of universal satisfaction of which are well defined), there may be no unique best UPA-C. Consider UPA-C#2 and UPA-C#3:

	Whiff	*Poof*
(UPA-C#2)	If Poof pushes, push.	If Whiff pushes, push.
	If Poof does not push, push anyway.	If Whiff does not push, push anyway.

(Note that UPA-C#2 is actually a UPA, but that is all right. The point of moving to UPA-C's was to expand the range of possible universal prescriptions, not to make ineligible for consideration any prescription which did not make some agent's obligation vary with the other's behaviour. In any event, we could make the point we propose to make with UPA-C#2 and UPA-C#3 by relying only on UPA-C's which are not UPA's. We could use UPA-C#3 and the 'mirror image' of UPA-C#3 which is mentioned in connection with the indeterminacy of the theory called 'RU', further on.)

	Whiff	*Poof*
(UPA-C#3)	If Poof pushes, push.	If Whiff pushes, push.
	If Poof does not push, don't push.	If Whiff does not push, push anyway.

It is obvious that UPA-C#2 can be universally satisfied in

only one way, by both agents' pushing. The consequences of universal satisfaction of UPA-C#2 are well defined and are valued at ten units. UPA-C#3 can also be universally satisfied in only one way. If Whiff and Poof both push, both satisfy UPA-C#3. If Whiff pushes and Poof does not, neither satisfies UPA-C#3. If Poof pushes and Whiff does not, Poof satisfies UPA-C#3, but Whiff does not. If neither pushes, Whiff satisfies UPA-C#3, but Poof does not. In sum, UPA-C#3 is universally satisfied only if both push. The consequences of universal satisfaction of UPA-C#3 are well defined, and are the same as the well-defined consequences of universal satisfaction of UPA-C#2, which are also the best consequences possible. Since COP-C directs each agent to satisfy the UPA-C which has best consequences when universally satisfied, COP-C provides no ground for choosing between UPA-C#2 and UPA-C#3. Indeed, COP-C involves a non-referring definite description.

It is tempting to try to ignore this difficulty, on the ground that all the equally good 'best' determinate UPA-C's will call for the same pattern of behaviour when they are universally satisfied. But if we make this move, we have abandoned the whole point of introducing UPA-C's in the first place, which was to deal with the possibility of less-than-universal satisfaction. To put the point more concretely: We introduced UPA-C's in hopes of improving the consequences of Whiff's behaviour when Poof does not push. Now that UPA-C's are allowed, what does COP-C actually require Whiff to do when Poof does not push? We have already pointed out that UPA-C#2 and UPA-C#3 have the same, well-defined, best possible consequences when they are universally satisfied. As far as COP-C is concerned, there is no preferring one to the other. But when Poof is not pushing, UPA-C#2 tells Whiff to push, and UPA-C#3 tells Whiff not to push. What COP-C tells Whiff to do is anybody's guess.

We have identified two difficulties with COP-C. First, it assumes that the consequences of universal satisfaction of UPA-C's are always well defined, which is not the case. Second, it assumes that there is a unique UPA-C the universal satisfaction of which produces best possible consequences.

This is not the case, even if we consider only determinate UPA-C's and even, remember, in a case in which there is a unique best pattern of behaviour (in effect, a unique best UPA).

We can eliminate the logical difficulties of COP-C by revising it in the manner suggested by Gerald Barnes,[3] who proposes a theory he calls 'RU':

RU: An act is right if and only if it conforms with an ideal set of rules; an ideal set of rules is any set of rules such that if everyone always did, from among the things he could do, what conformed with that set of rules, then at least as much good would be produced as by everyone's always conforming with any other set of rules.

Barnes's discussion of RU makes it clear that by a 'set of rules' he means what we have called a UPA-C. First, we note that RU does not allow as an ideal set of rules any UPA-C which is indeterminate, since universal satisfaction of such a UPA-C would not guarantee at least as much good as would be produced by universal satisfaction of some determinate UPA-C whose universal satisfaction produced the best consequences. The first difficulty of COP-C is not confronted explicitly, but it is sidestepped. Second, RU very carefully avoids any assumption that there is a unique best determinate UPA-C. That is the point of requiring each agent to follow 'an ideal set of rules'.

RU still has serious problems, however. What does RU require Whiff to do when Poof does not push? We have already shown in effect that both UPA-C#2 and UPA-C#3 are ideal sets of rules. Both are determinate, and the well-defined consequences of universal satisfaction of either are the best consequences possible. But UPA-C#2 tells Whiff to push, and UPA-C#3 tells Whiff not to push, when Poof is not pushing. Since RU tells Whiff only to follow *an* ideal set of rules, Whiff satisfies RU whatever he does. The situation is not the same as with COP-C, which tells Whiff to follow *the* best UPA-C, which turns out to be a non-referring description. There is no logical difficulty with RU. But it seems doubtful that a theory (such as RU) which leaves Whiff a free hand when Poof does not push is what the proponent of rule-utilitarianism really wants.

RU has another problem. It is indeterminate, even though

none of the relevant UPA-C's is. We have just observed that because UPA-C#3 is an ideal set of rules, Whiff satisfies RU if he does not push when Poof does not push. But the whole situation is symmetrical, so we can infer that Poof satisfies RU if he does not push when Whiff does not push. (The reader who is suspicious of arguments from symmetry can verify this claim by writing out the UPA-C which results from reversing all the names in UPA-C#3. This new UPA-C can be shown to be an ideal set of rules, just as UPA-C#3 is, and it will direct Poof not to push if Whiff does not push.) What all this means is that if neither pushes, both satisfy RU. This may seem surprising. We might expect that if both satisfied RU, then both would satisfy an ideal set of rules and best possible results would be produced. But the argument just suggested is fallacious. If both satisfy RU, each satisfies *some* ideal set of rules. There is no guarantee, however, that both satisfy the *same* ideal set of rules, and it is only their satisfying the same ideal set of rules that would ensure best possible results. In fact, if neither pushes, each satisfies *an* ideal set of rules (and therefore RU), but the ideal sets of rules in question are different.

We have established that if neither pushes, both satisfy RU. It is also obvious that if both push, both satisfy RU. (If both push, they both satisfy UPA-C#3, for example.) Therefore RU is universally satisfiable by different patterns of behaviour which have consequences of different value. RU is indeterminate.

The difficulty cannot be avoided by adding to RU a requirement that each agent follow the same ideal set of rules everyone else is following. Suppose that in our current example Poof does not push. We know that there is no way Whiff can behave so that he and Poof are both following the same ideal set of rules, because if Whiff and Poof were both following the *same* ideal set of rules they would both be pushing. Therefore a command to Whiff to follow the same ideal set of rules as Poof would require the impossible when Poof does not push. The proponent of RU plainly envisions that everyone who follows RU will follow the same ideal set of rules, but RU does not guarantee this, and it seems clear that it could not do so without reverting to COP.[4]

Let us quickly summarize our results to this point: COP has PropCOP (by courtesy of our exclusion of cases involving multiple best patterns of behaviour). That is to say, if everyone satisfies COP, best possible results will be achieved. COP does not have PropAU. It is not the case that any individual who satisfies COP must produce the best results possible given the behaviour of others. It is natural to think we can improve on COP by allowing UPA–C's (conditional rules, in effect). This move, which produces COP–C, might be expected to remedy COP's failure to have PropAU. But COP–C is beset by logical difficulties. RU (Barnes's theory) eliminates COP–C's logical problems, but even so, RU turns out to have neither PropCOP nor PropAU. It does not have PropCOP because it is indeterminate. It does not have PropAU because, as we have seen, it allows Whiff either to push or not-push when Poof is not-pushing. These shortcomings of RU are manifested even in a case involving a unique best pattern of behaviour.

Despite its failings, RU is as good a statement as there is of a rule-utilitarian theory which is intended to be judged by the consequences of universal satisfaction (as opposed to general acceptance, or whatever). RU is Brandt's famous 'specious rule-utilitarianism', shorn of a linguistic peculiarity of Brandt's formulation, and presented without Brandt's (erroneous) argument that the theory is equivalent to AU.[5] The only other variant of rule-utilitarianism which might plausibly be offered as a theory to be judged by the consequences of universal satisfaction is Lyons's 'primitive rule-utilitarianism'.[6] Lyons regards that theory as equivalent to utilitarian generalization, so we shall let the treatment of utilitarian generalization in the next chapter suffice for discussion of primitive rule-utilitarianism.

The difficulties uncovered in this chapter result from a basic incoherence in any sophisticated rule-utilitarianism. The sophisticated rule-utilitarian wants to consider conditional rules, which are designed to deal with the problem of *less-than-universal* satisfaction. On the other hand, he attempts to select the best rules on the basis of the consequences of the rules' being *universally* satisfied. This represents a natural attempt to combine the intuition that a theory should have

PropAU (which pulls in the direction of allowing conditional rules) and the intuition that a theory should have PropCOP (which pulls in the direction of testing sets of rules by their consequences if universally satisfied). But this way of combining the intuitions, as we see, does not work.[7]

We have not, to be sure, proved rigorously that no amount of clever reconstruction of COP–C or RU could make this approach work. We shall prove that claim rigorously in Chapter 7, provided that 'clever reconstruction' is limited to the creation of theories which are exclusively act-oriented.[8] In the intervening chapter we shall see that certain interpretations of utilitarian generalization constitute analogous attempts to combine the two fundamental consequentialist intuitions, and we shall see that these attempts fail as well.

UTILITARIAN GENERALIZATION

In this chapter I propose to do for utilitarian generalization what I did in the last chapter for rule-utilitarianism. My ultimate goal is to make it plausible that no version of utilitarian generalization can have both PropCOP and PropAU, and to suggest that sophisticated versions of utilitarian generalization suffer from the same sort of basic incoherence that we found in sophisticated versions of rule-utilitarianism.

Consider the following principle:

(UG) An act is right if and only if the consequences of its being performed by the agent and all other agents similarly situated are at least as good as the consequences of any other available act's being performed by the agent and all other agents similarly situated.

UG is intended to capture traditional utilitarian generalization, which we shall explicate so far as necessary as we go along.[1]

Stating UG in terms of all agents 'similarly situated' eliminates one problem which has been extensively discussed. UG is often stated as requiring an agent to do the act which has best consequences when done by himself and everyone else who has the opportunity to do that act. If UG is stated in that fashion, then the question arises whether the same number of other agents are in a position to do each of the acts available to the agent in question.[2] It is clear, however, that agents who are similarly situated have the same range of acts available to them.[3]

Let us now apply UG to the following example, which we have already used in connection with the symmetry counterargument to the claim that AU is indeterminate in Chapter 2.

		Poof	
		Push	Not-Push
	Push	3	4
Whiff			
	Not-Push	4	0

What does UG require of Whiff in this example? First, we observe that Whiff and Poof are similarly situated. The example is perfectly symmetrical. Now, if Whiff and everyone else similarly situated push, the consequences have a value of three units. If Whiff and everyone else similarly situated not-push, the consequences have a value of zero units. UG therefore directs Whiff to push. Similarly, UG directs Poof to push. UG is universally satisfied if and only if Whiff and Poof both push.

We see that UG does not have PropCOP. Universal satisfaction of UG does not guarantee the best possible results, which are achieved only if one party pushes and the other does not. UG also does not have PropAU. When both parties push, Whiff satisfies UG, but he does not produce the best consequences he could produce in the circumstances. For purposes of PropAU, Whiff's circumstances include the fact that Poof pushes, and Whiff would produce best consequences by not-pushing. (We have implicitly assumed that randomized acts are not available to Whiff and Poof. The availability of such acts would affect neither the conclusion that UG fails to have PropCOP nor the conclusion that it fails to have PropAU. This is shown in a note.[4] For the remainder of the chapter, we shall ignore the possibility of randomized acts in the text. Occasional notes will show that admitting randomized acts would affect none of our main conclusions.)

If David Lyons had never produced his famous argument for the extensional equivalence of UG and AU, we could stop right here. But the claim that UG and AU are extensionally equivalent obviously entails that UG has PropAU, since AU does. UG does not have PropAU, and UG and AU are not extensionally equivalent. It will be illuminating to see where Lyons goes wrong. Note that even if UG and AU were extensionally equivalent, UG would not have PropCOP, since AU does not have PropCOP. But we are not interested merely in finding some flaw in UG. We want to know whether there is any hope of repairing that flaw without introducing others.

Lyons states his version of utilitarian generalization somewhat differently from UG.[5] He does not use the phrase 'similarly situated'. None the less, it is clear what Lyons's first objection would be to our argument that UG requires Whiff to push. It would be that we have failed to take account of all the circumstances which determine Whiff's 'situation'. Specifically, he would point out that what Poof does affects the consequences of Whiff's act (which is true), and he would conclude that the relevant description of Whiff's situation must include a specification of Poof's behaviour. The same, of course, goes for Poof's situation.

This sounds plausible, but it will not do. If we interpret 'situated' as Lyons suggests, then the identity of the agents Whiff is similarly situated with depends on how Whiff himself behaves. Suppose that in our example Poof pushes. Whiff's situation is clear. Regardless of how Whiff behaves, his situation is that the only other agent is pushing. But Poof's situation varies with Whiff's behaviour. If Whiff pushes, Poof's situation is that the only other agent is pushing. If Whiff does not push, Poof's situation is that the only other agent is not pushing. We see that if Whiff pushes, Whiff and Poof are similarly situated. If Whiff does not push, they are not. The identity of the agents Whiff is similarly situated with depends on Whiff's behaviour because Whiff's behaviour affects others' situations and therefore affects whether others' situations are or are not the same as Whiff's. Since UG is expressly designed to deal with cases involving causal interaction—cases in which one agent's act is a causally relevant feature of the others' circumstances—this dependence of the identity of the agents Whiff is similarly situated with on Whiff's own behaviour will be present in every case of the sort UG is primarily designed to deal with.

We should perhaps qualify the claim of the previous paragraph slightly. Whether the identity of the agents similarly situated with Whiff *always* depends on Whiff's behaviour depends on just how far we take Lyons's approach. Thus, suppose we are dealing with a grass-walking case. Does the specification of Whiff's circumstances include a specification of the exact number of other agents who are crossing the grass, or does it merely include some statement about the relation of that number to the 'threshold' at which significant damage to the grass takes place (assuming there is such a threshold)? If each agent's circumstances include a specification of the exact number of others who walk on the grass, then obviously Whiff's behaviour *does* affect the circumstances of other agents and *does* affect whom Whiff is similarly situated with. However, if each agent's circumstances include only more general threshold-related information then all we can say is that *sometimes* the overall situation will be such that Whiff's behaviour affects the identity of the other agents he is similarly situated with. This will happen when Whiff is making a decision right at the threshold (roughly speaking).

Lyons does not notice that his approach makes the identity of the agents Whiff is similarly situated with depend on Whiff's behaviour. (In Lyons's terms, the point would be not that Whiff's behaviour affects the identity of the agents he is similarly situated with, but that Whiff's behaviour affects the identity and number of agents who are in a position to do the same fully described act as Whiff.) I think this point makes it clear that Lyons has misconstrued traditional utilitarian generalization. The traditional theory assumes that Whiff can decide who else is similarly situated, or who else is in a position to do the same act as himself, without reference to his own behaviour.[6]

So far I have argued that Lyons misconstrued traditional utilitarian generalization. Even if I am right, it might still be the case that Lyons has inadvertently suggested a way to improve traditional utilitarian generalization. In order to see whether that is so, we consider what happens if we try to plug into UG a Lyons-inspired notion of 'similarly situated'.

The first question that arises is the question previously noted about whether each agent's circumstances include a complete description of others' behaviour, or just a description in terms of proximity to various thresholds. For purposes of the present discussion, we shall assume the circumstances include complete descriptions. The principal reason is that in most cases there is no point at which the entire benefit or the entire damage from the relevant concerted behaviour appears all at once. The marginal benefit or damage varies with the number of participants in the behaviour in question, but it is not ordinarily zero everywhere except at a single point. (In this respect, voting cases are exceptional.) We cannot consider all possible Lyons-inspired notions of 'similarly situated'. The notion which involves complete descriptions seems the most plausible, and that is the one we shall use.[7]

Since, on our current interpretation of 'similarly situated', the identity of the agents similarly situated with Whiff depends on Whiff's behaviour, we must revise UG so that it speaks of agents who *turn out* to be similarly situated with Whiff given some specified choice on Whiff's part. With this in mind, we discover two obvious ways to plug the new notion of 'similarly situated' into UG. The statements which follow of the two resulting theories are unwieldy. What the statements actually say is not terribly complicated, and should be adequately illustrated by the ensuing discussion. To make the statements as clear as possible, we arbitrarily assign to the agent whose act is under discussion the name 'Alice'.

(UG′)   An act *a* by an agent Alice is right if and only if the consequences of its being performed by Alice and all other agents who turn out to be similarly situated with Alice if Alice does *a* are at least as good as the consequences of any other available act's being performed by Alice and all other agents who turn out to be similarly situated with Alice if Alice does *a*.

(UG″)   An act *a* by an agent Alice is right if and only if the consequences of its being performed by Alice and all other agents who turn out to be similarly situated with Alice if Alice does *a* are at least as good as the consequences of any other available act *b*'s being performed by Alice and all other agents who turn out to be similarly situated with Alice if Alice does *b*.

Roughly speaking, UG′ determines whether a particular act by Alice is right by identifying the class of agents who turn out to be similarly situated with Alice if she does that act and then asking whether that act is in fact the best act for Alice and all the members of that class to do. Under UG″, each possible act of Alice is associated with the class of agents who turn out to be similarly situated with Alice if she does that act, and the consequences of each act's being performed by Alice and all the agents in its associated class are then compared.

First, we consider UG′. In our current example, represented by the array

		Poof	
		Push	Not-push
	Push	3	4
Whiff			
	Not-push	4	0

what does UG′ require Whiff to do if Poof pushes? If Whiff pushes, then Poof is similarly situated with Whiff. The class of 'Whiff and all agents similarly situated' turns out to be Whiff and Poof. The consequences of Whiff and Poof's both pushing are better than the consequences of Whiff and Poof's both not-pushing. Therefore Whiff's pushing is right according to UG′. If Whiff does not push, then Poof is not similarly situated with Whiff. (Remember that Poof is pushing throughout this paragraph.) The class of 'Whiff and all agents similarly situated' turns out to be Whiff alone. The consequences of Whiff's not-pushing are better than the consequences of Whiff's pushing. Therefore, Whiff's not-pushing is right according to UG′. In sum, if Poof pushes, any act by Whiff is right according to UG′. This is plainly undesirable.[8]

There is worse to be said of UG′. Consider our standard example from earlier chapters:

		Poof	
		Push	Not-push
	Push	10	0
Whiff			
	Not-push	0	6

Suppose, in this situation, Poof does not push. What does UG′ require of Whiff? If Whiff pushes, then the class of 'Whiff and all agents similarly situated' turns out to be Whiff alone. The consequences of Whiff's pushing are inferior to the consequences of Whiff's not-pushing. Therefore, Whiff's pushing is not right according to UG'. If Whiff does not push, then the class of 'Whiff and all agents similarly situated' turns out to be Whiff and Poof. (Remember that Poof is not-pushing throughout this paragraph.) The consequences of both Whiff and Poof not-pushing are inferior to the consequences of both Whiff and Poof pushing. Therefore, Whiff's not-pushing is not right according to UG'. In sum, if Poof does not push there is no way Whiff can satisfy UG'.[9] This is intolerable. UG' will not do.

If we now turn our attention to UG'', we shall see that it is extensionally equivalent to AU. We begin by asking if there is some other way to characterize the class of 'all other agents who turn out to be similarly situated with Alice if Alice does a'. There is. This class is precisely the class of other agents who do a. (The reader may have noticed that in the discussion of examples under UG', Poof always turned out to be similarly situated with Whiff if and only if Whiff did what Poof was doing. This was no accident.) Consider any agent other than Alice, such as Ben. Alice's circumstances comprise the behaviour of everybody-except-Alice-and-Ben, plus the behaviour of Ben. Ben's circumstances comprise the behaviour of everybody-except-Alice-and-Ben, plus the behaviour of Alice. Plainly, Alice's and Ben's circumstances are the same if and only if their behaviour is the same.[10]

We have observed that the class of other agents who turn out to be similarly situated with Alice if Alice does a are just the class of other agents who do a. What follows about the consequences of a's being performed by Alice and all other agents who turn out to be similarly situated with Alice if Alice does a? What follows is that the consequences of a's being performed by Alice and the members of the specified class are just the consequences of a's being performed by Alice and the class of other agents who do a, which are obviously just the consequences of Alice's doing a. Similarly, the consequences of b's being performed by Alice and all other agents who turn out to be similarly situated with Alice if Alice does b are just the consequences of Alice's doing b.

To put the point another way, UG" seems to incorporate the traditional utilitarian generalizer's notion that we should hypothetically vary a class of acts, but the 'what if''s that UG" invites us to consider—'what if the class of agents who turn out to be similarly situated with Alice if she does *a* all did *a*', 'what if the class of agents who turn out to be similarly situated with Alice if she does *b* all did *b*', and so on—are not 'what if''s at all, so far as the agents other than Alice are concerned. They are all necessarily true. The agents who turn out to be similarly situated with Alice if she does *a do* do *a*. That is the condition for their being similarly situated with her. The agents who turn out to be similarly situated with Alice if she does *b do* do *b*. That is the condition for their being similarly situated with her. And so on. For all its apparent complication, UG" says in effect that an act is right if and only if its consequences are as good as the consequences of any alternative. UG" is equivalent to AU.[11]

It may be thought that this demonstration that UG" is equivalent to AU buttresses Lyons's claim of extensional equivalence. I am willing that it should be taken that way, provided two points are kept in mind. First, the equivalence of UG" and AU does not affect my earlier claim that Lyons misconstrued traditional utilitarian generalization. The notion of 'similarly situated' employed in UG" is not the traditional notion. UG" is not equivalent to UG. Second, my demonstration that UG" is equivalent to AU has nothing in common with Lyons's argument for extensional equivalence. In particular, it does not depend, as Lyons's argument does, on any claim about the attribution of the consequences of a class of acts to the individual acts making up the class. The whole point of my demonstration is that UG" does not really require the consequences of any *classes* of acts to be compared, since no *class* of acts is hypothetically varied in applying UG". As we hypothetically vary Alice's act in the course of applying UG" to her decision, the class of other agents to whom she is assimilated by UG" varies as well, and other agents move in and out of the relevant class. But there is no other agent, and therefore no class of other agents, whose act is ever hypothetically varied along with Alice's.[12]

I emphasized in the previous paragraph that my argument for the equivalence of UG″ and AU has nothing in common with Lyons's argument for the extensional equivalence of utilitarian generalization and act-utilitarianism. A great deal has been written about Lyons's argument, and I believe it is now generally understood that the argument fails. But to my mind there is no completely satisfactory refutation of Lyons in the literature.[13] It would not be useful to attempt at this point the ideal refutation of Lyons. I shall, however, devote one paragraph (the next) to an explanation of what I regard as Lyons's central error. If a one-paragraph treatment is too concise to be helpful, there will at least be no great cost.

Lyons insists that we should consider only acts fully described in terms of their causally relevant properties. In the cases utilitarian generalization was invented to deal with, the acts of various agents interact in the production of consequences, so the fully described acts available to each agent depend on what the others do. Now, Lyons's central premiss is that the consequences of a class of fully described acts must be attributable, without deficiency or excess, to the fully described acts considered individually. This premiss is not merely false. It is nonsense. Our standard notion of consequences, which Lyons employs, involves hypothetical variation of whatever we are investigating the consequences of. We cannot sensibly speak of the consequences of a class of fully described acts, because we cannot hypothetically vary more than one fully described act at a time. We can hold everybody-but-Jones's acts constant, and hypothetically vary Jones's fully described act as we please. But if we try to vary Smith's act concurrently with Jones's, we end up varying the fully described acts Jones has to choose from. In brief: Consequences are defined in terms of hypothetical variation. The consequences of a class of acts are identified by hypothetical variation of that class of acts. It is possible hypothetically to vary a class of acts, but it is possible only if the acts in question are *not* fully described. Lyons's notion of the consequences of a class of fully described acts is incoherent.[14]

(Although I have criticized Lyons rather strongly in this chapter, I should like to express my opinion that he made a great contribution. It was he more than anyone else who persuaded utilitarians to rise above the battle of example and counterexample and to investigate fundamental questions about the structure of utilitarian theories.)

In a sense, my one-paragraph refutation of Lyons merely repeats what we have already learned by considering UG' and UG''. Those theories resulted from an attempt to fit Lyons's notion of 'similarly situated' into the traditional framework of utilitarian generalization, represented by UG. But the attempt produced on the one hand a thorough monstrosity, UG', and on the other hand a theory, UG'', which was equivalent to AU and which effectively abandoned the core idea of utilitarian generalization, the hypothetical variation of classes of acts. The problem, I suggest, is the same as the problem with COP-C and RU. The appeal of Lyons's approach is the appeal of PropAU. We take the agent's fully described circumstances into account in hopes of producing a theory which allows each agent to make the best of others' actual behaviour. But Lyons's notion of 'similarly situated' does not mesh properly with the traditional focus on the consequences of a class of acts (by the agent and all others similarly situated), which is a response to the appeal of PropCOP. This is the second attempt we have seen to combine the intuition that a theory should have PropAU and the intuition that a theory should have PropCOP. Like the first attempt, this attempt seems doomed to failure.

Despite its flaws, UG is an attractive theory in certain respects. In Chapter 12 I shall suggest that the central question in formulating a consequentialist theory is the question of how each agent should view the behaviour of others. I shall compare the views of others' behaviour which are embodied in the traditional consequentialist theories with the view embodied in co-operative utilitarianism, which I regard as superior. We shall see that the view of others' behaviour embodied in UG is very similar to the view of other's behaviour embodied in co-operative utilitarianism. UG also can be interpreted so as to represent a sensible response to the *practical* problem faced by agents in a situation like the principal example of this chapter—agents who are symmetrically situated but who can achieve best possible results only by behaving differently. Chapter 11 compares the responses to this practical problem of UG, AU, and co-operative utilitarianism.

THE IMPOSSIBILITY OF AN
ADEQUATE TRADITIONAL THEORY

In this chapter I shall prove a number of theorems about adaptability, PropAU, and PropCOP, and about a new property I shall call 'exclusive act-orientation' which I regard as characterizing the class of 'traditional' consequentialist theories. First, I shall prove that adaptability entails both PropAU and PropCOP. Next, I shall present an intuitive argument that adaptability is stronger than the conjunction of PropAU and PropCOP. (A proper proof of this claim is deferred to a later chapter.) Finally, and most importantly, after defining exclusive act-orientation, I shall prove that *no exclusively act-oriented theory can be adaptable.* (Indeed, I shall prove along the way the stronger claim that no exclusively act-oriented theory can have both PropAU and PropCOP.)

The proof that no exclusively act-oriented theory can be adaptable, or can even approach adaptability to the extent of having both PropAU and PropCOP, is the culmination of our investigation of the traditional consequentialist theories. It amounts to a proof that no traditional theory, and no newly invented theory of the same general type, can be fully adequate when judged by the consequences of satisfaction of the theory. On the one hand, we shall see that AU, RU, UG, and all the variants of those theories we have considered are exclusively act-oriented.[1] I believe it will seem plausible that exclusive act-orientation characterizes a class of theories which includes, in addition to the widely discussed theories just named, all other theories we would regard as being in the same mould. On the other hand, I have already suggested in the Introduction, anticipating the propositions to be proved in this chapter about the relationship of adaptability to PropAU and PropCOP, that adaptability is the ultimate desideratum in a theory which is to be judged by the consequences of agents' satisfying it.

We have seen in Chapters 5 and 6 that some of the standard moves in discussions of rule-utilitarianism and utilitarian generalization represent attempts to create adaptable theories, or at least theories which have both PropAU and PropCOP. The proof that there cannot be an adaptable exclusively act-oriented theory makes it clear that the attempts which produced COP-C, RU, UG', or UG" were doomed from the start. No progress can be made on the project which inspired those attempts unless we consider theories which are fundamentally different from the traditional theories. No progress can be made unless we turn to theories which are not exclusively act-oriented.

Before I set about proving the claims I have listed, I remind the reader of the definitions of PropAU, PropCOP, and adaptability. 'The theory T has PropAU' was defined to mean: 'For any agent, in any choice situation, if the agent satisfies T in that situation, he produces by his act the best consequences he can possibly produce in that situation.' In other words, a theory T has PropAU if and only if any agent who satisfies T in any choice situation is guaranteed to produce the best consequences he can produce in that situation. 'The theory T has PropCOP' was defined to mean: 'If all agents satisfy T in all choice situations, then the class of all agents produce by their acts taken together the best consequences that they can possibly produce by any pattern of behaviour.' In other words, a theory T has PropCOP if and only if universal satisfaction of T (satisfaction by all agents all the time) would guarantee the best consequences that any pattern of behaviour by the universe of agents could possibly produce. 'The theory T is adaptable' was defined to mean: 'In any situation involving choices by any number of agents, the agents who satisfy T in that situation produce by their acts taken together the best consequences that they can possibly produce by any pattern of behaviour, given the behaviour of agents who do not satisfy T.' In other words, a theory T is adaptable if and only if the agents who satisfy T, whoever and however numerous they may be, are guaranteed to produce the best consequences possible as a group, given the behaviour of everyone else. In connection with both PropAU and adaptability, the behaviour of agents other than the individual or group who satisfy T is taken to be either the actual behaviour of other agents whose behaviour the individual or group cannot influence, or the dispositions to behave[2] of other agents whose behaviour the individual or group can influence. In connection with PropCOP this point does not arise, since PropCOP speaks only to a situation in which all agents satisfy T.

The proof that adaptability entails PropCOP is completely trivial. Suppose there is a theory T, which is adaptable. Now suppose that all agents satisfy T. If all agents satisfy T, then the class of agents who satisfy T is the entire universe of agents. Because T is adaptable, this class of agents produce the best consequences possible collectively. But if the entire universe of agents produce the best consequences possible collectively, then best possible consequences overall are produced. In short, if a theory T is adaptable, then if everyone satisfies T, best possible consequences overall are produced. In other words, if a theory T is adaptable, it has PropCOP.

The proof that adaptability entails PropAU is one step more complicated. Suppose there is a theory T, which is adaptable. Suppose also that Hypatia satisfies T. If Hypatia satisfies T, then obviously she is a member of the class of agents who satisfy T. Because T is adaptable, that class of agents produce the best possible consequences collectively. So Hypatia is a member of a group which produces best possible consequences as a group. From that it follows, as we proved in Chapter 3, that Hypatia herself satisfies AU, or in other words produces the best consequences possible in her own situation. In short, if a theory T is adaptable, then any agent who satisfies T produces the best consequences possible in his or her situation. That is to say, if a theory T is adaptable, it has PropAU. (We see now why the consistency claim of Chapters 3 and 4 is essential to the essay as a whole. This claim is essential to the proof that adaptability entails PropAU.)

It may seem that the proof that adaptability entails PropAU, simple as it was, was more complicated than necessary. Could we not have gone directly from the proposition that Hypatia satisfies T to the proposition that she herself produces best consequences in her situation? Strictly speaking, we could not.

Our definition of adaptability says that the class of *all* agents who satisfy T in any situation produce best consequences by their behaviour taken together. If Hypatia is not the only satisfier of T, then the definition of adaptability says nothing, on its face, about whether Hypatia herself produces best consequences.

It is worth noting that the same proposition which allows us to reach a conclusion about Hypatia's behaviour, namely the consistency claim of Chapter 3, allows us to show that our definition of adaptability is equivalent to another possible definition. We might have said that a theory T was adaptable if *every* class of agents who satisfy T in any particular situation (that is, the class of all agents who satisfy T in that situation, and every subclass of that class) produce the best consequences possible given the behaviour of people outside the class. This seems as if it might be an even stronger and more appealing property than adaptability as we have defined it. But in fact this definition is no stronger. The two definitions are equivalent. Obviously, if *every* class of agents who satisfy T produce best possible consequences given the behaviour of non-members of the class, then the class of *all* agents who satisfy T produce best possible consequences given the behaviour of non-satisfiers. The reverse is also true. If the class of *all* agents who satisfy T produce best consequences, then *every* class of agents who satisfy T produce best consequences, since each class of agents who satisfy T is a subclass of the class of all agents who satisfy T, and (as we proved in Chapter 3) all subgroups of any group which produces best consequences produce best consequences also.[3]

If we had started with the (apparently) broader definition of adaptability, then the proof that adaptability entails PropAU would have been simpler. But it would not have been appropriate to start with the broader definition. The appeal of the broader definition depends on the assurance provided by Chapter 3 that there can be no conflict between the production of good consequences by large groups and by smaller included groups or individuals. In addition, the most important division in the universe of all agents is the division highlighted in our original definition of adaptability, that is, the division between the satisfiers of T and the non-satisfiers. The full significance of this observation will become clear only after I have presented co-operative utilitarianism, the one adaptable theory we shall consider.

I have shown that adaptability entails both PropCOP and PropAU. As to the claim that adaptability is stronger than the conjunction of these properties, that seems intuitively obvious. Is it not clear that a theory might have the property that if everyone satisfies it they produce best possible results overall, and also have the property that if any individual satisfies it she produces best results as an individual, and yet not have the property that any *two* agents who satisfy it when some other agent is not satisfying it produce the best possible results as a pair? (Of course, the 'two agent' property does not follow from the 'single agent' property because of the indeterminacy of AU.) But a theory such as the one described would have PropCOP and PropAU without being adaptable. If the theory were adaptable it would have the property that any two agents who satisfied it produced the best possible results as a pair.

What I have just said is persuasive enough. It is not a proof. It invites the reader to agree that there can be a theory like the one described, but it does not produce one. The only example of such a theory I have come up with is an artificially hobbled version of co-operative utilitarianism, which I shall describe after co-operative utilitarianism itself has been introduced and discussed.[4]

We turn now to the demonstration that no exclusively act-oriented theory can be adaptable. The reader might reasonably expect that I would begin with a definition of exclusive act-orientation. I shall not begin that way, however. For reasons which will become clear, I am never going to produce a definition of exclusive act-orientation which is both precise and completely general. The basic difficulty is that while there are many cases in which it is clear what sort of directions may be given by the kind of theory I refer to as exclusively act-oriented, there are some troublesome cases where the import of exclusive act-orientation may become vague. I shall therefore proceed as follows. I shall begin by indicating in an intuitive way what I mean by exclusive act-orientation in general. Having done that, I shall consider a specific sort of case in which the application of the intuitive notion of exclusive act-orientation does not seem problematic, and I shall specify precisely what counts as exclusive act-orientation in the context of that sort of case. I shall then have in effect a precisely specified necessary condition for exclusive act-orientation, and it is on this necessary condition that I shall base a rigorous proof that an exclusively act-oriented theory cannot be adaptable. Although I have felt compelled to explain why, in a manner of speaking, I am going to back into the crucial proof, I hope the approach will seem less circuitous in the execution than in this synopsis.

First, I note a feature which is common to the standard consequentialist theories. AU, RU, and UG share a common picture of the sort of situation moral theories are supposed to deal with, and of how they deal with them. Consider once again our most favoured example.

		Poof	
		Push	Not-push
	Push	10	0
Whiff			
	Not-push	0	6

This array represents a moral choice situation to which each of AU, RU, and UG can be applied. Furthermore, what each of those theories does is to specify for each agent some subset of the set of acts ('pushing' and 'not-pushing') available to him, such that the agent satisfies the theory in question if and only if he does an act from the specified subset. The specified subset for any agent may of course depend on the other agent's behaviour, and it may in some circumstances be the whole set.

Thus, AU makes its direction to Whiff depend on what Poof does. If Poof pushes, then the subset from which AU requires Whiff to choose is the subset consisting of the act 'push'. If Poof does not push, then the subset from which AU requires Whiff to choose is the subset consisting of the act 'not-push'. But there is always some subset of the available acts such that Whiff satisfies AU if and only if he does an act from that subset. RU identifies different subsets from those identified by AU, at least in some circumstances. We saw in Chapter 5 that if Poof does not push, then the subset from which RU requires Whiff to choose is the subset consisting of the acts 'push' and 'not-push'. Although it may seem counter-intuitive, we showed that Whiff satisfies RU (while Poof does not push) if and only if he does an act from that (improper) subset.[5] UG is different still. We have not previously discussed the application of UG to this example, but it is clear that UG directs Whiff to push regardless of what Poof does, so that even if Poof does not push, the subset from which Whiff is required to choose is the subset consisting of the act 'push'. AU, RU, and UG identify different subsets of the available acts from which Whiff is required to choose when Poof not-pushes, but each theory identifies some subset and then is satisfied by Whiff if and only if he does an act from the subset.

A theory need not operate in this way. Consider a version of rule-utilitarianism which selects as the relevant set of rules the set which it would have best consequences for everyone to try to satisfy. There is still a question whether this version of rule-utilitarianism requires each agent actually to *satisfy* that set of rules, or whether it requires each agent only to *try* to satisfy that set of rules. If we had decided that the crucial set of rules was the set it would be best for everyone to try to satisfy, it would not be implausible to go on and say that what each agent was required to do was to *try* to satisfy that set of rules. Observe, however, that a theory which said this would be quite different from AU, RU, and UG. Such a theory would *not* select a subset of the acts available to the agent and say that the agent satisfied the theory if and only if he did an act from that subset. An agent would satisfy such a theory if and only if he tried to satisfy the relevant set of rules. So long as he tried to do this, it would not matter what act he eventually did.

It might be objected that 'trying to satisfy the set of rules it would be best for everyone to try to satisfy' is itself an act available to the agent, and that even the version of rule-utilitarianism currently under consideration therefore selects a subset of the available acts and says that the agent satisfies the theory if and only if he does an act from that subset. It seems, however, that this act of 'trying to satisfy . . .' is a different sort of act from the acts of 'pushing' and 'not-pushing', or 'walking on the grass', 'not walking on the grass', 'punishing an offender', and so on. Each of these latter descriptions ('pushing' and so on) refers to a fairly specific complex of behaviour. 'Trying to satisfy the set of rules it would be best for everyone to try to satisfy' does not. Furthermore, descriptions like 'pushing' are in terms closely related to the features of the acts which actually account for their particular consequences. 'Trying to satisfy . . .' is not.

Even if 'trying to satisfy . . .' is an act of a sort, I suggest that it is not the sort of act with which traditional consequentialist theories are ordinarily concerned, at least in their objective forms. I do not say that this narrow view of the sort of acts which are relevant is necessarily a virtue of traditional theories. Merely that it is a feature of traditional theories.[6]

Of course, I have not offered any precise distinction between acts like 'trying to satisfy the set of rules it would be best for everyone to try to satisfy', which ordinarily are not relevant to traditional theories, and acts like 'pushing', which ordinarily are. How, for example, do we classify an act like 'trying to high-jump 7 feet'? Even though this is described as an act of trying, it has more in common with 'pushing' than with 'trying to satisfy the set of rules it would be best for everyone to try to satisfy'. 'Trying to high-jump 7 feet' refers to a fairly specific complex of behaviour. It might also be that it is precisely the *trying* that produces good consequences. For example, the agent might be a talented young high-jumper who is making a videotape of his technique in a practice session to review with his coach.

Despite the fact that we have drawn no precise distinction between acts like 'pushing' and acts like 'trying to satisfy the set of rules it would be best for everyone to try to satisfy', I think the discussion so far has identified in a general way a feature that is common to traditional consequentialist theories. These theories generally regard the agent as having a choice from a list of acts like pushing—acts described fairly concretely and in terms as close as possible to the consequence-producing features of the acts—and they specify some subset of the acts on this list (which subset may depend on how other agents behave) such that the agent satisfies the theory if and only if he does an act from that subset. Traditional theories ordinarily do *not* require acts like 'trying to satisfy . . .' any set of rules or any theory.

It is worth noting that traditional theories also do not ordinarily require any particular decision procedure. Act-utilitarians may have something to say about how an agent should try to identify the act AU requires in various circumstances. But objective AU, generally speaking, does not. I say 'generally speaking' because there are certain cases, such as the 'mad telepath' cases discussed in Chapter 10,[7] in which traditionalists might want to insist that their theories do speak to the question of what decision procedure an agent should use. But such cases are pathological. AU is satisfied by Whiff in our standard example if and only if he not-pushes, when Poof not-pushes, regardless of how he decides what to do.[8] Parallel assertions are true of RU and UG.

In sum, whether an agent satisfies a traditional consequentialist theory depends, ordinarily, on what he does from a list of acts like 'pushing' and not on what he tries to do or how he decides what to do. This is the feature of traditional theories I refer to by saying they are 'exclusively act-oriented'. Hereafter I shall use the phrase 'traditional theories' to refer not only to theories which are time-honoured or well known, but to all possible consequentialist theories which share this feature of the much-discussed traditional theories such as AU, RU, and UG. I think it is fair to say that consequentialists interested in the consequences of satisfaction of theories have considered only theories which are 'traditional' in this broad sense.

I have now described the intuitive notion of exclusive act-orientation. To say that a theory is exclusively act-oriented, or 'traditional' in our broad sense, is to say that whether an agent satisfies the theory ordinarily depends only on what he does from a list of acts like 'pushing' and 'not-pushing'. This is not a precise definition of exclusive act-orientation. I doubt that I could be much more precise at this level of generality, and I shall not attempt it. Instead, as I have already explained, I shall turn my attention to a particular case in which the import of exclusive act-orientation seems clear, and I shall specify precisely how a theory must deal with that case if it is to count as exclusively act-oriented.

The particular case is of course our standard Whiff and Poof example:

		Poof	
		Push	Not-push
	Push	10	0
Whiff			
	Not-push	0	6

It seems clear that any traditional theory would view each of Whiff and Poof as having just two choices in this example. The choices are 'pushing' and 'not-pushing'. In some contexts it might be suggested that the appropriate descriptions are of the form 'push while Poof is pushing', 'push while Whiff is not-pushing', and so on. That does not alter the fact that in any fully described situation in which either Whiff or Poof might find himself in this example, he has, on any traditional view, two choices, one of which, however it is described, is in effect to push, and one of which is not to. Here is the basis for our precise necessary condition for exclusive act-orientation: *Any exclusively act-oriented theory must, in this example, on any assumption about Poof's (Whiff's) behaviour, identify some non-empty subset of the set of acts comprising 'pushing' and 'not-pushing' such that Whiff (Poof) satisfies the theory if and only if he does some act from that subset.* This necessary condition for a theory's being exclusively act-oriented I shall refer to, for expository convenience, as the 'partial definition' of exclusive act-orientation.

Observe that under the partial definition, the subset identified for one agent by an exclusively act-oriented theory does not have to vary with the other agent's behaviour (though it may). Nor does the subset have to be a proper subset of the set of available acts (an exclusively act-oriented theory may in some circumstances identify as the relevant subset the whole set, in effect leaving the agent a completely free hand). The subset *does* have to be non-empty. If an exclusively act-oriented theory selected the empty subset on any assumption about Poof's (Whiff's) behaviour, then it would direct Whiff (Poof) to do the impossible. (Selecting the empty subset is not the same as directing the agent not to push. 'Not-pushing' is an act for our purposes. Selecting the empty subset is directing the agent to neither push nor not-push, which he cannot do.) AU, RU, and UG all satisfy the partial definition of exclusive act-orientation.[9] It seems plausible to suppose that any other theory we would regard as 'traditional' in its general approach would satisfy the partial definition also.[10]

No theory which satisfies the partial definition of exclusive act-orientation can be adaptable. The proof of this claim is a *reductio,* and begins forthwith. Suppose there is an adaptable theory T which satisfies the partial definition. Suppose further that Poof does not push. Since T satisfies the partial definition, there is some non-empty subset of the set of acts 'pushing' and 'not-pushing' such that Whiff satisfies T (while Poof does not push) if and only if he does an act from that subset. Call the subset S. We can deduce what S must be from the assumptions we have made about T. We know that Whiff satisfies T if and only if he does an act from S. So, if Whiff does an act from S, he satisfies T. Since T is adaptable, T has PropAU. That means that any agent who satisfies T produces the best possible consequences in his circumstances. If Whiff produces best possible consequences in his circumstances, which include Poof's not-pushing, he must not-push. Therefore, if Whiff satisfies T, he not-pushes. Remembering what we have already established, that if Whiff does an act from S, he satisfies T, we can conclude that if Whiff does an act from S, he not-pushes. But remember also that S is non-empty. The only non-empty set such that if Whiff does an act from that set he not-pushes is of course the set consisting of the act 'not-pushing'. Therefore S consists of the act 'not-pushing'. In sum, if Poof does not push, then Whiff satisfies T if and only if he (Whiff) not-pushes also.

What we have just proved about Whiff we could also prove about Poof. Given our assumptions about T, if Whiff does not push, then Poof satisfies T if and only if he (Poof) does not push.

But now, suppose that both Whiff and Poof not-push. We have demonstrated that each of them satisfies T, when the other not-pushes, if and only if he not-pushes. Therefore, when both not-push, both satisfy T. But then universal satisfaction of T does not guarantee the production of the best possible consequences. T does not have PropCOP. Adaptability entails PropCOP, so if T does not have PropCOP, T is not adaptable. That is a contradiction. We conclude that a theory which satisifies the partial definition of exclusive act-orientation cannot be adaptable. QED.

Three questions arise: (1) What is really going on in the proof just presented? (2) Does the argument prove anything of interest beyond the Whiff and Poof example? (3) Does the proof suggest that the partial definition was stronger than it looked, perhaps inappropriately strong for a condition which is supposed to be satisfied by all traditional consequentialist theories? These questions are obviously interrelated.

What is going on in the proof is this. We select a case which meets the following requirements: (a) it is clear what the relevant possible acts for each agent are for purposes of any traditional theory; (b) AU is indeterminate; and (c) it is true of the inferior pattern of universal satisfaction of AU (or of some inferior pattern of universal satisfaction of AU) that AU directs each agent to do precisely what he does in that pattern, given the behaviour of the other agents. (The last requirement excludes cases in which the only inferior pattern(s) of universal satisfaction of AU are pattern(s) in which some agent is left some degree of freedom of choice by AU, given the way the others are behaving. As stated, this requirement is stronger than is necessary to make the proof work, but the proof will not work in every case in which AU is indeterminate, as we show in a note.[11]) Because we have selected a case in which it is clear what the relevant possible acts are for purposes of traditional theories, we can formulate a partial definition of exclusive act-orientation tailored to the case in question. Having done that, we focus on some inferior pattern of universal satisfaction of AU in which each agent is required by AU to do just what he does in that pattern, given the others' behaviour. If that pattern of behaviour is realized, then each agent's behaviour is just the behaviour any theory with PropAU must require of him, given the way the others behave. Any theory with PropAU must require that behaviour; and any theory with PropAU which also satisfies the partial definition of exclusive act-orientation relevant to the case in question must be *satisfied* by that behaviour. (It may seem that the statement that the theory must be satisfied by the behaviour adds nothing to the statement that the theory must require the behaviour. But in fact it adds something very important. In effect, the partial definition, by saying that the theory must identify a set of acts such that the agent satisfies the theory *if* and only if he does an act from that set, prevents the theory from requiring anything *beyond* the act it must require if it is to have PropAU, anything such as trying to follow some theory or adopting some decision procedure. The importance of this restriction will be revealed in later chapters.) It follows from what we have said so far that any theory which has PropAU and which satisfies the relevant partial definition of exclusive act-orientation must be satisfied by the behaviour of every agent in the inferior pattern of universal satisfaction of AU we have focused on. Any such theory is universally satisfied in this inferior pattern. Therefore it does not have PropCOP. In other words, no theory which satisfies the relevant partial definition and has PropAU can have PropCOP. No theory which satisfies the relevant partial definition can be adaptable.

This paraphrase of the proof makes two things clear. First, we did not prove just that a theory which satisfied our partial definition could not be adaptable. We actually proved that a theory which satisfied the partial definition could not have both PropAU and PropCOP, a somewhat stronger claim.[12] Second, the argument of the proof will work in a much broader class of cases than the Whiff and Poof case we have been discussing. For example, it will work in the voting case if we assume: (1) that we can agree that every traditional theory must identify for each agent in any possible situation some subset of the set of acts 'voting' and 'not-voting' such that that agent satisfies the theory if and only if he does an act from the identified subset;[13] and (2) that AU is indeterminate; and (3) that in some inferior pattern of universal satisfaction

of AU every agent is required by AU to do just what he does.[14]
These assumptions all seem very plausible. So do parallel
assumptions about resource-conservation cases and tax-paying
cases, about agreement-keeping and punishing, and so on. In
other words, the argument we used in the Whiff and Poof
example can be used to show that in most of the cases traditionally associated with the debate among consequentialists,
a theory which focuses solely on the sort of acts traditional
theories have regarded as relevant cannot be adaptable.

We have answered the questions about what is going on in
the proof and about whether the proof is relevant beyond the
Whiff and Poof example. The remaining question is whether
the partial definition is too strong. I do not believe it is. The
partial definition excludes theories which state the agent's
obligation in terms of trying to follow some theory or other,
or in terms of adopting some decision procedure, but we have
already argued that no traditional theory is thereby excluded.
The partial definition also excludes certain gimmicky theories
like a theory which says to each of Whiff and Poof in our
standard example: 'If your opposite number pushes, push. If
he not-pushes, then not-push while thinking of a number
greater than any number he thinks of while he not-pushes.'
Or, to make it clear that the gimmick need not be a mental
act: 'If your opposite number pushes, push. If he not-pushes,
then not-push by removing your finger farther from your
button than he removes his finger from his.' If we assume
that neither the agents' arithmetical fancies nor the enthusiasm
with which they not-push affects the consequences of their
behaviour, then these latest theories are adaptable, at least as
far as this one case is concerned. Any individual agent who
satisfies one of these theories makes the same choice with
regard to pushing or not-pushing as his opposite number, and
therefore produces the best consequences possible in his situation. But the only pattern of behaviour in which both agents
can satisfy either theory is the pattern in which both push,
because if both not-push, then each is required to do something
else besides merely not-pushing which is so defined that they
cannot both satisfy the further requirement at the same time.
Similar gimmicky theories can be constructed which are

adaptable in all possible cases. Such theories do not, however, satisfy the partial definition in the Whiff and Poof case, nor would they satisfy the parallel partial definitions in other cases. That is a point in favour of the partial definitions, not a point against them. We have discovered no reason to think our partial definition of exclusive act-orientation in the Whiff and Poof case was too strong.

I shall conclude this chapter by expanding on what I have already said about the significance of the proof that no exclusively act-oriented theory can be adaptable, but first I note four points about the notion of exclusive act-orientation and about the content of the proof which may forestall certain misunderstandings:

(1) An exclusively act-oriented theory can have a subjective counterpart. For example, an act-utilitarian might believe that each agent has a *subjective* obligation to do the act which would have best consequences if his factual beliefs were true. This is irrelevant to the question of what constitutes satisfaction of the exclusively act-oriented objective AU.

(2) A *non*-exclusively act-oriented theory can be fully objective in the sense that what it requires of an agent does not depend in any way on what the agent believes. For example, a theory which specified a certain decision procedure for Whiff to follow in our example and which required Whiff to apply that procedure correctly in all respects would be non-exclusively act-oriented, but it would be thoroughly objective provided the correct sequence of steps in the decision procedure did not depend on the content of Whiff's antecedent beliefs. The theory might even require Whiff to adopt certain beliefs in the process of applying the procedure. Even this, still provided that the beliefs to be adopted did not depend on Whiff's antecedent beliefs, would not make the theory subjective in any standard sense in which some theories are said to impose subjective obligations.[15]

(3) The proof that no exclusively act-oriented theory can be adaptable does not show that no theory at all can be adaptable. Essential use is made of the exclusive act-orientation of T in the course of establishing that any agent satisfies T if he does the act that AU requires. The adaptability of T entails

that T must require the act AU requires, or in other words that T can be satisfied *only if* that act is done. But it is the exclusive act-orientation of T that entails that T cannot require anything beyond that act, and therefore that T is satisfied *if* that act is done.[16]

(4) We make no implicit claim, and it is clearly not the case, that every non-exclusively act-oriented theory is adaptable. For example, the version of rule-utilitarianism that requires each agent to try to satisfy the set of rules it would be best for everyone to try to satisfy, though it is not exclusively act-oriented, could hardly be claimed to be adaptable. An agent might satisfy this theory, by trying to identify and do what would be required of him by the relevant set of rules, but fail utterly in his trying and do a perfectly horrendous act.

As we observed at the beginning of this chapter, the proof that no exclusively act-oriented theory can be adaptable, or can even approach adaptability to the extent of having both PropAU and PropCOP, makes it clear that attempts to improve traditional theories along traditional lines can never produce a completely satisfactory theory. COP-C, RU, UG′, and UG″ are not even first steps in the right direction. The only first step which might be useful is the abandonment of exclusive act-orientation.

The proof that no exclusively act-oriented theory can be adaptable could be viewed as showing that any consequentialist theory must to some extent be defective from a consequentialist point of view. I do not view exclusive act-orientation as an essential feature of an acceptable moral theory, but presumably some readers will feel that it is essential. Such readers must resign themselves to the fact that any theory which passes muster on this count will fail on some other. Either it will not have PropAU, or it will not have PropCOP. This is a weaker blow to consequentialists' hopes than any of the arguments that various forms of consequentialism are 'self-defeating' would be if they were valid.[17] The 'self-defeat' arguments purport to show that universal satisfaction of various forms of consequentialism would *necessarily* produce bad results. I have shown only that satisfaction of a consequentialist theory cannot *guarantee* the best possible results from both individual and collective behaviour, so long as only exclusively act-oriented theories are considered. Still, that is a significant blow. It shows that the most desirable consequentialist programme cannot be realized by a traditional theory.

Our proof also says something about the usefulness of arguing against consequentialist theories by describing cases in which the theories produce 'counterintuitive' results. If we regard as cases involving counterintuitive results both (a) cases in which a theory requires an act that does not itself have best consequences and (b) cases in which universal satisfaction of a theory does not guarantee best possible consequences, then we have shown that *every* traditional theory produces counterintuitive results in some cases. That means that defenders of one traditional theory must do more than just describe some cases in which another theory they disfavour produces counterintuitive results if they are to accomplish anything which can really strengthen the appeal of their own preferred theory.

There is one final point to be mentioned. This point anticipates the material on co-operative utilitarianism, which begins in the next chapter. There is a sense in which co-operative utilitarianism dictates a decision procedure for each agent to follow. Of course, I do not claim that co-operative utilitarianism is exclusively act-oriented, so the fact that it can be viewed as dictating a decision procedure raises no difficulty on that account. It may seem to some readers, however, that in excluding from the range of 'traditional' theories theories which dictate decision procedures, I have drawn a somewhat *ad hoc* distinction in order to be able to go through the proof of the present chapter and thus set the stage for the appearance of co-operative utilitarianism as the *deus ex machina* which will save the consequentialist programme from inevitable defeat.

There are two reasons why this criticism would be unfair. First, the distinction is not *ad hoc*. I think it is a feature of traditional objective theories (and co-operative utilitarianism is an objective theory, even though it is not exclusively act-oriented) that in the sort of cases I have been discussing they do not impose requirements on the agents' decision processes. They impose requirements only on the agents' ultimate behaviour.

Second, no exclusively act-oriented theory could be made into an adaptable theory even by the addition of a 'perfect' decision procedure for that theory. Consider AU. Suppose we were aware of a decision procedure for identifying the act(s) which satisfied AU in any situation, costlessly and infallibly. Any agent who wanted to satisfy AU would have only to apply this procedure and be assured of correct results. Let us call the procedure D(AU). Consider now the theory AU* which requires of each agent that he apply D(AU) and do what it tells him to do. Is AU* adaptable? No. Suppose Whiff and Poof both not-push, in our standard example. Each satisfies AU. Has each satisfied AU*? We cannot say, just on the basis of the information that both not-push, since that says nothing about whether they applied D(AU). But certainly each *may* have satisfied AU*. Each may have applied D(AU) and have done what it directed. After all, what D(AU) does is to identify the act (unique, in this situation) which satisfies AU. Since Whiff and Poof are both satisfying AU, they may both, for all we know, have applied D(AU) and therefore have satisfied AU*. But that means that AU* may have been universally satisfied, even though inferior results are being produced. AU* does not have PropCOP any more than AU did.

The reader may not be satisfied with the argument just given. Have I really said enough about D(AU) to exclude the possibility that if both parties follow D(AU) successfully they are somehow constrained to reach the pattern of behaviour in which both push? Surely not, since I have said almost nothing about D(AU). In response, let me clarify the point I am trying to make. My point is not that any particular candidate for D(AU) fails to generate an adaptable AU*. My point is that we can imagine a D(AU) which functions perfectly in terms of identifying the act required by AU, but which does not generate an adaptable AU*. It follows that any D(AU) which generates an adaptable AU* must do something *more* than merely identify the right act according to AU. Any decision procedure on which we can base an adaptable theory must be something more than a perfect decision procedure *for AU*.

Essentially the same argument can be used to show that *no*

exclusively act-oriented theory could be converted into an adaptable theory just by the addition of a perfect decision procedure for that theory. Consider any exclusively act-oriented theory T, a costless and infallible decision procedure D(T) for identifying the act T requires, and T*, which directs each agent to apply D(T) and to do what it tells him to do. Now, because T is exclusively act-oriented, it cannot be adaptable. We have already proved that. If T is not adaptable, there is some possible situation and some pattern of behaviour such that if that pattern of behaviour is realized there is a collection of agents (which may be only a single agent) who satisfy T but who do not produce best consequences possible as a group. But those same agents who satisfy T without producing best possible consequences might have satisfied T* also. Since all D(T) does is identify the act required by T, each of the agents in question might, for all we know, have followed D(T) and therefore have satisfied T* as well as T. But if those agents might have satisfied T* without producing best possible consequences, T* is no more adaptable than T. The point, as with the earlier argument concerning AU, is that D(T) cannot be the basis for an adaptable theory unless it does something more than merely identify the act required by the exclusively act-oriented T.[18]

What all this means is that it is not just the exclusion of decision procedures which accounts for the non-adaptability of exclusively act-oriented theories. The problem is more basic. The problem is the assumption that what the theory should require, and therefore what a decision procedure for the theory should attempt to identify, is simply acts like 'pushing'. It is not obvious what else a theory could plausibly require. Co-operative utilitarianism is one suggestion about 'what else'.

CO-OPERATIVE UTILITARIANISM
INTRODUCED

According to the theory I call 'co-operative utilitarianism' (hereafter 'CU'), what each agent ought to do is to *co-operate, with whoever else is co-operating, in the production of the best consequences possible given the behaviour of non-co-operators.* I shall spell out what this statement of CU means in two stages. First, I shall explain the basic notion of co-operation which is embedded in CU. That is, I shall explain what it means for a *group* of agents to be co-operating. I shall discuss explicitly only what it means for a group of agents to be co-operating in the production of best possible consequences, but I believe that all co-operation, in whatever project or in pursuit of whatever goal, can be analysed along essentially the same lines. Second, I shall consider what it means for an *individual* agent to co-operate *with whoever else is co-operating.* The shift of focus from defining co-operation by a group to describing what an individual must do who wants to co-operate but must first identify the other agents available for him to co-operate with is an important step. It is an essential step if we are to build an acceptable moral theory on the notion of co-operation. Unfortunately, it gives rise to some complex logical problems, as we shall see.

I shall argue that CU is an adaptable theory. I do not claim that it is the only possible adaptable theory, though it is the only plausible adaptable theory I am aware of. Since I claim that CU is adaptable, I obviously do not claim that it is exclusively act-oriented. This point deserves to be stressed at the outset. As the analysis of co-operation will make clear, co-operation, as I view it, is *not* merely a matter of correct ultimate behaviour. It is not merely a matter of pushing or not pushing under the right circumstances in our Whiff and Poof examples. Correct behaviour is required, but certain attitudes and beliefs are required as well. This, incidentally, explains why I do not state CU in a form analogous to the other theories so far considered, the formulations of which have all begun 'An act is right if and only if . . .'[1] A non-exclusively act-oriented theory cannot be stated this way without distortion of emphasis.

Since I have stressed that CU is not exclusively act-oriented, I should stress that CU *is* fully objective. I noted at the end of Chapter 7 that a non-exclusively act-oriented theory can be objective. CU is an example. Although the agent is required by CU to have certain attitudes and beliefs, the attitudes and beliefs that are required do not depend on the antecedent beliefs of the agent in question.[2] Note that while CU is an objective theory, it has a natural subjective counterpart (or perhaps a range of natural subjective counterparts of varying degrees of subjectivity) just as other objective utilitarian theories do. In this chapter, designed to *introduce* CU, I shall not always be careful about the distinction between CU and its subjective counterpart(s). I shall sometimes speak loosely or metaphorically about what CU requires, and it may seem to the reader that I am describing a subjective theory. If the reader will keep in mind that a theory can be objective even though it is not exclusively act-oriented, and if he will keep in mind that I sometimes speak imprecisely, he should not find anything I say impossible to reconcile with the idea that CU is objective. In Chapters 9 and 10 I shall be careful about the distinction between CU and its subjective counterpart(s). Any doubts raised in this chapter about the objectivity of CU should be dispelled.

The discussion of what it means for a group of agents to co-operate in the production of the best consequences possible is based, predictably, on our favourite example:

		Poof	
		Push	Not-Push
	Push	10	0
Whiff			
	Not-Push	0	6

We add to the description of this example one new assumption. We shall assume that in the situation represented by the above array, self-interest directs each agent not to push, no matter what the other does. This is a new assumption, but it is consistent with the original description of the example, which said nothing at all about the consequences of various patterns of behaviour for the interests of Whiff and Poof themselves.

We begin our analysis of co-operation by looking at the variety of ways in which Whiff and Poof can *fail* to be co-operating in the production of the best consequences possible. First, suppose that Poof is simply selfish, and decides not to push. If Poof thinks and behaves thus, he obviously is not co-operating in the production of best possible consequences. Furthermore, there is no way Whiff, however unselfish *he* may be, can co-operate with Poof in the production of best possible consequences. Whiff can make the best of Poof's unco-operativeness by not-pushing himself. (In doing so, he would not merely 'make the best' of Poof's behaviour from his own point of view. If Poof does not push, then not-pushing is the best thing for Whiff to do in terms of *overall* consequences.) Alternatively, Whiff could behave as he would behave *if* he and Poof were co-operating in the production of best possible consequences, by pushing, though there is really nothing to recommend this course of action, unless perhaps Poof can be persuaded by Whiff's example to be more co-operative in the future. But there is no way Whiff can co-operate with Poof while Poof is selfishly not-pushing. Selfish behaviour on the part of Poof makes co-operation impossible.

In fact, it is not even necessary to the breakdown of co-operation identified in the preceding paragraph that Poof should not push. Suppose that Poof is motivated solely by self-interest, but suppose also that he is misinformed about the situation. He believes that the self-interested thing for him to do is to push, and that is what he does. Now, if Whiff is unselfish he will push also, and best possible results will be achieved, but it seems clear that Whiff and Poof will not have co-operated. Poof's attitude is inconsistent with his being counted as a co-operator. He behaves as he would behave if he were co-operating, but that is the result of ignorance, not of an attempt to co-ordinate his behaviour with Whiff's in pursuit of a jointly valued outcome. Poof is not co-operating;

and because Poof is not co-operating, Whiff is not co-operating with him. Whiff's motives are pure. Indeed everything about Whiff's attitude and behaviour is unexceptionable. But he is not co-operating with Poof because Poof is not co-operating with him.

We could make the example more extreme. We might assume that *both* Whiff and Poof are selfish and misguided in the way Poof was just assumed to be. If this were the case, then both would push, and best possible results would again be produced. It would be even clearer, however, that there was no co-operation going on. We might describe the situation in which both parties are selfishly motivated but end up pushing as a result of ignorance as one in which the parties 'co-operate in spite of themselves', but if we said that we would plainly mean that they produced the desirable results of co-operation despite the absence of genuine co-operation.

Already we see that co-operation is not simply a matter of engaging in the correct behaviour, that is, the correct alternative from the set 'pushing' or 'not-pushing'. In order for an agent to be co-operating, he must be attempting to achieve a jointly valued outcome by co-ordinated behaviour. And in order for one agent to be co-operating with a second, the second must be a co-operator himself.

Improper motivation is not the only source of breakdowns in co-operation. Suppose Poof wants to co-operate, but he is misinformed about the consequences of various possible patterns of behaviour for himself and Whiff. Specifically, suppose Poof believes that the best pattern is the one in which neither agent pushes. Counting on Whiff's participation in this pattern Poof not-pushes. At this point the only sensible thing for Whiff to do, assuming he is properly motivated and fully informed, and assuming the situation will not be repeated sufficiently often so that he should attempt to educate Poof, is to not-push also. It is clear that neither Whiff nor Poof is co-operating in the production of best consequences possible. Poof is trying to co-operate. Whiff is making the best of the unfortunate situation created by Poof's mistaken belief. But there is no co-operation between Whiff and Poof, despite their good motives.

Once again, the same point could be made even in a situation in which both parties ended up pushing. Suppose Poof wants to co-operate and believes that the best joint pattern of behaviour is the pattern in which he pushes and Whiff does not. In this situation, Poof will push. Whiff, if he is attempting to produce best consequences overall and if he is well informed, both about the basic situation and about what Poof is doing and why, will push also. Best possible results will be achieved. But not, surely, by co-operation. Poof does not understand the situation and would disapprove of Whiff's behaviour. If Poof knew Whiff was pushing, he would presumably regard himself as making a valiant but futile solo effort. Whiff has behaved unexceptionably in all respects. But he has not co-operated with Poof because Poof has not co-operated with him. Poof has tried to co-operate. He has even been led, by happy accident, to behave as he would behave if he and Whiff really were co-operating. Whiff has taken advantage of this happy accident to see to it that the best consequences possible are produced. But to say all that is not to say that Whiff and Poof have co-operated.

For co-operation to occur, more is required even than proper motivation and correct understanding of the basic situation. Suppose Poof is well motivated and understands the basic situation, but suppose he believes (erroneously) that Whiff is selfish and will not-push for that reason. Having this belief about Whiff, Poof not-pushes. As usual, all Whiff can do, even if he is in fact unselfish and well informed, is to make the best of the situation by not-pushing.

This mode of breakdown of co-operation, like the others, can occur even though both parties push and best results are produced. Suppose Whiff and Poof both want to co-operate. Both understand the consequences of various patterns of joint behaviour. But Poof erroneously believes (1) that Whiff is selfish and (2) that Whiff erroneously believes that self-interest requires him (Whiff) to push. Believing all of this, Poof will push. Whiff, if he figures out what Poof will do and why, will push also. Best results will be achieved. But not by co-operation. Poof does not regard Whiff as a co-operator, and so does not regard himself as co-operating with anyone. Therefore he is not co-operating, and therefore Whiff is not either. The case could be made more extreme by assuming both parties suffer from the same sort of misapprehension about the other that we have hitherto attributed only to Poof. If that were the case, then both would push and best results would be achieved. We could even say that best results would be achieved on account of the attempts of both parties to produce best results. But we would not characterize what occurred as co-operation. As we have noted previously, we might say that the parties had managed to co-operate in spite of themselves, but that would amount to an admission that true co-operation did not occur.

It should be apparent that we could continue this catalogue of possible modes of breakdown of co-operation indefinitely. Co-operation might break down because Poof, though well intentioned and well informed about the basic situation and aware that Whiff was trying to co-operate, mistakenly believed that Whiff did not understand the basic situation. Or it might break down because Poof, though aware that Whiff was properly motivated and informed about the basic situation, erroneously believed that Whiff erroneously believed that Poof was selfish, or misinformed. And so on.

Co-operation involves a potentially infinite hierarchy of reciprocal beliefs. Seemingly, if Whiff and Poof are to co-operate, each must be attempting to produce a jointly valued outcome by co-ordinated behaviour; each must be correctly informed about the consequences of various patterns of joint behaviour; each must be aware that the other is properly motivated and well informed; each must be aware that the other is aware that he (the first of the pair) is properly motivated and well informed; and so on. False beliefs at any level of this hierarchy will prevent the existence of co-operation even if they do not prevent the achievement of best possible consequences. What is true for a group of two is true for larger groups as well. For any group, of whatever size, co-operation involves the same sort of potentially infinite hierarchy of intertwined beliefs connecting all the members of the group, in addition to proper motivation and correct basic information on every agent's part. And, lest we forget, co-operation *also* requires correct behaviour by each agent. This might be

thought to follow from proper motivation and all those correct
intertwined beliefs. Strictly speaking, it does not. There is
always the possibility that a properly motivated and completely well-informed Poof might not-push because of a slip
of the finger, or because of a sudden seizure. In any case, the
requirement of correct behaviour is sufficiently important to
be mentioned separately.

What I have said about the infinity of ways in which co-
operation can break down, and about the potentially infinite
hierarchy of beliefs which is involved, might lead one to
wonder whether co-operation can ever be achieved. It is at
least doubtful that any agent can actually entertain the infinite
set of beliefs which we have outlined. I suggest that co-operation can occur none the less. It is true that there are an infinite
number of ways in which co-operation can fail, and that there
is a potentially infinite set of beliefs which the most completely informed co-operators might have. But something less
than this infinity of beliefs will suffice. As long as each putative co-operator is properly motivated and has some minimum
complement of correct beliefs from the lower levels of the
hierarchy (say perhaps a correct understanding of the basic
structure of the case and an awareness that the others are
properly motivated and understand the basic structure of the
case), and as long as none of the putative co-operators entertains any *false* beliefs from a higher level of the hierarchy,
then we should be willing to say that they are co-operating,
provided of course that each does the right act (the act required
of him in the best pattern of behaviour for the group) into
the bargain. Of course, the more relevant correct beliefs the
parties have, the more sophisticated is their co-operation, in
a sense. But the important thing, so long as the parties share
a certain minimum corpus of correct beliefs, is that no one
should entertain a false belief about someone else's beliefs
and therefore positively misapprehend what is going on.

I anticipate three principal objections to my analysis of
co-operation. First, there will be some readers to whom it still
appears that the hierarchy of beliefs is irrelevant, and that the
correct analysis is the straightforward claim that co-operation
(within any particular group) breaks down if and only if

somebody fails to do his part in the best pattern of behaviour for the group. Without really adding anything to what I have already said, I would point out that the examples so far discussed argue strongly against the 'only if' half of this claim, and to some extent against the 'if' half. As to the 'only if'—remember the simple case in which both Whiff and Poof are purely selfish, but in which both are misinformed and both push, in the mistaken belief that doing so will serve their own interests. Because both push, both do their parts in the best pattern of behaviour for the group. Yet this is surely not a case of co-operation, except perhaps 'co-operation in spite of themselves'. Therefore it is not the case that co-operation breaks down only if some member of the group fails to follow the best pattern of behaviour for the group. Other cases we have already discussed make the same point, but this case is the clearest.

As to the 'if' claim—it is true that co-operation breaks down if some member of the group does not follow the best pattern. Even so, if we consider the question of *how* exactly co-operation has broken down in such a case, we find that we must look at more than the parties' ultimate acts. Remember the case in which Poof alone is selfish and well informed, and not-pushes. If the well-motivated Whiff is aware of what Poof is doing and why and makes the best of the situation by not-pushing himself, then if we ask about each agent only whether he pushed or not, each will have behaved the same way. It is true that there is no co-operation, and that Whiff is not co-operating with Poof any more than Poof is co-operating with Whiff. But it is also true that the responsibility for the failure of co-operation rests entirely with Poof. We must look beyond the parties' acts in order to know what has really happened with regard to the failure of co-operation. All of this confirms the idea that co-operating is more than a matter of simply behaving correctly.

Turning to the second objection, it might be suggested that co-operation is really a matter of behaving according to an agreed plan. There are two principal defects of this suggestion. First, it seems clear that co-operation can occur in the absence of any agreement. If Whiff and Poof are presented with our standard example and have no opportunity to confer, but if each is well intentioned and well informed and confident of the other's goodwill and ability to understand the situation, and confident that the other has confidence in him, and so on, then we would expect them to arrive at the behaviour of pushing together, and we would have no doubt that in doing so they were co-operating. Second, it is doubtful that even if Whiff and Poof had an agreement, this agreement would *displace* co-operation (in our sense, which does not require an agreement) as an explanation for successful co-ordination. The discussion of agreements in Chapter 2 established that in an important sense there might be no ground for criticizing either Whiff or Poof for his *individual* behaviour if both of them violated the agreement. That suggests that there is an element of co-operation required even in the joint following of an explicit agreement. Often each party to an agreement follows the agreement only because he expects the other to, and because he expects the other to expect him to, and so on. In short, while agreements can be useful to co-operators,[3] co-operation in our sense is often the precondition for making use of an agreement. Agreements cannot be regarded as a sufficient alternative to co-operation such as we have described.

Finally, it may seem to some readers that while my analysis is unexceptionable, it is an analysis not of 'co-operation' but of 'co-ordination'. My analysis requires the parties to have the same goal. The goal need not be the production of best possible consequences. But the goal must be shared. It might be suggested that this commonality of purpose is not present in all cases we would regard as involving co-operation. Thus, if two agents confronted with a (genuine) prisoners' dilemma manage to resist the appeal of their dominant self-interested strategies and to bring about the jointly preferred but unstable symmetric outcome, would we not say that they had co-operated, even though they had different maximands? I do not know if we would all say that, but some of us would, surely. And to that extent my definition of 'co-operation' may be too narrow. I could say that it takes only a slight extension to make my analysis cover the case of the co-operating prisoners. Even if the prisoners have different maximands, they cannot solve the dilemma without recognizing that they share the dilemma and have parallel interests in overcoming it. But I shall not press that line.

Instead, I shall concede that 'co-operation' may be a broader term than I suggest in one respect and explain why I none the less prefer 'co-operation' to 'co-ordination' as the name for the phenomenon I am analysing. To me, 'co-ordination', while it may tend more to suggest the existence of a single goal and may be more apt in that respect, also suggests a primary focus on the parties' ultimate behaviour—on whether Whiff and Poof in our example push their buttons or not. 'Co-operation' seems better suited to indicate the importance of the parties' motivation and mutual awareness. The phenomenon I am concerned with is the joint promotion of common goals by agents who are mutually aware. There is no word which is incontestably the right one for this phenomenon. I hope my use of 'co-operation' does not seem inappropriate to most readers. Even more, I hope those to whom it does seem inappropriate will take note of these paragraphs and remember as we proceed what I mean.

Turning to a different matter, the reader may have noticed a strong similarity between my analysis of co-operation and David Lewis's analysis of convention.[4] Lewis and I share a common inspiration in the work of Thomas Schelling.[5] In effect, Lewis regards using a language as a pure co-ordination game among the speakers of the language, and I regard behaving morally as being, *in part,* a pure co-ordination game among the class we might refer to as the 'competent agents of good-will'. Of course there are differences between Lewis's analysis of convention and mine of co-operation. For example, Lewis's definition of convention requires a regularity of behaviour in a recurrent situation, whereas co-operation in my sense can occur in a situation which has neither precedent nor sequel. Still, there is a definite resemblance, which I have no wish to minimize.

Despite the resemblance, there is an extremely important difference between what I have to say and what Lewis and Schelling have said. The difference concerns issues that are left *after* we have defined co-operation. I shall spend the rest of this chapter, and the next two chapters as well, discussing how one agent should decide which other agents to regard as participants in the co-operative venture. Lewis and Schelling do not reach this question. They both discuss pure co-ordination problems in contexts where they assume that all the agents involved are motivated to try to co-ordinate and understand the structure of the problem. Neither of these circumstances can be taken for granted by a moral agent who is trying to figure out, in some situation, which other agents he ought to regard as co-operators. An agent attempting to behave morally does not reach the stage where he may regard himself as a participant in a pure co-ordination game until he has determined just which other agents in the overall situation are also players in the pure co-ordination game. And the precise structure of the pure co-ordination game depends not only on the structure of the overall situation, but on who the players of the pure co-ordination game are.

I mentioned in the Preface that a number of writers have made suggestions which could be regarded as steps in the direction of CU. Specifically, a number of people have perceived, more or less clearly, that behaving morally is to some extent a matter of taking part in a pure co-ordination game involving the competent agents of good will.[6] But no one has confronted the problem of just how this class is to be defined and what one agent must do in order to figure out who else belongs.[7] As we shall see, there are some genuine difficulties.

I have explained what it is for a group of agents to co-operate in the production of best consequences possible. I must now explain what it means for an *individual* to 'co-operate, with whoever else is co-operating, in the production of the best consequences possible given the behaviour of non-co-operators'. An initial difficulty is this. The analysis of what it is for a group to co-operate emphasizes that co-operation is very much a *group* activity, depending on a shared attempt to co-ordinate behaviour and on a hierarchy of intertwined beliefs. It might seem that no sense at all can be made of an injunction to an individual to co-operate. We can deal with this problem by saying that the injunction to an individual to co-operate is just an injunction to take part in the group activity which constitutes co-operation, but then it appears that any one agent's ability to satisfy the injunction depends on the attitudes, beliefs, and behaviour of other individuals. If that is so, then others' unwillingness to co-operate might make co-operation by some willing agent logically impossible. This is troublesome, since it is clear that a moral theory (such as CU) ought to be viewable as giving directions to each individual (not just to groups), and that the directions ought to be ones that each individual can (as a matter of logical possibility) satisfy somehow whatever other agents do.

In fact, the injunction to 'co-operate, with whoever else is co-operating . . .' is interpretable as an injunction directed to individuals, and one which each individual can satisfy regardless of the attitudes, beliefs, and behaviour of other agents. The phrase 'with whoever else is co-operating' is the key.

What CU contemplates that each agent should do is roughly the following: *First,* he should be willing to take part in a joint attempt to produce the best consequences possible by co-ordinating his behaviour with the behaviour of other agents who are also willing. That is, he should hold himself ready to do his part in the best pattern of behaviour for the group of co-operators, whoever precisely the other members of that group turn out to be. *Second,* he should consider the other agents involved in the co-ordination problem he is making a decision about and determine which of those other agents are available to be co-operated with. Another agent is 'available to be co-operated with' if he (the other agent) is prepared to take part in a joint attempt to produce best possible consequences, and if he understands the basic situation, and if he correctly identifies everyone else who is willing to take part in the joint attempt and who understands the situation, and so on. *Third,* he should ascertain how other agents who are *not* (for whatever reason) available to be co-operated with are behaving or are disposed to behave.[8] *Fourth,* he should identify the best possible pattern of behaviour for the group of co-operators (that is to say, the group consisting of himself and other agents who have been identified as available to be co-operated with) given the behaviour (or dispositions to behave) of the non-co-operators. *Fifth,* he should do his part in the best pattern of behaviour just identified.

To summarize, the follower of CU begins by holding himself ready to co-operate with whoever else is willing and able to co-operate. He then identifies the other co-operators and does his part in the best possible pattern of behaviour for the class of co-operators (including himself) in view of the behaviour of the non-co-operators.[9]

We see that the injunction to 'co-operate, with whoever else is co-operating . . .' can be viewed as an injunction addressed to each agent individually. Furthermore, the sketch of what is involved in co-operating with whoever else is co-operating makes it clear that an agent can satisfy the injunction even if no other agent is available to be co-operated with. If one agent decides correctly that no other agent is available to be co-operated with, then that agent ascertains the behaviour (or dispositions to behave) of *all* other agents, and then identifies the best 'pattern of behaviour' for the group consisting solely of himself, given everyone else's behaviour, and then adopts that 'pattern'. The agent who finds no one else available to be co-operated with ends up co-operating with the empty class, or in effect simply satisfying AU.

The phrase 'co-operating with the empty class' may sound odd in connection with our usual notion of co-operation, and no one need use the phrase who does not like it. But it does emphasize that my sketch of what it means to 'co-operate, with whoever else is co-operating . . .' provides a perfectly natural extension of the idea of co-operating with whoever else is available to cover the case where no one else is available at all. The important thing is that the injunction to co-operate with whoever else is co-operating is addressed to individuals and is satisfiable by any individual regardless of the attitudes, beliefs, and behaviour of others. When I say it is satisfiable by any individual, I mean of course that it is always logically possible for any individual to satisfy it, whatever the attitudes and behaviour of the others. I do not mean that it is always obvious to any agent what he must do to satisfy CU. There is no plausible theory such that it is always obvious what one must do to satisfy it.

My suggestion that an individual may end up 'co-operating with the empty class' is reminiscent of a passage where Colin Strang says of a lone would-be co-operator: '[He] isn't expected to be heroic or to do, or even attempt, the impossible. If two are needed to launch and man the lifeboat, the lone volunteer can only stand and wait: *he also* serves. The least a man can do is offer and hold himself ready, though sometimes it is also the most he can do.'[10] The first requirement of CU is precisely that each agent 'hold himself ready'. He must offer to co-operate, in a sense, though the offer need not in general be publicly expressed.

The five-step sketch of what is involved in following CU brings to mind the passage I have already quoted from Harrod's classic article, 'Utilitarianism Revised'. Speaking of whether a utilitarian should follow a practice the general following of which would be desirable but which may not be generally followed, Harrod says:

I believe that, where the practice is not general, a second refining process is required. Will the gain due to its application by all conscientious, *i.e.*, moral, people *only* be sufficient to offset the loss which the crude utilitarian principle registers? It may be objected to this that there are no moral people, but only more or less moral people. To meet this, for the word moral in the second refining principle, say people sufficiently moral to act disinterestedly in this kind of case.[11]

In our terms, Harrod is suggesting that each agent should decide who else is prepared to co-operate in the practice and should then decide whether the practice is a good one for that group to adopt. Harrod goes on to note that the question of who is 'sufficiently moral' will be complex, but he suggests that only a rough approximation to the correct answer is necessary in practice. I agree. (The use of rules of thumb in connection with CU is discussed in later chapters.[12]) Harrod also suggests that 'implicit calculations of this kind are actually carried out in the most ordinary affairs of everyday life by moral men'.[13] Again, I agree.

Returning to the consideration of CU itself, the sketch of what is involved in following CU provides the basis for a heuristic argument to the effect that CU is adaptable. Let us see how the group of agents who satisfy CU in some situation make their decisions and how they end up behaving, by simply describing their progress through the steps of the process we have outlined. We need a name for the group of agents who satisfy CU, and we shall call the group 'S', to emphasize that we are speaking of the group of agents who *satisfy* CU. Not the group who *try* to do what CU requires, but the group who *succeed*. (Although this is probably unnecessary, I note that there is no connection between the 'S' of this chapter and the 'S' of Chapter 7 beyond the fact that 'satisfy' and 'subset' start with the same letter.)

Now, what do the members of S, the satisfiers of CU, do? First, each member of S holds himself ready to do his part in the joint attempt to produce best consequences. Second, each member of S correctly identifies all the other agents who are willing to take part in the joint attempt, and who are adequately informed, and who correctly identify others who are well motivated and well informed, and so on. At this stage, corresponding to the second step of the sketch, the members of S all identify each other as the class of agents available to be co-operated with, since it is precisely the members of S who are both willing and able to do what is required of them in the effort to co-operate. Third, the members of S all correctly ascertain the behaviour (or dispositions to behave) of non-members of S. Fourth, the members of S all correctly identify the best pattern of behaviour for the members of S given the behaviour of non-members. Fifth, the members of S all do their part in that pattern. If the members of S all do their part in the best pattern of behaviour for the members of S given the behaviour of non-members, it is clear that the members of S produce the best consequences possible as a group. In short, the group of agents who satisfy CU in any situation produce the best consequences possible as a group. In other words, CU is adaptable.

The argument just given that CU is adaptable has one flaw. There is an air of sleight-of-hand at the point where I assert that the members of S, severally attempting to decide who else is well motivated and well informed and so on, all manage to identify each other as the class of agents available to be co-operated with. If the members of S do in fact identify each other at this stage, then the rest of the argument for the proposition that the members of S produce the best consequences possible as a group is straightforward and unproblematic. But it is essential that the members of S identify each other at the point where each decides who else is available to be co-operated with.

Consider what can happen if the members of S do not identify each other correctly. If any member of S includes in what he takes to be S (the class of agents available to be co-operated with) an agent who is not in fact a member of S, then he will formulate and follow the best plan of behaviour for a group which includes an agent who may not follow the plan at all, and the member of S in question may therefore act in a way that does not produce best possible results given others' actual behaviour. Alternatively, if any two members of S exclude each other from what they (individually) take to be S, then the members of S may fail to co-ordinate among themselves. Suppose that in our standard Whiff and Poof example it can happen that consistently with CU each of Whiff and Poof somehow comes to regard the other as a non-co-operator. If this happens and both not-push, both satisfy CU. Each does the best act possible given the behaviour of the other, whom he regards, and by hypothesis correctly regards so far as CU is concerned, as a non-co-operator. But they do not produce best possible results as a group.[14] The same sort of failure of co-ordination among members of S could occur in any other case where the members of S split up into two or more subgroups, with the members of each subgroup regarding non-members of that subgroup as non-co-operators. In sum, it is essential that the members of S identify each other correctly if they are to be certain of producing best possible results as a group.

Once we realize the importance of the step at which the members of S identify each other, three difficulties appear:

First, each member of S must decide which other agents are properly motivated, and are well informed, and correctly identify other agents who are willing and well informed, and so on. This 'and so on' covers a potentially infinite hierarchy of intertwined beliefs. It is natural to wonder whether 'and so on' does not conceal some logical difficulty, either some unavoidable circularity in the decision process of each individual which is introduced by his considering others' beliefs about his own beliefs, or perhaps a need for an infinite series of steps which no agent is in a position to complete.

Second, if the members of S really are to identify each other at this step, then in addition to considering other putative co-operators' willingness, general understanding of the situation, and beliefs about other putative co-operators, each member of S must also decide whether other putative co-operators will correctly ascertain the behaviour of *non*-co-operators at the later step where that is required. (Membership in S depends on satisfaction of CU and therefore depends on negotiating *all* steps correctly. A member of S risks including in what he takes to be S some non-members of S unless he checks that each person he regards as a member of S succeeds at the later step of CU referred to.) This raises another possible circularity. Is it acceptable for the members of S to inquire into the success of other putative members in ascertaining the behaviour of non-members of S *as part of the process of determining who the members are*? It seems as if the non-members must already be identified, in which case the members are already identified as well.

Third, we recall that co-operation requires, in addition to appropriate attitudes and beliefs, appropriate behaviour. The members of S are agents who satisfy CU, and since the last step of CU is a direction to do one's part in a certain pattern of behaviour, the members of S must apparently, in order to identify each other, consider each other's ultimate behaviour as well as each other's attitudes and beliefs. Each member of S must somehow satisfy himself that no other agent he regards as a member of S will have good intentions and all the right beliefs, but will have a seizure at the last minute and do the wrong thing. However, if each member of S must consider the ultimate behaviour of every other member, then each member of S apparently acts on information which would be sufficient to tell him what to do to satisfy AU, and we are led to wonder whether CU really differs from AU, or whether its claimed superiority over AU is an illusion.

The natural way to respond to these difficulties, especially those involving possible circularity or infinite regress, would be to spell CU out in still greater detail. If I set about elaborating the five-step sketch of CU, with special attention to the process by which the members of S identify each other, I could eventually produce a satisfactory elaboration, along with a persuasive argument that CU as elaborated was adaptable and that the logical difficulties were only apparent. That is roughly the path I shall follow, but not exactly.

In the next chapter I shall consider a series of formally stated decision procedures for an agent faced with a moral decision. The first decision procedure will look much like the five-step sketch of CU from this chapter, though it will be simpler and will *not* have the property that the agents who follow it successfully are guaranteed to produce the best consequences possible. I shall elaborate that decision procedure in stages until I have produced a procedure I shall call 'P' which has all the logical properties we want in CU. Specifically, P satisfies the following requirements: (1) it is a procedure for each agent to follow individually; (2) it can (logically speaking) be followed successfully by each agent regardless of what the others do; (3) it can (logically) be successfully followed simultaneously by any number of agents, from none to the entire universe of agents (this point is noted because of the gimmicky adaptable theories mentioned in Chapter 7, which under certain circumstances can be satisfied by only one individual); (4) it is non-circular; (5) it requires of any agent only a finite number of steps; (6) each agent who follows it successfully identifies as the class of agents he is 'co-operating' with just the class of other agents who follow it successfully; and (7) the agents who follow it successfully produce the best possible consequences as a group given the behaviour of the agents who do not follow it successfully. Such of the claims about P as are not obvious from the face of the eventual statement of P I shall prove rigorously. Indeed, that is the point of shifting attention from CU to P. The discussion of P will constitute a rigorous demonstration of the logical possibility of a theory which lives up to my claims for CU.

The reader may wonder about the relationship of P to CU.

If P has all the properties we want in CU, why do I not simply present P as the required spelling-out of CU? The answer, roughly, is that P is *too* detailed. It is a precisely described model or realization of CU, but it is only one among many possible models or realizations. P illustrates how CU works. It will provide the basis for a full statement of CU in Chapter 10. And the detail in the statement of P is necessary to the rigorous proof that P works. But the detail of P is more than is necessary to capture the basic ideas of CU. I cannot be more specific about the relationship of P to CU until P itself has been discussed. I shall return to this topic in due course.

I have indicated how I will deal with the first two of our three difficulties, involving the spectres of circularity and infinite regress. The discussion of P in the next chapter will also shed some light on the third difficulty, the possibility that application of CU requires as much information as would be required by application of AU. The discussion will make clear that it is not really true that each member of S must know how the others will behave. What each member of S needs to know about each other member of S is just that each other member will eventually act on the best plan *as he* (the other member) *sees it* when he comes to the last step of the sketch of CU. It is not necessary for one member of S to know what other members will do under any other description than this. Of course, other stages of the process have the effect of checking that all the members of S eventually reach correct conclusions about how they should act. Still, the only thing one member of S need ever know about other members' behaviour as such is that the other members behave consistently with their own conclusions about how they should behave. It is obvious that a theory which is to be adaptable must provide each agent who satisfies the theory with some firm handle on all other agents' behaviour under some description. What each member of S knows about the behaviour of other members of S would seem to be the least that could possibly suffice, and it is markedly different from what one agent needs to know about others' behaviour in order to apply AU.

As the final episode in this introduction to CU, I should like briefly to compare CU with the other consequentialist theories we have investigated. What I have to say will to some extent anticipate the discussion of Chapter 12, in which I argue that CU embodies a more satisfactory answer than any other consequentialist theory to the question of how each agent should view others' behaviour. I introduce the topic now in order to suggest that CU is an intuitively attractive theory, quite aside from its adaptability. The material of the next two chapters is rather technical. I hope by pausing here for some comment on the intuitive appeal of CU to forestall the reader from deciding that the whole theory is too convoluted to be worth worrying about.

First, if we take it as provisionally granted that CU manages to be adaptable without involving any hidden logical defect, it is worth inquiring why CU succeeds where other theories which have tried to combine PropAU and PropCOP, such as COP-C, RU, UG', and UG'', fail. The answer is that CU combines PropAU and PropCOP in a very different way from these other theories.

The other theories take it for granted that each agent must respond to the ultimate behaviour (such as 'pushing' or 'not-pushing') of all other agents. By saying each agent must respond to the ultimate behaviour of all others, I do not mean that every agent must act after every other. I mean that in principle what is required of one agent depends on a complete specification of the ultimate behaviour of every other. COP-C and RU provide for this by allowing conditional prescriptions; UG' and UG'' provide for it by making the description of each agent's situation include a reference to every other agent's behaviour. Having made this bow in the direction of PropAU, these theories attempt to build in PropCOP by focusing on the best set of prescriptions for everyone to follow or the best act for every agent similarly situated to perform. In effect, these theories assume both that *no one* other than the agent who is applying the theory can be counted on to behave as he ought (since the agent must respond to everyone else's behaviour) and that *everyone* can be counted on to behave as he ought (since it is on that assumption that the best prescriptions or the best act are chosen). It is no wonder these theories are unsatisfactory.

CU, by contrast, assumes very sensibly that some agents can be counted on to do their part in producing best possible consequences, and that some can not. What each agent is instructed to do is to figure out which other agents fall into each category. Each agent is then required to join with the other agents who can be counted on to do their part in responding to the behaviour of those agents who can not. The agents who can be counted on to do their part are not required to worry about responding to the behaviour of others who can be counted on. Co-ordination among the co-operators is achieved just because they *do* all do their part. That, roughly, is where PropCOP comes in. An optimal response by the co-operators to the non-co-operators is achieved because the co-operators are required to respond as a group to the behaviour of those who do not co-operate. That, roughly, is where PropAU comes in. The whole approach is more sensible than the approach of COP–C, RU, UG′, or UG″, once we see what those theories really involve.

I have noted one way in which CU's approach to the question of how each agent should regard others' behaviour is more sensible than the approach of traditional theories. There is another aspect of the difference which will receive considerably more attention in Chapter 12, but which is worth introducing here. One of the basic facts about the world is that there is a multiplicity of moral agents. This strongly suggests that the business of behaving morally ought to be viewable as a community enterprise. If we have a consequentialist theory, then the business of producing good consequences ought to be viewed as a community undertaking. CU brings this feature of the moral life much more clearly to the fore than other forms of consequentialism.

As far as AU is concerned, each agent regards others' behaviour as on a par with the winds and the tides (or at least, on a par with natural phenomena, though not necessarily phenomena which cannot be influenced by the agent in question). The agent applying AU regards everyone else's behaviour or dispositions to behave as part of the circumstances. At the most fundamental level, there is no reference to the desirability or even the possibility of co-operation in pursuit of a common goal. Rule-utilitarianism (in the pure form represented by COP) and UG in effect instruct each agent to ignore the others entirely. There is some reference to the desirability of co-ordination, since each agent is to behave according to a pattern, or to perform an act, which would be best for everyone. In the final analysis, however, each agent is required only to do his part in a hypothetical co-operative effort which is doomed by its unrealistic assumption of universal participation before it begins. The agent is excused from the messy business of finding out who his fellow co-operators really are. RU, COP–C, UG', and UG'' combine the defects of AU and of COP and UG, as they attempt to combine the virtues.

CU is the one theory which emphasizes that those agents who are prepared to behave morally are engaged in a common undertaking which requires a shared recognition of the need for co-ordination and a shared willingness to go beyond ideal rules and counterfactual assumptions. In short, CU is the one theory which recognizes that co-operation is the heart of the matter.

THE LOGICAL POSSIBILITY OF 'CO-OPERATING . . .'

In this chapter I shall develop the decision procedure P which models CU and which establishes the logical possibility of a theory with the properties I have claimed for CU. I shall not repeat here the full list of properties P is to have.[1] The central problem, clearly, is to produce a P which is adaptable without involving either circularity or infinite regress. (Strictly speaking, 'adaptable' has been defined with reference to moral theories, not decision procedures. I shall use both 'adaptable' and 'satisfy' in connection with decision procedures, in the obvious senses. An agent will be said to satisfy a decision procedure if he applies it correctly in all respects; and a decision procedure will be said to be adaptable if the class of agents who satisfy it produce the best consequences possible as a group given the behaviour or dispositions to behave of agents who do not satisfy it.)

As I mentioned in the Preface, some of the arguments about P are extremely complex. The most difficult arguments, which belong logically in the middle of this chapter, I have removed to an Appendix. Although I indicate in the text the point where the Appendix logically belongs, I recommend that the reader proceed straight through the chapter without referring to the Appendix. Indeed, I recommend that the reader continue on and finish the essay before referring to the Appendix. The Appendix contains proofs of some claims made in the text, claims which are fully intelligible without their supporting arguments. This chapter and the next are sufficiently complicated without those proofs. After he has finished the essay, the reader can review this chapter and take on the Appendix if he chooses.

One point should be emphasized before we begin. I have spoken of P as a decision procedure, and there is a sense in which it is just that. On the other hand, P is not at all the sort of thing we usually have in mind when we speak of decision procedures in connection with moral theories. Ordinarily, if we are looking for a decision procedure, what we want is a decision procedure *for* some already accepted theory. That is, we have a theory about what acts are right or wrong, but it is not possible in practice to identify right acts by direct appeal to the theory, and the decision procedure is intended as a solution to this practical difficulty. Thus, act-utilitarian rules of thumb are part of a decision procedure for AU, which is thought to be incapable of being applied directly to every moral choice. P, however, is *not* a decision procedure of this sort. It is not a decision procedure *for* any independent theory or criterion of right behaviour. P not only identifies, it *defines* the 'right' act. The right act (according to P) is just the act eventually directed by P when P is actually applied correctly.[2]

As we shall see, P is complex and would be very difficult to apply in most cases. It is important to understand that this is irrelevant, in view of my purpose in presenting P. If I were looking for a decision procedure to deal with the practical difficulties of some already accepted theory, then obviously I would require a decision procedure which could be applied in practice. But P, as I have just explained, is not a response to the practical difficulties of some other theory. It is therefore not required that P be easy to apply in practice. My object in discussing P is to demonstrate the logical possibility of a theory with the virtues I have claimed for CU. The practical difficulty of applying P is beside the point. Of course, concern about the practical difficulty of applying CU is very much to the point, and the reader may reasonably suspect in light of the complexity of P that CU is going to have some problems when it comes to practical application. How CU is to be put into practice is a matter I shall discuss in Chapters 10 and 11.

I could simply produce P at this point, but it will be more instructive if I lead up to it by considering a series of inadequate procedures, specifically, a series of procedures which are *not* adaptable. Considering these inadequate procedures will make it clear why P is complex. I shall refer to these inadequate procedures as 'FS#1' (for 'False Start #1'), 'FS#2', and so on. Note that the FS's may have some problems, such as possible circularities, which I do not bother to comment on. The FS's are of interest because they are not adaptable, whatever their other deficiencies.

Consider first a procedure which resembles the five-step sketch of CU in Chapter 8, with the step at which one follower of CU attempts to identify other followers somewhat simplified.

FS#1 1. Be willing to do whatever is required of you by step 5 below.

2. Identify other agents who are attempting to follow this procedure (FS#1), and who are willing to do whatever is required of them by step 5 below. Call the class of agents so identified 'C'.

3. Call the class of agents consisting of the complement of C, less yourself, '-C'. Ascertain how persons in -C are behaving.

4. Call the class of agents consisting of C plus yourself 'C+'. Ascertain the best pattern of behaviour for the members of C+ given the behaviour of members of -C.

5. Do your part in the best pattern discovered in step 4.

The following comments on the interpretation of FS#1 are relevant to the interpretation of all the procedures considered in this chapter, that is to say, all the FS's and P itself:

First, note that the agent applying FS#1 is not a member either of the class he calls 'C' or of the class he calls '-C'. C and -C are complements *relative to the class of other agents*. In the class of all agents, including the agent applying FS#1, the complement of -C is C+, which is C plus the agent in question. (The whole taxonomy involving C, -C, and C+ is more complicated than we need for FS#1, but it will be necessary in FS#2 and later procedures, which will involve loops and the progressive exclusion of agents from C as the procedure is applied.)

Second, the 'behaviour' of members of -C, mentioned at step 3, is either their actual behaviour or their dispositions to behave in response to influence from the members of C+.[3]

Third, the 'best pattern of behaviour' for members of C+ mentioned in step 4 is the best logically and causally possible pattern of behaviour. Also, I assume that whenever an agent is required to ascertain the best pattern of behaviour for the members of C+, there is a unique best pattern. This assumption will be continued right through the initial proof that P is adaptable. After that proof has been given, I will point out how P could be modified to deal with multiple best patterns of behaviour.

Fourth, all of the references to the attitudes, beliefs, or behaviour of other agents are to be construed as tenseless. Thus the question of how the members of -C 'are behaving' is really the question of how they have behaved, are behaving, or will behave. The same is true of inquiries into what agents in C 'are attempting' or 'are willing' to do. It follows that the instruction at step 2 to 'identify' the other agents who make up C and the instruction at step 3 to 'ascertain' how the members of -C are behaving cannot and do not require a contemporaneous inspection of the relevant phenomena. In all the FS's and in P, words like 'ascertain' and 'identify' should be taken to mean simply 'formulate and entertain a correct belief about (the identity of)'. How the beliefs are arrived at is irrelevant. (I shall comment further on this point presently.)

Fifth, no specification is given in FS#1 of the universe of agents which the agent looks to at steps 2 and 3 when he divides the universe of other agents into C and -C. Theoretically, the relevant universe of agents is all agents who have any moral decision to make at any time. As a practical matter, an agent attempting to apply a procedure of the general type of the FS's or P should commence by identifying the other agents who are involved in the same co-ordination problem as himself. To make such a step part of the procedures, however, would complicate both the statements of the procedures, and the eventual proof that P is adaptable. Since my interest in these procedures is purely theoretical, and since it does not matter to the adaptability of P if the agent regards the entire universe of other agents as potential co-operators, I shall leave the FS's and P to operate in this broadest possible context. Note that I shall use Whiff and Poof examples to illustrate the failings of the FS's. Each example so used is to be regarded as representing a complete moral universe.

Finally, in any case in which it matters, the FS's and P are to be regarded as addressed to time-slices of agents, as opposed to agents-continuing-through-time.[4] This makes it unnecessary to worry about the question of whether an agent-continuing-through-time might correctly apply any one of the procedures, which are designed to promote co-ordination between himself and other agents, without co-ordinating the behaviour of his own time-slices. By regarding the procedures as addressed to time-slices, we shift to the procedures the burden of producing co-ordination among time-slices as well as among time-extended agents. This approach may seem to overlook some practical aids to co-ordination. Jones-on-Tuesday and Jones-on-Wednesday may not be quite as much in need of a definite procedure to bring about co-ordination between them as Jones and Smith are. But such practical aids can, theoretically, be dispensed with by the adaptable procedure P we eventually produce. If P is applied successfully by every time-slice of Jones, then all the time-slices of Jones will co-ordinate among themselves, *and* Jones-continuing-over-time will also co-ordinate successfully with any other time-extended agent all of whose time-slices successfully apply P.

So much for the interpretation of FS#1. Let us see now whether FS#1 is adaptable in the context of our standard Whiff and Poof example:

		Poof	
		Push	Not-Push
	Push	10	0
Whiff			
	Not-push	0	6

To ask whether FS#1 is adaptable is to ask whether the group of agents who satisfy it always produce the best consequences possible. We shall therefore consider various cases, involving different assumptions about who the satisfiers are.

If both Whiff and Poof satisfy FS#1, then it is easy to see that both end up pushing and best consequences are achieved. If both satisfy FS#1, then each is willing to do his part (step 1); each identifies the other as willing (step 2); each decides that –C is empty (step 3); each realizes that the best pattern of behaviour for the members of C+ is the pattern in which both push (step 4); and each pushes (step 5). So far so good.

Now suppose that one agent (say Poof) fails to satisfy FS#1. Will Whiff, who satisfies FS#1, behave in such a way as to produce the best consequences possible given the behaviour of Poof? It turns out that the answer to this question depends on just how Poof fails. If Poof is simply unwilling to have any part of FS#1, then Whiff will decide at step 2 that Poof does *not* belong in C;he will ascertain at step 3 how Poof is behaving; he will identify at step 4 the best act for himself in view of Poof's behaviour; and he will do that act at step 5. It will be the case that the class of agents who satisfy FS#1 (namely Whiff) produce the best consequences possible given the behaviour of the non-satisfiers.

Let me pause here to make a point which is of minimal importance to the discussion of FS#1, but which is very important to the understanding of P, and ultimately of CU. It may seem that when I say Whiff 'will ascertain at step 3 how Poof is behaving', I am assuming that Poof's behaviour influences Whiff's opinion about Poof's behaviour and thereby influences Whiff's behaviour, in violation of my standard assumption that in the Whiff and Poof examples neither agent is able to influence the other. This is not so. As I have noted, 'ascertain' in the context of FS#1 means only 'form and entertain a correct belief about'. To say that Whiff ascertains how Poof behaves is to say nothing about how Whiff's correct belief is formed. It may well be formed before Poof behaves, in which case it obviously cannot be influenced by Poof's behaviour.

It may seem that if I do not wish to assume any causal influence of Poof's behaviour on Whiff's beliefs, I should avoid words like 'ascertain' which suggest a causal connection. Perhaps I should say that Whiff is required by FS#1 to 'guess correctly' how Poof behaves. But if I do not want to presuppose causal connections, neither do I want to exclude them. 'Guess correctly' suggests that Whiff has no basis for his opinion about how Poof behaves, whereas he might have excellent evidence, either in the form of past experience with Poof or, in some cases, in the form of direct inspection of Poof's contemporaneous behaviour. What I need is a word which is totally neutral on the question of whether there are causal connections between one agent's behaviour and another's beliefs. Unfortunately, I have not been able to think of a word which is totally neutral. Only unwieldy phrases like 'formulate and entertain a correct belief about' seem totally neutral.

I shall therefore go on using words like 'ascertain' and 'identify', with the reminder that nowhere in this entire discussion, concerning all the FS's, and P, and CU, do I assume either the presence or the absence of causal connections affecting the agents' beliefs. Whether there are causal connections simply does not matter, in theory. (In practice, of course, it may matter a good deal.) To say that an agent satisfies one of the FS's, or P, or CU, is to say nothing about how that agent's beliefs are produced. It is only to say that he has correct beliefs about the required matters.

We have seen that if Poof fails to satisfy FS#1 by opting out entirely, then Whiff (who satisfies FS#1) will produce the best consequences possible given Poof's behaviour. Unfortunately, there are other ways for Poof to fail to satisfy FS#1. Suppose that both Whiff and Poof start out trying to follow FS#1. Each is willing to do his part (step 1). Each identifies the other as willing (step 2). Each decides that -C is empty (step 3). At step 4, Whiff correctly identifies the best pattern of behaviour for the members of C+ as the pattern in which both agents push, and he pushes (step 5). Poof, however, makes a mistake at step 4. He concludes that the best pattern of behaviour is the pattern in which Whiff pushes and he (Poof) does not. Accordingly, Poof not-pushes at step 5. In the situation we have just described, Whiff has followed FS#1 perfectly. But he has not acted in such a way as to produce the best possible consequences given Poof's behaviour. FS#1 is not adaptable.

FS#1 fails because there is no step at which satisfiers of FS#1 discover a breakdown of co-operation which results from somebody's making a mistake. Obviously what 'should' have happened is that when Poof made his error, Whiff should somehow have taken this into account and excluded Poof from the class of persons he (Whiff) assumed he was co-operating with. But there is no step in FS#1 which requires Whiff to check for the sort of error Poof made.

The remedy may seem obvious. If the difficulty is that FS#1 lacks a step at which followers of FS#1 check to see that other would-be followers of FS#1 make no mistakes at steps 2, 3, or 4, let us put in such a step. (Although we had Poof make his error at step 4, it is clear that an error at step 2, or at step 3 in a more complicated case, would have gone unnoticed by Whiff in the same way.)

FS#2 1. Be willing to do whatever is required of you by step 5 below.

    2. Identify other agents who are attempting to follow this procedure (FS#2), and who are willing to do whatever is required of them by step 5 below. Call the class of agents so identified 'C'.

    3. Call the class of agents consisting of the complement of C, less yourself, '–C'. Ascertain how persons in –C are behaving.

    4. Call the class of agents consisting of C plus yourself 'C+'. Ascertain the best pattern of behaviour for the members of C+ given the behaviour of members of –C.

    4'. Determine whether any member of C has made any error at step 2, 3, or 4. If some member of C has made an error at one of these steps, go to (a) below; otherwise go to (b).

        (a) Eliminate from C all current members of C who have made errors at step 2, 3, or 4. Call the resulting class 'C' for purposes of future steps. Return to step 3 and proceed as before.

        (b) Proceed to step 5.

    5. Do your part in the best pattern discovered in step 4.

FS#2 is identical to FS#1 except for the addition of step 4'. Step 4' introduces a loop into the procedure. After ascertaining the best pattern of behaviour for the current C+ at step 4, the agent pauses to consider whether anyone in his perceived C has made a mistake. (It may seem that this inquiry into whether any other agent 'has made' a mistake is inconsistent with my earlier statement that references to other agents' decision processes and behaviour are tenseless. There is no inconsistency. Briefly, 'has made a mistake' means 'makes (tenselessly) a mistake at a previous step'. If it is not obvious how 'previous' can be understood in an appropriately non-temporal fashion, I shall explain in detail in connection with P.) If someone in the agent's perceived C has made a mistake, the offending agent (or agents) is (are) dropped from C, and the loop is retraced. As the membership of C changes, so of course does the membership of –C and of C+. When the agent discovers at step 4' no member of his current C who has made a mistake, he goes to step 5 and does his part in the best pattern of behaviour for the current C+.

FS#2 represents some improvement over FS#1, but it still is not the case that the class of agents who satisfy FS#2 always succeed in producing the best possible consequences given the behaviour of the non-satisfiers. To see how FS#2 fails, suppose that Whiff and Poof are both trying to follow FS#2. Each is willing to do whatever is required of him. Each correctly includes the other in his initial C. Each decides at step 3 that –C is empty, and each correctly identifies the best plan at step 4. At step 4', Whiff considers Poof's work to date, observes that Poof has made no mistakes at steps 2, 3, or 4, and goes on to step 5, as he should; he pushes his button, and glows with satisfaction, having followed FS#2 to the letter. Poof, unfortunately, makes his first mistake at step 4'. He decides (erroneously) that Whiff has made a mistake at 4. He excludes Whiff from C; he returns to step 3; he decides (erroneously) that Whiff, on the basis of his supposed mistake at step 4, is going to not-push; he decides at step 4 (second time around) that he should therefore not-push; he arrives at 4' the second time, observes that C (as he sees it) is empty and therefore that no member of C has made any errors; and he goes on to 5, where he does not push. In the situation we have just described, Poof does not satisfy FS#2, but Whiff does. Even so, Whiff does not act in such a way as to produce the best consequences possible given Poof's behaviour, since Whiff pushes while Poof does not. FS#2 is not adaptable any more than FS#1.

The problem, of course, is that Whiff did not catch Poof's error at 4'. Errors at steps 2, 3, or 4 would have been caught by Whiff at 4'. But Poof did not make his error in the most convenient spot. Introducing 4' allows some errors to be caught, but it creates opportunities for new errors and provides no means of catching them. We could try to cure the problem by adding yet another step where each agent checks for others' errors at step 4'.

FS#3 1. Be willing to do whatever is required of you by step 5 below.

     2. Identify other agents who are attempting to follow this procedure (FS#3), and who are willing to do whatever is required of them by step 5 below. Call the class of agents so identified 'C'.

     3. Call the class of agents consisting of the complement of C, less yourself, '–C'. Ascertain how persons in –C are behaving.

     4. Call the class of agents consisting of C plus yourself 'C+'. Ascertain the best pattern of behaviour for the members of C+ given the behaviour of members of –C.

    4'. Determine whether any member of C has made any error at step 2, 3, or 4. If some member of C has made an error at one of these steps, go to (a) below; otherwise go to (b).

      (a) Eliminate from C all current members of C who have made errors at step 2, 3, or 4. Call the resulting class 'C' for purposes of future steps. Return to step 3 and proceed as before.

      (b) Proceed to step 4''.

    4''. Determine whether any member of C has made an error at step 4'. If some member of C has made an error at 4', go to (a) below; otherwise go to (b).

      (a) Eliminate from C all current members of C who have made errors at 4'. Call the resulting class 'C' for purposes of future steps. Return to step 3 and proceed as before.

      (b) Proceed to step 5.

     5. Do your part in the best pattern discovered in step 4.

It should come as no surprise that FS#3, even with its complicated double loop, fails to solve our problem. FS#3 does guarantee that anyone who follows it will catch anyone else's mistakes at 4'. But now there is a possibility that some agent will follow FS#3 perfectly *until* he makes a mistake at 4", just as all the other agents who have followed FS#3 perfectly up to that point are deciding that all mistakes have been caught and are moving on (quite properly as far as FS#3 is concerned) to step 5. If this happens, FS#3 can fail in essentially the same way as FS#2 before it.

Further attempts to patch up FS#3 in the manner so far considered would lead to an infinite series of error-catching steps, 4', 4", 4''' . . . Unless we assume that agents applying one of these procedures can get through an infinite number of steps, we must look elsewhere for a solution to our difficulties.

What we really need, it seems, is a step like the following, to be inserted into FS#2 in place of 4'.

> 4*. Determine whether any member of C has made any error at step 2, 3, or 4, or whether any member of C is making any error at this step (4*). If some member of C has made or is making any such error, go to (a) below; otherwise go to (b).
>
> (a) Eliminate from C all current members of C who have made or are making errors of the types just considered. Call the resulting class 'C' for purposes of future steps. Return to step 3 and proceed as before.
>
> (b) Proceed to step 5.

Step 4*, however, is patently circular. The correct decision for Whiff about whether to exclude Poof at step 4* depends on whether Poof makes an error at 4*. But the correct decision for Poof at step 4*—and therefore the correct answer to the question of whether Poof makes an error at step 4*— depends on whether Whiff makes an error at 4*. In short, what Whiff is required to do by step 4* cannot be determined without knowing what Whiff is required to do by step 4*. This is unacceptable. Indeed, I have introduced 4* primarily so that it can be contrasted with the error-checking steps of P, which will not involve any such circularity.

At this point the nature of the problem should be clear enough. Let us consider a procedure which has the properties we are looking for.

P   0.   Call the class consisting of all agents other than yourself 'C'.

1.   Eliminate from C any current member of C whose decision procedure is *formally* improper in any of the following ways:

(i)   the agent, after any application of step 4, fails to proceed to step 5;

(ii)   the agent, after any application of step 5, fails to proceed to whichever of step 2 or step 6 he is apparently required by step 5 to proceed to *in view of the belief he actually entertains* about the proposition step 5 requires him to formulate and entertain a belief about;

(iii)   the agent, after any application of step 6, fails to proceed to whichever of step 2 or step 7 he is apparently required by step 6 to proceed to *in view of the belief he actually entertains* about the proposition step 6 requires him to formulate and entertain a belief about;

(iv)   the agent, having arrived at step 7, either attempts some other step thereafter or acts otherwise than is required of him by the CBP (defined below) *as he saw it* on his last previous pass through step 4.

Call the resulting class 'C' for purposes of future steps.

2.   Call the class which consists of the members of C plus yourself 'C+'. Call the complement of C+ '–C'.

3.   Ascertain the behaviour of members of –C.

4.   Ascertain the best pattern of behaviour for the members of C+, given the behaviour of members of –C. Call this pattern the 'current best plan' (hereafter 'CBP').

5. Ascertain whether any member of C makes any error at, or fails to attempt, any previous step. If some member of C makes an error at, or fails to attempt, any previous step, go to (a) below; otherwise go to (b).

   (a) Eliminate from C all current members of C who make an error at, or fail to attempt, a previous step. Call the resulting class 'C' for purposes of future steps. Return to step 2 and proceed as before.

   (b) Proceed to step 6.

6. Ascertain whether any member of C attempts step 2 again. If any member of C attempts step 2 again, go to (a) below; otherwise go to (b).

   (a) Eliminate from C all current members of C who do *not* attempt step 2 again. Call the resulting class 'C' for purposes of future steps. Return to step 2 and proceed as before.

   (b) Proceed to step 7.

7. Do your part in the CBP.

This is the point at which the Appendix should be considered, eventually. I repeat my recommendation that the reader ignore the Appendix until he has read the rest of this essay. The Appendix consists of: (1) comments on the interpretation of P in addition to the earlier comments made in connection with FS#1; (2) an extended argument showing why there are no latent circularities in P; (3) a proof that P is adaptable; (4) in the course of the proof that P is adaptable, a proof that P cannot require an infinite number of steps; and (5) a proof that the agents who satisfy P identify each other as the class of 'co-operators'. In sum, the Appendix demonstrates that P has all the properties we wanted it to have. Most importantly, P involves no circularity and is adaptable.

If we ignore the details which are discussed in the Appendix, the broad outlines of the operation of P are easy to grasp intuitively. The main object for each agent is to identify the class C of other agents with whom he can 'co-operate' by acting on the best plan of behaviour for the group consisting of the members of C plus himself. How do the agents who satisfy P accomplish this? Each agent who satisfies P starts (at step 1) by excluding from the class of putative co-operators agents who are going to come to the final stages of the process and then either make some howling formal error or just decide to ignore what they have done so far and act on a momentary impulse. The agent does not consider at this point the *substantive* correctness of any other agent's beliefs at any stage of the process, but he excludes from the class of putative co-operators other agents who cannot be counted on to avoid certain specified *formal* errors. The agent then ascertains the behaviour of the agents currently regarded as non-co-operators (that is, the members of –C) and formulates the best plan of behaviour for the class currently regarded as co-operators (C+). (Recall that I am still assuming there is always a unique best plan.) The agent then considers whether the other putative co-operators have done everything right so far. If they have not, he eliminates those who have made errors, ascertains the behaviour of the agents just eliminated, and formulates the best plan for the now slightly smaller class of putative co-operators. When the agent discovers that all the other putative co-operators have done everything right so far, he considers whether they are all terminating their decision processes at this point. (This is step 6.) If everyone else in the class of putative co-operators is stopping, he stops. If someone else is going on, then there is a chance that someone has made a last-minute error or that someone will make an error further on, so he goes on. He also eliminates from the class of putative co-operators all other agents who do *not* go on, since these agents cannot be counted on to catch any last-minute or future errors by other putative co-operators. Through all of this process, an agent who satisfies P never eliminates from the class of putative co-operators as he sees it any other agent who satisfies P. (An agent who satisfies P eliminates only agents whom he is required by P to eliminate; therefore, as can be seen by inspection of P, he eliminates only agents who make some mistake in applying P; therefore he eliminates no other satisfier of P.) Eventually, the agents who satisfy P all stop together and act on the same best plan of behaviour and achieve the best results possible as a group.

This heuristic summary of the operation of P suggests two points for further comment. First, note that an agent who satisfies P never inquires directly into the ultimate behaviour (such as 'pushing' or 'not-pushing') of other agents who satisfy P. No satisfier of P ever inquires into the ultimate behaviour of another satisfier of P at step 3, because no satisfier of P ever assigns another satisfier of P to his –C. The only reference any satisfier of P ever makes to the ultimate behaviour of other satisfiers of P is at step 1 (iv), where he ascertains that other agents regarded as co-operators (members of C) can be counted on to act on the CBP *as they see it* when they are done with applying P. I shall comment on the precise relation of P to CU in the next chapter, but I note here that this feature of P fits in with certain observations I made about CU in Chapter 8. I suggested that the successful co-operative utilitarian would require less information, or in any event quite different information, about the ultimate behaviour of the other co-operators than he would need if he were applying AU. And I suggested further that that was one of the reasons CU represented a 'sensible' approach to other agents' behaviour. Each satisfier of CU identifies the others who can be counted on to do their part in whatever turns out to be the best plan for the group of co-operators, and then worries no further about how the others so identified ultimately behave.

Second, it seems appropriate to comment on the question of just how it happens that the satisfiers of P all stop together. The main reason P 'works' while the later FS's do not is the inquiry by each agent at step 6 of P into whether the other putative co-operators are stopping or not. FS#2 and FS#3 fall down because the satisfiers of those procedures may decide (correctly) to exit from the procedure while someone they regard as a co-operator goes on through another loop, during which he may make any sort of mistake. The importance of the fact that the satisfiers of P stop together is apparent. The question is, how do they manage it?

As they wend their way through P, the satisfiers of P must eventually reach a point where everyone but the satisfiers of P has been eliminated from the class of putative co-operators. (Roughly, this means that everyone who makes any mistake is eventually found out. That this happens is proved in the Appendix.) Now, suppose that the satisfiers of P have reached this point—all the non-satisfiers have been eliminated—and they arrive for the first time thereafter at step 6. What should they do? The answer is, it does not matter whether they go on to step 7 or back to step 2, provided they all do it together. If they all go on to step 7, they will all be acting correctly. If they all go back to step 2, they will also all be acting correctly. (I assume there is more than one satisfier of P. If there is only one, then he must go to step 7.) Whether any *individual* agent should go back to step 2 depends entirely on what other agents do. The result is that while P gives perfectly definite instructions to any individual agent, given the decision-processes of others, P does not give definite instructions to the group as a whole about when to stop. There is a sense in which we cannot explain by reference to P how the group as a whole manage to stop together.

Observe that the oddity in P we have just described does not amount to a logical circularity. If Jones and Smith, having made no eror thus far, arrive at step 6 together after eliminating everyone else from the class of putative co-operators, then whether Jones *should* return to step 2 (according to P) depends on whether Smith *does* return to step 2; but what Smith *does* does not depend logically either on what Jones does or on what Jones should do. (The matter of possible circularities is fully discussed in the Appendix.)

The situation of the satisfiers of P is analogous to the situation of a group of agents who manage to universally satisfy AU in a situation in which AU is indeterminate. Remember Whiff and Poof in our standard example. AU gives perfectly definite directions to each individual, given the behaviour of the other, but AU does not give any definite direction to them as a pair. As a pair, they can universally satisfy AU in two quite different ways. We cannot explain by reference to AU how they manage to satisfy AU *together,* if they do, as of course they may.

As a matter of fact, this inability completely to explain universal satisfaction will be a feature of any theory which makes the behaviour required of one agent depend on the behaviour of others and which can be universally satisfied in some cases in more than one way. In light of the discussion in the first part of this essay, I think I am justified in suggesting that this oddity about universal satisfaction will be a feature of any plausible consequentialist theory. It therefore should not trouble us overmuch that it is a feature of P. Universal satisfaction of P at least brings a solid return for whatever oddity it involves. The group of agents who satisfy P, however they manage it, produce best possible consequences as a group. No traditional theory can claim that.

It is time now to tie up a loose end, the matter of multiple best patterns of behaviour. I shall not explain in detail how we would revise P in order to handle multiple best patterns of behaviour. Roughly, what we would do is this. We would alter step 4 so that the agent identifies at that step not the best pattern of behaviour for C+, but the best patterns. After checking at step 5 for errors by other agents, the agent would move to a new step at which he selects some best pattern as a tentative plan for the members of C+. He would then check to see whether other members of C+ have all attempted that step and selected the same tentative plan. If they have not, the agent returns to step 2 without eliminating anyone from his C. If they have all selected the same tentative plan, the agent goes to a step corresponding to step 6 of the original P and exits from the procedure (if all goes well) in the same manner as from the original P.[5] It might take a number of tries for the satisfiers of P all to come up with the same tentative plan for C+, but they would eventually do it.[6]

This brief treatment of the problem of multiple best patterns of behaviour may seem to widen manyfold the already wide gap between P and any sort of *practical* decision procedure. There is no question that the specified mode of dealing with the problem is not even remotely practical in most cases. I shall devote Chapter 11 to discussing how CU deals with the problem of multiple best patterns of behaviour on a practical level.

I have now described a procedure, P, which has all the logical properties claimed for CU. P is addressed to individuals; it is satisfiable (logically) by any one agent regardless of what the others do; it is satisfiable by any number of agents together; it involves no circularity; it requires of each agent only a finite number of steps; any agent who satisfies it identifies as the class of 'co-operators' just the other agents who satisfy it; and it is adaptable. We are ready to move on to the question of what the discussion of P tells us about CU.

THE THEORY OF CO-OPERATIVE UTILITARIANISM

If we wish to know what the discussion of P tells us about CU, we must begin by recalling where we had got to in the discussion of CU at the end of Chapter 8. We had discussed CU in two guises. According to the original statement of CU, CU directs each agent to 'co-operate, with whoever else is co-operating, in the production of the best consequences possible given the behaviour of non-co-operators.' According to a more expansive five-step sketch of CU, CU directs each agent to: (1) hold himself ready to do his part in the co-operative venture; (2) identify the other co-operators; (3) ascertain the behaviour of the non-co-operators; (4) identify the best pattern of behaviour for the co-operators; and (5) do his part in that best pattern. It was the five-step sketch that made us wonder whether the original statement of CU concealed some logical pitfall, especially with regard to the identification of other co-operators.

The discussion of P demonstrates that there is no insuperable logical difficulty in a theory of the sort represented by the original formulation of CU. Furthermore, the discussion of P makes clear that the five-step sketch captures the basic point of such a theory, which is that each agent should decide explicitly which other agents are available to be co-operated with, and should then join in an optimal-response by the co-operators to the behaviour of the rest. On the other hand, comparison with P reveals that the five-step sketch is a bit misleading as to the mechanics of the process. P shows us that the middle three steps of the five-step sketch must in a sense all go on at the same time. The loops in P are essential. It is possible, of course, that in some case the satisfiers of P might go right straight through from step 0 to step 7 without ever repeating a step; but the possibility of looping back, and the associated idea of a progressive whittling down of the class of putative co-operators, are necessary to the adaptability of P. If CU is to be adaptable, then the neat linear appearance of the five-step sketch must be an over-simplification.

At the point near the end of Chapter 8 where I broke off the discussion of the logical difficulties raised by the five-step sketch, I suggested that I could, by elaborating the sketch, eventually produce a satisfactory spelling out of CU and a persuasive, if unrigorous, argument that CU was indeed adaptable. We have now arrived, by a somewhat different route, at the point for setting forth the spelled-out CU. Obviously, the spelled-out CU will follow the general outline of P. Indeed, I have virtually described the spelled-out CU already, in the course of the heuristic summary of the operation of P in Chapter 9.

What CU requires each agent to do is the following: He must hold himself ready to take part in a co-operative effort. He must identify others who are willing and able to do their part. (The 'able' here does not refer to physical ability, since no agent's 'part' could be something he was physically unable to do. It refers to psychological ability—freedom from last-minute backsliding, conative disruptions, or whatever—which might or might not be thought to be already covered by the agent's 'willingness', depending on how we interpret that.) He must ascertain the behaviour or dispositions to behave of the *non-co-operators* who have been identified thus far (that is, the agents who are *not* willing and able to do their part), and he must ascertain the best pattern of behaviour for the co-operators in the circumstances. He must then decide whether anyone he currently regards as a co-operator has made any mistake so far. If any putative co-operator has made a mistake, then all who have made mistakes are eliminated from the class of putative co-operators, and the process of identifying the best behaviour for the (reduced) class of co-operators is repeated. And so on, until it is discovered that no putative co-operator has made a mistake. At this point the inquiry shifts to the question of whether the putative co-operators are all terminating their investigations into each others' decision-making. If any putative co-operator is not terminating his investigation here but is going on to another round of checking on his fellow co-operators, then the agent in question goes on also, to be sure of catching any last minute errors the others might make. Only when the agent in question discovers that the putative co-operators are all stopping does he stop and do his part in the current best plan.

The spelled-out CU is complicated. I shall comment presently on how the follower of CU deals with this in practice. For the moment, I note that the convolutions of CU result quite naturally from the fact that CU represents what an individual agent must do if he is to ensure that he ends up participating with as many other agents as possible in the sort of multi-layered activity involving reciprocal beliefs that we have discovered co-operation to be. Co-operation is a complex activity. 'Co-operating with whoever else is co-operating', since it involves not only co-operating but also ascertaining who else is available to be co-operated with, is inevitably more complex still.

I shall not stop to argue that CU, as spelled out, is adaptable. The proof that P is adaptable provides a model for as brief or as extended an argument concerning CU as the reader might want. In essence, CU works just the way P does. The only difference is that CU is not as precise and detailed as P.

I stated P in as much detail as I did in order to make the absence of any circularity or other logical difficulty as clear as possible. But note that P is not the only procedure I could have used in the demonstration of the logical possibility of a theory with the properties claimed for CU. I could have used instead of P any number of other procedures constructed along the same lines, differing only in insignificant ways in the ordering and definition of certain operations. This fact is what I was referring to when I said in Chapter 8 that P would be a model or realization of CU, but not simply a spelling out. What is implicit in the original statement of CU is not the precise detail of P, but the general approach represented by the latest spelling out of CU. In particular, what is implicit is the idea that one should start by regarding all other agents as potential co-operators and should then gradually exclude from the class of putative co-operators agents who turn out not to be available to be co-operated with on account of improper motivation, misinformation, faulty identification of other potential co-operators, or whatever. This general approach is what P and all the possible alternatives to P have in common.

Aside from clarifying how CU works and reassuring us about the adaptability of CU, the discussion of P suggests a number of other observations about CU. Some of the comments which follow would be rather cryptic if they dealt with matters not previously discussed, but in fact each comment has a precise parallel in some part of the discussion of the FS's or P in the preceding chapter.

First, although CU dictates a decision procedure, it is like P in not being a decision procedure *for* some independent criterion of right action. The right act according to CU is just the act which the agent who successfully follows CU is eventually directed to do.[1] This feature of CU is essential to its adaptability, since we established at the end of Chapter 7 that no exclusively act-oriented theory could be made adaptable even by the addition of a 'perfect' decision procedure for that theory.

Second, in the context of any problem in which the question arises whether CU is addressed to time-slices or to time-extended agents, CU, like P, should be regarded as addressed to time-slices.

Third, although CU as stated does not include an initial step at which the agent restricts the relevant universe of other agents to those who are involved in a co-ordination problem with himself, such a step could be included without creating any serious logical difficulties, and CU with that initial step would reflect what any follower of CU would do in practice. I shall continue to omit mention of this step when I sketch the operation of CU, but I shall assume that CU is always applied to a universe of agents restricted to those involved in whatever co-ordination problem is under consideration.

Fourth, although I have used words like 'ascertain' in spelling out CU, I do not mean to imply that the agent's beliefs about others' decision processes or behaviour must be caused by the others' decision processes or behaviour. In order to satisfy CU, an agent has only to formulate and entertain correct beliefs about certain matters and to act upon those beliefs. How the required beliefs can be arrived at is a pressing practical question. But how they are arrived at is irrelevant to whether an agent satisfies CU. No causal connections are presupposed.

Fifth, just as I prove in the Appendix that the agents who satisfy P recognize each other as the 'co-operators', so I could show that the satisfiers of CU identify each other correctly. This is not essential to the adaptability of CU. It would do no harm for the satisfiers of CU to regard as co-operators nonsatisfiers who ultimately behaved according to the best pattern of behaviour for themselves and the satisfiers combined (given the behaviour of everyone else). Still, the original heuristic argument for the adaptability of CU depended on the assertion that the satisfiers of CU would correctly identify each other, and it is nice to know that even that argument, though oversimplified, was not far off base.

Sixth, the discussion of P confirms that the satisfiers of CU can get along with minimal attention to each others' ultimate behaviour ('pushing' or 'not-pushing' or whatever). No co-operator needs to know more about the ultimate behaviour of another co-operator than that he (the other) can be counted on to act in accordance with his own eventual conclusions about how he should act.[2]

Seventh, CU shares the odd feature of P which we noted near the end of Chapter 9: we cannot completely explain, just by reference to CU, how the satisfiers of CU all manage to satisfy it together. CU, like P, gives perfectly definite directions to each individual co-operator, given the decision-processes of the others. But it leaves some leeway with respect to the precise point of termination of the mutual checking process by the group as a whole. As I have noted,[3] this oddity or something analogous to it will be a feature of any plausible consequentialist theory, so its presence as a feature of CU is not a reason for dissatisfaction.

Eighth, if CU is to deal with cases involving multiple best patterns of behaviour, then the spelling out I have done so far is still not quite adequate. CU needs to be further elaborated along the lines suggested for the modification of P at the very end of Chapter 9. Instead of ascertaining the best pattern of behaviour, the follower of CU must ascertain the best patterns. He must then select a tentative plan for co-operation, check to see if other putative co-operators have selected the same tentative plan, and so on. The basic idea of CU is unchanged, although the impracticality of the decision procedure CU requires is increased considerably. The peculiar practical problem raised by multiple best patterns of behaviour is, as I have noted before, the topic for Chapter 11.

In the remainder of this chapter, I shall consider some possible objections to CU. The first objection, and the most obvious, is that CU is too complicated to be put into practice. 'Can it possibly be the case', the reader has no doubt been saying to himself, 'that every agent attempting to make a moral decision is required to go through a process as intricate as the fully spelled-out CU?' The answer, I suggest, is: 'Theoretically, yes. Practically, of course not.'

In practice, agents who want to make decisions in the spirit of CU should take some shortcuts, just as agents following other theories use rules of thumb. The adherent of CU should ordinarily follow a procedure which only approximates CU, and which is rather like FS#1 in Chapter 9. Holding himself ready to do his part, he should begin by attempting to identify the other agents who are willing to co-operate. He should then adopt some view about the behaviour of the non-co-operators; determine as best he can the appropriate pattern of behaviour for the would-be co-operators; and act accordingly.

Ordinarily, of course, the agent who adopts this simplified procedure will not satisfy CU. For one thing, he may make a mistake of some sort at one of the steps where he attempts to ascertain the identity of the other would-be co-operators, the behaviour of the non-co-operators, and the best pattern of behaviour for the co-operators. Furthermore, even if the agent in question makes no mistake at any of these steps, he still will not have satisfied CU if any of the *other* would-be co-operators makes a mistake at one of them, since CU would require him to go back and eliminate any would-be co-operator who had made a mistake. For that matter, he will not have satisfied CU even though no other would-be co-operator makes a mistake of the sort mentioned, if some other would-be co-operator decides to run through another loop of CU 'just in case', since CU then requires all agents to go through the loop again. Overall, it is unlikely that the agent who attempts to follow the simplified procedure I have described will end up satisfying CU in a case of any complexity.

It is worth noting, however, that the agent who adopts the simplified procedure *might* satisfy CU. Indeed, it is not unlikely that he should do so in a sufficiently simple case. *If* the agent correctly identifies the other would-be co-operators, and the behaviour of the non-co-operators, and the best pattern of behaviour for the would-be co-operators; and *if* the other would-be co-operators also negotiate these steps correctly; and *if* the would-be co-operators all stop without retracing the loop, and do their part; *then* all of the would-be co-operators will have gone through essentially the sequence of steps CU requires. If each would-be co-operator relies explicitly, or can be regarded as relying implicitly, on the assumption that the others make no mistakes and on the assumption that they terminate their decision processes at the first opportunity, then all the would-be co-operators satisfy CU. And, of course, they produce the best consequences possible as a group.

Consider our standard Whiff and Poof case. If each of the pair is willing to co-operate; if each decides the other is willing to co-operate (whether on the basis of prior experience or of general trust in his fellow-man); if each is aware that the best pattern of behaviour is the pattern in which both push; if each assumes that the other identifies him as a co-operator and understands the basic situation; if each assumes that the other will look no further into the situation than this; and if both push; *then* both, by following the simplified procedure, satisfy CU. And of course they produce best consequences possible. It may seem that this brief tale does little to demonstrate the virtue of CU, since it establishes only that in one case CU produces the same result as a bit of common sense. But my purpose here is not to demonstrate the virtue of CU. My purpose in this paragraph is to emphasize how simple the simplified procedure for CU may turn out to be. Where common sense is adequate, the simplified procedure for CU is at least no more complicated.

The use of the simplified procedure is analogous to the use of rules of thumb by adherents of AU, or RU, or UG″, or whatever. (Rules of thumb are most often discussed in connection with AU, but any theory which makes what one agent ought to do depend on what everyone else is doing needs rules of thumb quite as much as AU does.) Agents who adopt rules of thumb, like agents who adopt the simplified procedure, will often fail to satisfy the theory they are trying to approximate. On the other hand, they may manage to satisfy the theory they are trying to approximate (their target theory, as we might call it), and any agents who do manage to satisfy their target theory are guaranteed the benefits of whatever desirable properties that theory may possess—PropAU, adaptability, or whatever. Whether or not they satisfy their target theory, agents who adopt well-chosen rules of thumb (like agents who, wishing to follow CU, adopt the simplified procedure) are acting in the spirit of their theory while coping with practical difficulties as best they can.

Note incidentally that just as a follower of any other theory should ignore what is ordinarily a good rule of thumb when he has information which makes that rule of thumb inapposite, so should the follower of CU adopt some different and closer approximation to CU when he has relevant information which the simplified procedure does not allow him to use, such as knowledge that some other would-be co-operator misapprehends the consequences of various patterns of behaviour. Whatever rules or procedures are suggested as practical aids should obviously be used with discretion.

It must be admitted that an agent who adopts the simplified procedure for CU is less likely to satisfy CU than an agent who adopts a good act-utilitarian rule of thumb is to satisfy AU. But if there is greater likelihood of going wrong in attempting to satisfy CU, that is because of the features of CU which make it a more powerful theory than any traditional theory. It is also worth noting that some of the ways of going wrong in attempting to satisfy CU (such as failing to eliminate a non-co-operator who ends up behaving as if he were a co-operator) do not lead to behaviour which has inferior consequences. Only satisfaction of CU can ensure the benefits of satisfying

CU, but failure to satisfy CU does not by any means ensure that the benefits are lost.

The simplified procedure for CU, supplemented by whatever rules of thumb can be devised for dealing with the specific issues that must be faced even in applying the simplified procedure, and supplemented also by the suggestions for dealing with multiple best patterns of behaviour which I shall discuss in the next chapter, constitutes a reasonable practical embodiment of the central idea of CU.

One further point about the simplified procedure. It may seem that an agent cannot, as a practical matter, apply even the simplified procedure in a very complicated case. Suppose the agent is confronted with a grass case involving hundreds or thousands of persons, or a voting case involving millions. It seems that we cannot plausibly contemplate that he should even *attempt* to identify the other would-be co-operators, and so on. The difficulty is not just that he will probably make some mistake if he tries to apply the simplified procedure. The difficulty is that we can hardly imagine him even *trying* to apply it.

There is a solution to this problem. The fact is that the agent does not really need to worry about which other *individual* agents are would-be co-operators, and so on. All he really needs to do, and all we should construe the simplified procedure to require of him, is to consider other agents in subclasses of agents who are similarly situated with each other.[4] Each agent should begin by ascertaining how many agents there are in each subclass of other agents similarly situated with each other. He should then ascertain how many agents in each subclass are would-be co-operators; how many non-co-operators in each subclass will do each of the acts available to the members of that subclass; and so on. In sum, all the agent needs to consider is the *number* of other agents from various subclasses who have various inclinations and who behave in various ways. CU itself (and not just the simplified procedure) could be revised so that the agent considers only the numbers of other agents in various analogously defined subclasses of other agents, and CU so revised could still be shown to be adaptable.[5] The simplified procedure is therefore fully in the spirit of CU even if we regard it as requiring only an attempt to ascertain *how many* agents from each subclass of agents similarly situated are would-be co-operators, and so on. That sort of attempt is surely not out of the question.[6]

I turn now to a different objection to CU. I have been discussing the objection that CU is too complicated to be put into practice. But it might be thought that the fully spelled-out CU cannot represent even what is required of an agent in theory. It might be suggested that, because many agents could not correctly apply the fully spelled-out CU if they tried, even a *theoretical* requirement of applying CU violates the postulate that 'ought implies can'.

Now, what CU requires each agent to do is to entertain a certain succession of beliefs, and then, eventually, to do some act. There is no ought/can problem about the act that is eventually required, since the only acts that are considered in formulating the best pattern of behaviour for the co-operators are acts that the agents in question can perform. If there is any problem, it must be in the requirement of certain beliefs.

CU will often require an agent to formulate beliefs about various propositions without adequate evidence, which is to say in circumstances where the agent is likely to be mistaken. An agent who tries wholeheartedly to satisfy CU may well fail. In a case where such an agent fails, there is a sense in which the agent cannot satisfy CU. But the sense in which the agent cannot satisfy CU is not the sense that is relevant to the dictum 'ought implies can'. The problem is not that the agent is incapable of entertaining the relevant beliefs. It is rather that he is unable to identify correctly the beliefs he ought to entertain. The situation is precisely analogous to a case in which an agent who attempts to apply AU, or RU, or UG″, is unable to identify the right act. It is often impossible, practically speaking, for an agent applying one of those theories to identify the act the theory requires. In a sense, the agent cannot satisfy the theory. But so long as the required act would be within the agent's capacity to perform if it were once identified, then the ought/can postulate is satisfied. Similarly, in the case of CU, the difficulty of identifying the required beliefs is irrelevant. It is enough that the agent would be capable of entertaining the required beliefs if he somehow managed to identify them.

I do not think the mere entertaining of the beliefs required by CU presents a serious challenge to the intellectual competence of any agent who meets the minimum standards for moral personhood. CU is simply not *that* complicated.[7] It might appear that there is a special difficulty because the agent is required not merely to formulate and contemplate certain propositions but actually to *believe* them. We do not have exactly the same sort of control over what we believe that we have over what we do. Even this is not a serious problem. CU can be construed, without affecting its adaptability, to require only that the agent formulate the required propositions and act on them. No special attitude or commitment, of the sort which raises doubts about whether we can believe what we choose, is necessary.

There is one genuine problem with CU in this area. Agents applying CU who are involved in the same co-ordination problem do not necessarily act simultaneously. There may be causal connections between their decision processes and behaviour, even though CU does not presuppose such connections. As it happens, causal connections, which are never theoretically necessary to the satisfactory operation of CU, can turn out to be an embarrassment. Suppose that Whiff acts before Poof. Whiff is required by CU to formulate certain beliefs about Poof's decision processes. It is possible that there should be causal connections between Whiff's decision processes and behaviour and Poof's which make it the case that whatever Whiff believes will be wrong. Thus, it is possible that if Whiff believes Poof is willing to co-operate, that will cause Poof not to be willing, but that if Whiff believes Poof is not willing, that will cause Poof to be willing after all. In such a situation, it is causally impossible for Whiff to satisfy CU, since Whiff cannot have a correct belief about whether Poof is willing to co-operate. CU violates the postulate that 'ought implies can'.

I am not certain how best to respond to this objection. One thing that can be said is that cases involving the sort of perverse causation I have described are presumably rare and seem appropriately regarded as pathological. Also, any plausible adaptable theory is going to have the same problem CU has with such cases. We know that an adaptable theory must be non-exclusively act-oriented. Any plausible adaptable theory, it seems, must require some kind of mental process involving beliefs about other agents analogous to those required by CU. But then any plausible adaptable theory will have analogous shortcomings. (Furthermore, while exclusively act-oriented theories, which require no beliefs, avoid the theoretical ought/can objection, cases in which it is causally impossible for an agent to have correct beliefs about the future can pose a serious *practical* problem for the agent attempting to implement any consequentialist theory, even one which is exclusively act-oriented.)

One way to deal with the current problem would be to say that if Poof exhibits the sort of perverse responsiveness to Whiff which I have described, then Poof is not a 'real' co-operator *in any event*. We could recast CU so that each agent excludes from the class of putative co-operators other agents who are disposed to exhibit any variety of this perverse responsiveness. This would preserve the adaptability of CU while eliminating the ought/can objection. But the remedy may seem too drastic. Unless we are committed to strong notions about free will, it seems hard on Poof to exclude him from the class of co-operators (and to regard him as a non-satisfier of CU) because of perverse ways he might respond under certain circumstances, even though, as things actually develop, he is as co-operative as could be wished.

Alternatively, we might replace CU with the requirement that each agent 'satisfy CU if possible'. This would eliminate the ought/can objection, since Whiff would automatically 'satisfy CU if possible' in any case in which satisfaction of CU turned out to be causally impossible. The revised theory would not be adaptable, since it would be possible to 'satisfy CU if possible' without satisfying CU. But the revised theory would be equivalent to CU, and therefore would be adaptable, in all but the pathological cases under consideration.

My only firm conclusions are the following: First, the present difficulty with CU, while it is troublesome, is not a devastating objection. Second, the whole matter deserves some further thought.[8]

I turn now to another objection to CU, perhaps the most interesting. Recall that in the Introduction I defined PropAU, PropCOP, and adaptability in such a way that the consequences of any required decision procedure are ignored in deciding whether a theory has one or more of those properties.[9] (To be more precise, what are ignored are any consequences of the decision procedure *except for* the consequences of the acts chosen by applying the procedure. These consequences are themselves indirect consequences of the application of the procedure.) Because traditional theories like AU, RU, and so on, do not require any particular decision procedure, ignoring the consequences of any required decision procedure did not affect the argument or the conclusions of the first half of this essay. But CU does require a particular decision procedure. In proving that P (and by extension CU) was adaptable, I assumed implicitly that each agent was faced with a list of possible acts. I assumed that the consequences of all possible patterns of behaviour by the universe of agents which could be constructed from the acts on the various lists were specified. And I proved that whatever set of agents satisfied P (or CU) would achieve the pattern of behaviour for themselves as a group which had best possible consequences, in terms of the specification of consequences of overall patterns already assumed, given the behaviour of the non-satisfiers of P (or CU). I did *not* take into account any possible consequences which might flow directly from the application of the decision procedure P (or CU) required. The possibility of such consequences does not upset the argument that CU is adaptable, given the way I defined adaptability. But it does suggest a new objection to CU. The new objection is that if CU is adaptable only by virtue of my not considering certain consequences of the application ɔf CU, then the argument in favour of CU based on its adaptability is significantly weakened.

I believe this objection has considerably less force than may at first appear. In order to explain why, it will be necessary to look more closely at the consequences which the definition of adaptability excludes and at the nature of the problem the exclusion raises.

There are basically two sorts of consequences excluded by the definition of adaptability which may cause problems. First, any attempt to apply CU consumes some resources in the form of the agent's time and mental energy. We can imagine a case in which the consequences of the best possible ultimate behaviour are so little better than the consequences of the alternatives that it would not be worth the agent's while to apply CU. In such a case, the agent who applies CU will produce worse consequences *overall* (that is, considering both the consequences of the ultimate behaviour and the cost of applying CU) than the agent who does not. To illustrate the other sort of problematic consequences, suppose we add to our standard Whiff and Poof hypothetical a third party, a mad telepath who will monitor Whiff's decision process and will plant a bomb in Macy's if he discovers Whiff applying CU. Even if the benefit from Whiff's applying CU would outweigh the cost of applying it in the absence of the mad telepath, we can assume that the damage which would be caused by an explosion in Macy's exceeds any possible benefit from Whiff's and Poof's ultimate behaviour of pushing or not-pushing their buttons. Once again, Whiff will bring about worse consequences *overall* if he applies CU than if he does not. It will become clear further on why I have separated these two types of direct consequences of the application of CU. For now, note that the basic problem the direct consequences create is the same in each case. They give rise to situations in which it has worse consequences overall to apply CU than not to apply it.

There are two obvious ways in which we might attempt to revise CU so that there cannot be situations in which it has better consequences overall not to apply CU. Neither of these obvious attempts succeeds, but they are worth pausing over.

First, we might suggest that CU need not really require the decision procedure at all. We might suggest that all CU has to require of each agent is that he do the *act* which he would be directed by CU to do *if* he correctly applied the decision procedure. This would eliminate the current difficulty. If agents did not actually have to go through the decision procedure, then any bad consequences of actually going through it would be avoided. Unfortunately, this modification of CU would destroy CU's adaptability. We know this must be true, because a theory which says to each agent 'Do the act which . . .' is exclusively act-oriented and therefore cannot be adaptable; but it is worth seeing how the modified CU would fall down in a specific example.

Consider once more our standard Whiff and Poof hypothetical. Suppose that neither Whiff nor Poof is willing to co-operate, and that both are in fact going to not-push, motivated by self-interest. Now, if Whiff successfully applied CU, he would discover Poof's unco-operativeness, and he would eventually be directed to not-push in response to Poof's behaviour. Therefore, when both not-push out of self-interest, Whiff in fact does the act which CU would direct him to do if he applied CU. The same is true of Poof. When both Whiff and Poof not-push out of self-interest, Poof also does the act CU would direct if he applied it. In sum, when both not-push out of self-interest, each satisfies the injunction 'Do the act which you would be directed by CU to do if you applied it.' But they produce inferior consequences as a pair. The 'exclusively act-oriented analogue of CU', as we might call this injunction, is no more adaptable than any other exclusively act-oriented theory.

The point is that what CU requires of one agent depends not merely on what other agents do but on how they decide what to do. CU requires each agent to co-operate *with other co-operators,* which is to say, with other agents whose decision processes take a certain form. Given all the facts about Whiff's decision process and ultimate behaviour, it may make no difference to Poof's ultimate behaviour whether he (Poof) applies CU or merely does the act he would do *if* he applied CU. But whether Poof applies CU affects what CU requires of Whiff. It is this interaction between the requirements imposed on the agents' decision processes, along with the fact that we are concerned with the results of satisfaction of theories by groups and not just by individuals, that makes it impossible to replace CU with its exclusively act-oriented analogue.[10]

The second obvious way of trying to avoid the conclusion that applying CU may sometimes have worse consequences overall than not applying it requires us to consider a hierarchy of decisions for each agent. This needs some explaining. Suppose that Whiff and Poof are faced with the usual buttons. Whiff has a decision to make, which is whether to push his button or not. This I shall call the first-level decision. Now, if Whiff is concerned only with the consequences of his pushing the button or not, then he should apply CU to the first-level decision. CU is adaptable, unlike any other theory that has ever been described. CU guarantees the best possible results, individually or, if Poof applies CU also, collectively, from the behaviour with regard to the buttons. On the other hand, it may be the case that the cost in time and energy of applying CU to the problem of the buttons is greater than the benefit which can be achieved by any possible choice about whether to push. Or it may be that there is a mad telepath who will blow up Macy's if Whiff applies CU. If these conditions obtain, or even if they may obtain, then in principle Whiff ought *not* to be concerned solely with the consequences of his pushing the button or not. He ought also to be concerned with the direct consequences of whatever decision procedure he adopts for deciding what to do about the button. In short, Whiff faces another significant decision. He must choose between applying CU to the first-level decision, applying AU to the first-level decision, making the first-level decision by flipping a coin, and so on. This I shall call the second-level decision.

Observe that CU can be applied to the second-level decision as well as to the first-level decision. If CU is applied to the first-level decision, the relevant list of possible acts for Whiff is: '(1) push; (2) not-push'. The relevant consequences (which depend of course on how Poof behaves) are those specified in our original description of the problem. If CU is applied to the second-level decision, the relevant list of possible acts for Whiff is: '(1) make the first-level decision by applying CU; (2) make the first-level decision by applying AU; (3) make the first-level decision by flipping a coin . . .' The relevant consequences of each possible choice at the second level are the consequences of the act that will be chosen at the first level (pushing or not) *plus* any direct consequences of applying to the first-level decision the procedure chosen in the second-level decision. Thus, if there is in fact a mad telepath who will blow up Macy's if Whiff applies CU to the first-level decision, then application of CU to the second-level decision will direct Whiff *not* to apply CU to the first-level decision. Or if it is merely the case that applying CU to the first-level decision is too much trouble in view of the possible gains from co-ordination, then once again application of CU to the second-level decision will direct Whiff *not* to apply CU to the first-level decision.

It may seem that our problem is solved. If all we are worried about is the consequences of Whiff's and Poof's ultimate behaviour with regard to the buttons plus the direct consequences of any decision procedure they use to make the first-level decision about the buttons, then all we have to do is instruct them to start by applying CU to the second-level decision, and everything will work out. But there is a catch. Suppose it is more trouble than it is worth to apply CU to the *second-level* decision? Or suppose the mad telepath will blow up Macy's if either agent applies CU to the second-level decision? If either of these conditions obtains, then it will have worse consequences overall to apply CU to the second-level decision than not to. The original difficulty has reappeared at the next higher level of decision.

We could of course cure the difficulty that appears at the second level by instructing each agent to begin by applying CU to the third-level decision (concerning what decision process to use in making the second-level decision). But then there is a new problem: it may be more trouble than it is worth to apply CU at the third level, or the mad telepath may be as upset by use of CU at the third level as by use at the second level or the first.

Plainly we cannot solve the problem we started with by appeal to this hierarchy of decision levels. Each time one problem is solved, a new one is created. It is worth noticing that CU can, in principle, be applied at any level in the hierarchy of decisions. And even if we focus on higher-level decisions, CU's adaptability is a point in its favour, since there may be co-ordination problems at levels above the first. Thus, it may be worth while for Whiff to apply CU to the first-level decision if and only if Poof does so as well; or the mad telepath may be offended only if Whiff and Poof use different decision procedures for the first-level decision. Both of these possibilities create co-ordination problems at the second level, and CU is adaptable in dealing with co-ordination problems at that level just as it is adaptable in dealing with co-ordination problems at the first level.[11] Still, the ultimate difficulty remains. CU is adaptable at whatever level we apply it. But adaptability is not quite the perfect property. The consequences that are relevant to deciding whether CU is adaptable never include the direct consequences of applying CU to the particular decision in issue.

CU is not perfect, and it is apparently not perfectible. In defence of CU, I shall argue in what follows for three claims: (1) *No* theory can be perfect, from the point of view of a consequentialist who is interested in the consequences of satisfaction of theories (that is, from the point of view we have adopted in this essay). (2) CU in fact comes 'tolerably close' to perfection. (3) CU comes closer to perfection than any exclusively act-oriented theory. The first claim can be established conclusively. The second and third claims admit only of arguments which are persuasive, but not conclusive.

With regard to the first claim, we know from Chapter 7 that an exclusively act-oriented theory cannot be adaptable. But a theory which is not adaptable cannot be perfect from the point of view we have adopted. A theory which is not adaptable does not deal adequately even with the simple straightforward cases discussed in the first half of this essay—Whiff and Poof at their buttons, grass-walking, and so on. Therefore no exclusively act-oriented theory can be perfect. But no non-exclusively act-oriented theory can be perfect either, for just the reason CU is not perfect. Any non-exclusively act-oriented theory requires the agent to do *something more* than just perform an act from the list of acts which the agent is viewed as choosing between, and whose consequences are considered in deciding whether the theory applied is adaptable. Whatever this 'something more' is, there is always the possibility that there will be a mad telepath in some situation who will blow up Macy's in response to that 'something more'. No exclusively act-oriented theory can be perfect; and no non-exclusively act-oriented theory can be perfect. In sum, no theory at all can be perfect. What we obviously want is a theory which is both adaptable and exclusively act-oriented. But that, as we know, is impossible.

With regard to the second claim, that CU comes tolerably close to perfection, there are two points to be made. First, there are very few cases in which the decision procedure CU requires would have significant direct consequences (consequences which are not consequences of the act chosen) aside from the cost in time and energy. We can imagine mad telepaths, but we encounter them rarely. Second, the cost in time and energy of applying CU is likely to be small or even negligible compared to the overall benefits of adaptability. This is so whether we consider what the cost is in theory or what it is in practice. In practice, as we have seen, the agent who wishes to act in the spirit of CU will ordinarily follow a procedure which is a considerably simplified approximation to CU. Surely the cost of following the simplified procedure will be very small compared to the benefits of co-ordination which a reasonable approximation to an adaptable theory promises. In theory, to be sure, CU is more complicated and may require the agent to entertain a large number of beliefs about various propositions. But then, CU says nothing in theory about how these beliefs are to be discovered. The only resources of time and energy which are required *in theory* for the satisfaction of CU are the time and energy necessary to *entertain* the relevant beliefs, not the time and energy that would be necessary to discover them. The time and energy necessary merely to entertain the beliefs required by CU are negligible. In sum, whether we focus on the theory or the practice of CU, the sorts of consequences which account for the imperfection of CU can be neglected in all but very unusual cases.

I turn now to the third claim, that CU comes closer to perfection than any exclusively act-oriented theory. I cannot prove this claim rigorously because the defects of CU on the one hand and of exclusively act-oriented theories on the other are of different sorts. CU is superior in those cases in which there are no mad telepaths or similar horribles, and in which the advantages of co-ordination are large enough to outweigh the cost of following CU. Exclusively act-oriented theories, since they do not require any decision procedure,[12] are superior in those cases in which there *are* mad telepaths or in which the advantages of co-ordination are so small that it is not worth even making an effort to follow CU.

What I have already said in connection with the second claim tends to support the third claim as well. If mad telepaths are rare, and if the advantages of co-ordination are generally large enough to justify following CU, then the cases in which CU is superior are more numerous than the cases in which exclusively act-oriented theories are superior.

There is a further important point. The advantage which exclusively act-oriented theories have over CU in theory they may not really have in practice. The theoretical advantage is that, since they do not require any decision procedure, exclusively act-oriented theories can never be embarrassed by the consequences of a decision procedure. But consider the practical situation in connection with act-utilitarianism, for example. I have hypothesized previously a mad telepath who would blow up Macy's in response to Whiff's applying CU. It is quite as likely that there should be a mad telepath who would blow up Macy's in response to Whiff's applying any act-utilitarian rule of thumb, or even in response to Whiff's making a decision with the intention or the hope of satisfying AU. How, in practice, could an act-utilitarian Whiff deal with such a mad telepath? That is, how could Whiff avoid the bad consequences which would flow from the presence of such a mad telepath, given his own commitment to act-utilitarianism?

It is easy to say that Whiff should just go ahead and satisfy AU, since that can be done (in theory) without using any particular rule of thumb, and even without intending to satisfy AU. But we know that in practice an act-utilitarian Whiff must rely on rules of thumb much of the time, if he is to have any hope of satisfying AU. And the suggestion that Whiff should simply go about satisfying AU without intending to is a transparent evasion of the practical issue. The same sort of problem, obviously, can be created for any exclusively act-oriented theory by hypothesizing a mad telepath with the appropriate tendencies. Whatever theoretical advantage over CU exclusively act-oriented theories may enjoy, we see that the advantage largely disappears when we shift our attention from theory to practice. (The advantage may not disappear completely. If we restrict our attention to mad-telepath cases, the advantage of the exclusively act-oriented theory *does* disappear completely. The mad telepath is not more likely to object to CU than to object to attempts to follow any other theory. But the exclusively act-oriented theory may retain a slight advantage to the extent that following its rules of thumb is less burdensome than following the simplified procedure for CU. This advantage can hardly outweigh the advantage CU secures by its adaptability, but it prevents me from asserting that if we consider the practicalities of applying exclusively act-oriented theories they cease to look better than CU in any respect at all.)

Let me summarize briefly the discussion of the last few pages. Because the definition of adaptability excludes from consideration certain consequences of the application of various theories, CU, despite its adaptability, is not a 'perfect' consequentialist theory. There are cases in which it has worse consequences overall to apply CU than not to apply it. This defect in CU is incurable. On the other hand, we have shown that there *cannot be* a theory which is perfect in our sense. The ideal consequentialist theory— a theory which guarantees in all cases that the best possible consequences *all things considered* will be produced by whatever collection of agents satisfy the theory—is a logical impossibility. If every possible theory is imperfect, then there is good reason to believe that CU is the best theory possible. The cases in which it fails seriously (cases in which there are weighty direct consequences of the required decision procedure) are uncommon; and the cases in which it fails more commonly (cases in which the benefits from co-ordination are not worth the cost of following a reasonable approximation to CU) are not serious. Furthermore, the problem of possible direct consequences from whatever decision procedure is adopted, which is the source of CU's only deficiency, afflicts *all* moral theories in practice even if it is avoided by certain theories (those which are exclusively act-oriented) in theory. On the whole, CU still seems preferable to any other version of utilitarianism.

Before going on, I have one final observation concerning the problem of the direct consequences of applying CU. It is tempting to suggest that the problem of what to do when there is a mad telepath or the problem of what to do when it simply is not worth the effort to follow CU can be solved by 'common sense'. I think most consequentialists assume that there are many decisions which every agent can see are not worth a moment's reflection. And most consequentialists would also assume that if Whiff were aware of a mad telepath who would blow up Macy's in response to certain avoidable behaviour by Whiff, whether the behaviour were applying CU or using some standard act-utilitarian rule of thumb, then Whiff could figure out that he should avoid the behaviour in question.

. As I say, it is tempting to rely on 'common sense'. But I do not do so. The reason is that any appeal to common sense would be at odds with my own strictures against the 'obviousness' argument in Chapter 2. Appeals to common sense are likely to conceal genuine difficulties, and this is a case where the appeal would do just that. I *am* willing to claim that whatever 'common sense' can do for the adherent of any other theory it can do for the adherent of CU as well. To the extent that the act-utilitarian can decide by using common sense when a problem is not worth worrying about, or how a mad telepath may be circumvented, to that extent the co-operative utilitarian can do the same. In my view, however, we should just admit that we are in a theoretical box, from which there is no theoretical exit. No theory can deal completely adequately with the problem of when decision procedures required by that theory (whether required in theory or required as a practical matter) should be abandoned.

I have now completed the exposition of the theory of CU and the discussion of the objections to CU which that exposition brings to mind. In the remainder of this chapter I shall comment briefly on the relationship of CU to certain theories and arguments from the first half of the essay.

First, some readers may feel that the argument for the

adaptability of CU is uncomfortably like the snowball argument in defence of AU which I rejected in Chapter 2. There is an obvious resemblance between the hierarchy of assumptions which I show Narveson implicitly relies on[13] and the hierarchy of reciprocal beliefs which co-operators have about each other. There are crucial differences, however. For one thing, the snowball theorist, in order to make the snowball argument work, must begin by assuming that all agents (or some specified subset of the universe of agents) have the required motivation and beliefs. In the argument for the adaptability of CU, there is no such assumption. Whatever collection of agents successfully negotiate the process required by CU will end up with a certain number of correct beliefs about each others' motivation and knowledge, but no agent is assumed in advance to have the required beliefs. CU requires the relevant motivation and requires each agent's inquiry into others' motivation and beliefs. Successful application of CU generates the hierarchy of reciprocal beliefs instead of assuming it.

Furthermore, we saw that even if the snowball theorist's entire hierarchy of assumptions about the agents' motivation and general knowledge is conceded, the snowball argument still does not work unless it is assumed in addition that each agent will behave correctly in view of the actual behaviour of all other agents. In effect, the snowball theorist must assume that each agent's behaviour causally influences every other's behaviour.[14] The argument for the adaptability of CU does not depend on any such assumption of reciprocal causation. The snowball argument must be supplemented by an assumption about causation because of the 'individualism' of AU. Something is needed to link up the various acts, about which we know only that they satisfy AU and therefore that they have best consequences taken *individually,* into the best possible pattern of *collective* behaviour. CU does not share the individualism of AU. When the satisfier of CU finally acts, he is directed to do the act which is part of the best possible pattern of behaviour for the *group* of co-operators. Once the co-operators are identified, no assumption other than satisfaction of CU is required to guarantee that they produce the best possible collective behaviour.

Turning to a different matter, some readers may feel that CU is disquietingly reminiscent of the 'gimmicky' theories mentioned briefly in Chapter 7, such as the theory that says to each of Whiff and Poof, in our standard example: 'If your opposite number pushes, push. If he not-pushes, then not-push while thinking of a number greater than any number he thinks of while he not-pushes.' I noted that theories of this sort could be constructed which were adaptable in all cases, and it may seem that CU is merely such a generally applicable gimmicky theory, somewhat more attractively packaged than the theories mentioned in Chapter 7.

CU and the gimmicky theories of Chapter 7 do share a most important feature. They all require Whiff and Poof to do something beyond simply pushing the button or not. They are all *non*-exclusively act-oriented. Still, the suggestion that CU is gimmicky in the same way as the theories of Chapter 7 overlooks some important differences: (1) What CU requires besides pushing or not pushing, namely a certain decision procedure, is required of all agents all the time. Unlike the 'thinking of a greater number' ploy, CU's decision procedure is more than an *ad hoc* response to disfavoured behaviour by another agent. (2) What CU requires besides pushing or not-pushing is something that can be accomplished by any number of agents together, unlike 'thinking of a greater number'. (3) Unlike the 'greater number' requirement, the decision procedure CU requires does not make CU adaptable just by guaranteeing that the class of satisfiers of CU will be artificially limited to some class of agents who can be regarded as behaving acceptably given the behaviour of the rest. Instead, CU's decision procedure guides those who satisfy it to the desired behaviour. CU is a natural working out of a sensible approach to moral decision-making. The gimmicky theories are not.

There is one final matter. Some reader may feel moved to ask: 'If following CU is such a desirable thing, why can't AU, or RU, or any other theory, "co-opt" CU by simply adding to the list of acts regarded as open to the agent in any situation the act of "following CU"?' The response would be very much the same whichever theory attempted to co-opt CU in this manner, but AU is the easiest to deal with, so I shall focus on it. Let us consider the application to our standard Whiff and Poof example of a co-opting theory which I shall call AU′. AU′ is simply AU modified so as to regard each agent as having a choice between three acts—'push', 'not-push', and 'follow CU'. Now, what does AU′ require each agent to do? As usual, what Whiff is required to do depends on what Poof does. Let us assume that Poof is selfishly motivated and does not push. In this situation, AU′, which requires only that Whiff do an act with at least as good consequences as any other act on the relevant list of possibilities, will be satisfied by Whiff whether Whiff opts for 'not-push' or for 'follow CU' (which will lead to Whiff's not-pushing).[15] So, if Poof selfishly not-pushes, then Whiff satisfies AU′ if he not-pushes without bothering to follow CU. By the same token, if Whiff selfishly not-pushes, then Poof satisfies AU′ if he not-pushes without bothering to follow CU. But then if both agents selfishly not-push, both satisfy AU′. AU′ is not adaptable, and the attempt to modify AU in such a way as to co-opt CU has fallen through.

It might seem that the problem is in the formulation of AU′. There is something odd about positing a list of choices in which 'not-push' and 'follow CU' are regarded as alternatives, since choosing to follow CU may lead to not-pushing. Perhaps we should consider a theory I shall call AU″. AU″ is applied to the choice between alternatives such as 'follow AU', 'follow CU', and so on. Even if we ignore the oddity of the suggestion that AU″ should give the agent a choice between following AU and following other theories, AU″ does not solve the problem. If both agents choose to follow AU and end up not-pushing (as we know they may even though they both satisfy AU), then both have satisfied AU″. If Poof is following AU and not-pushing, then it makes no difference to the consequences of Whiff's decision whether Whiff chooses 'follow AU' or 'follow CU'.[16] Whiff therefore satisfies AU″ if he chooses to follow AU. Similarly, if Whiff is following AU and not-pushing, Poof satisfies AU″ if he follows AU. In sum, if both agents follow AU and not-push, both satisfy AU″, which turns out to be no more adaptable than AU′.

It should be clear what the problem is. The benefits of CU cannot be achieved within the context of other theories just by regarding 'follow CU' as a new alternative to be added to the list of possible acts, or possible modes of decision, or whatever. The benefits of CU are achieved by *requiring* agents to follow CU, not by merely allowing them to. Even regarding 'follow CU' as a *possible* choice would mean a significant change in the outlook of exclusively act-oriented theories. But even if the defender of a traditional theory were prepared to go so far, it would not be far enough.

There is one way in which the defender of a traditional theory might attempt to argue that his theory *required* following of CU without transparently abandoning the traditional theory in question. The move is most plausible if made by an act-utilitarian. Might not the act-utilitarian suggest that CU represents the *subjective* obligation AU should be construed to impose? In other words, might not the act-utilitarian suggest that an agent ought to adopt CU as a method of trying to identify the best act in the circumstances? This suggestion overlooks the fundamental difference between AU and CU. AU is exclusively act-oriented. Objective AU defines the agent's obligation in terms of acts like pushing, and the task for subjective AU, as traditionally understood, is to identify the right act so defined. CU recognizes that the agent's obligation cannot be satisfactorily defined in the way objective AU defines it. CU defines the right act only as the act chosen by a certain decision procedure. To regard CU as a procedure for finding the right act in the sense in which subjective AU might require a procedure for finding the right act is either to distort the idea of a subjective counterpart to the exclusively act-oriented objective AU or else to miss the point of CU.[17]

NOTES ON A PRACTICAL PROBLEM

In this chapter I shall offer a few observations about how followers of CU might deal in practice with cases involving multiple best patterns of behaviour. I shall not produce a comprehensive discussion of how CU is to be applied in practice, nor even a comprehensive discussion of how it is to be applied to the sort of case this chapter deals with. I shall make a beginning. In the process, I shall exploit some opportunities for comparisons between CU, AU, and UG.

In the first half of the chapter, I introduce three basic techniques, supplements to the simplified procedure of Chapter 10, which followers of CU might use to deal with the problem of multiple best patterns of behaviour. Lest there be any doubt, I do not claim that successful following of these techniques always leads to satisfaction of CU. These are practical techniques, for dealing as well as possible with practical problems. One of the techniques involves unequivocally abandoning the attempt to produce the best consequences theoretically possible, at the point where it becomes clear that that attempt is counterproductive.[1] In the second half of the chapter, I discuss the application of these techniques (and a further elaboration of one of them) to the problem of grass-crossing, which, as I have noted previously, is representative of a broad range of important problems, such as taxpaying, voting, and so on.

Throughout this chapter (except as specifically noted) *I assume that the agents involved in the examples are all would-be co-operators and have identified each other as such.* Thus, important preliminary steps in CU (or in the simplified procedure) are assumed already to have been negotiated. (In this connection, it is worth noting that for purposes of CU, the existence of multiple best patterns of behaviour for the entire universe of agents does not necessarily create any difficulty.

What *does* create a difficulty is the existence of multiple best patterns of behaviour for the class of putative co-operators. Near the end of the chapter, I shall have occasion to discuss an example where some agents are non-co-operators, and where there is a unique best pattern of behaviour for the co-operators, given the behaviour of the rest, despite the existence of multiple best patterns of behaviour for the entire universe of agents.)

Consider now a new Whiff and Poof example, which represents the simplest case in which the existence of multiple best patterns can create a genuine practical problem:

		Poof	
		Push	Not-push
	Push	10	0
Whiff			
	Not-push	0	10

Even if Whiff and Poof are both co-operatively inclined, both well informed about the basic situation, both aware of the other's willingness to co-operate and well-informedness, and so on, the doughty pair still have a grave problem. Should each individual push, or should he not? If communication is not allowed, and if there is no precedent or general custom to guide the pair, then it seems that as a practical matter each agent must choose on a whim whether to push or not, and the chances of co-ordinating and producing results with value 10 units are just 50 per cent.

I say 'it seems' in the preceding sentence advisedly. As Thomas Schelling has pointed out, in an elegant discussion on which I shall draw heavily,[2] there may be cues which make the chances of successful co-ordination much better than I have supposed. The point is most easily illustrated by considering a slightly different example. Suppose that instead of having a choice between pushing and not-pushing, each agent must write on a piece of paper either 'heads' or 'tails'. If both write the same word, then results with a value of 10 units are produced. If they write different words, then the results have value zero. This example is structurally identical to the button-pushing example. That is, it is identical if we consider only the schematic representations of the two situations, ignoring the 'labelling' of the available strategies as 'pushing', or 'heads', or whatever. Both examples are represented by the same array,

$$10 \quad 0$$
$$0 \quad 10.$$

Despite this, it seems clear that Whiff and Poof would have a much better than even chance of achieving the consequences with value 10 units in the heads/tails example. Each could write down 'heads' with considerable confidence that the other would do the same. It is not an easy matter to explain just why this is so, but it is so none the less. In the pair 'heads or tails', 'heads' sticks out. Whiff can name 'heads' because it sticks out, and because he expects that Poof will expect him (Whiff) to see that it sticks out and to name it for that reason, and so on. I do not claim, of course, that all pairs of would-be co-operators would succeed in the heads/tails example. There is no cut-and-dried logical argument for naming 'heads'. Some would-be co-operators would name 'tails'. Occasionally, two 'tails'-namers would even come together and manage to co-ordinate on 'tails'. Still, it is plain that in this situation most ordinary would-be co-operators could co-ordinate, usually by naming 'heads'.

It may seem that the high probability of co-ordination in the heads/tails example depends on the fact that an individual asked to name 'heads' or 'tails' independently of any attempt to make his choice agree with someone else's would name 'heads' more often than not, and on the exploitation of this fact by the would-be co-operators. No doubt this predisposition towards naming 'heads' even when nothing turns on it is part of the explanation of why 'heads' can be agreed on. But it is not the whole explanation. Consider another example. If we ask pairs of persons not totally ignorant of baseball to select the same individual (without communication, of course) from the trio of Ted Williams, Joe DiMaggio, and Sandy Koufax, and if we offer a suitable reward for success, any pair who are even slightly sophisticated about the nature of co-ordination problems will agree on Sandy Koufax. He doesn't fit. He is a pitcher, whereas the other two are great hitters (and, incidentally, outfielders). He is a National Leaguer, whereas the other two are American Leaguers. In this case the ability to co-ordinate clearly does not depend on the fact that people asked *individually* to select one of these three players would be more likely to select one than another, as they might be more likely to select 'heads' than 'tails'. There is no obvious prediction to make about a purely statistical bias in favour of Koufax or either of the others. Koufax emerges as the 'obvious' choice *only* when the context of the choice is an attempt to co-ordinate.

The point of the discussion so far is that real-world situations may include features which constitute important cues for agents who wish to co-ordinate their behaviour, even though the features in question are in a sense irrelevant to the consequences of various patterns of behaviour. It makes no difference in the heads/tails example whether both parties name 'heads' or both name 'tails', but the former pattern is much more likely to be achievable. Similarly, it makes no difference in the baseball-player example which of the three players both parties select, but there is only one of the three that there is any special reason to expect agreement on. This, then, is the first of the three techniques for co-operation in the face of multiple best patterns of behaviour—the recognition and exploitation of cues such as I have been discussing.

It should be obvious that there can be no general theory of what is a cue and what is not.[3] Almost anything could be a cue. Some features will be cues for some would-be co-operators and not for others. Plainly, cues are only useful if they are generally recognized by the parties faced with any particular problem, and if it is generally recognized that they will be generally recognized, and so on. I could give many more examples, illustrating the range of features that can sometimes be exploited as cues,[4] but I trust the basic point has been adequately made. Even if we cannot say exactly when some feature will work as a cue, nor exactly how it works when it does, the existence of the phenomenon is undeniable. Perceptive would-be co-operators can get a good deal of mileage out of this technique.

In the examples discussed so far in which there have been

cues to co-ordination, the cues have been aids to parties who wanted to behave the same. It is also possible to have cues which help parties similarly situated to behave differently. Recall an example we have already discussed in other contexts, represented schematically by the following array:

$$\begin{array}{cc} 3 & 4 \\ 4 & 0. \end{array}$$

If the choices in this situation are 'push' and 'not-push', then on the face of things, there is no way for the parties to decide who is to push and who is not to. Suppose, however, that the situation represented by this array occurs twice in succession. If the parties manage, by sheer luck, to behave differently in the first repetition, then they will have no difficulty at all behaving differently in the second. Each can simply repeat his earlier choice. There might be other cues in the situation which would allow a better than even chance of behaving differently even on the first repetition, but focusing on the second repetition allows us to make two points at the same time. The two points are (1) that it is possible to have cues which help the parties to behave differently, where that is what is desired, and (2) that an important source of cues in a great variety of situations is precedent.

I have shown that would-be co-operators may be aided by features of a situation which make some best pattern of behaviour 'stick out'. A related point is that in some situations a pattern which is not a best pattern at all may stick out. Consider a situation represented schematically by the following array:

$$\begin{array}{ccc} 2 & 0 & 0 \\ 0 & 3 & 0 \\ 0 & 0 & 3. \end{array}$$

In this situation there are two best patterns of behaviour, each of which produces results valued at three units. Unfortunately, it is not obvious how the parties can co-ordinate their behaviour on a particular one of these best patterns. If there are in fact no cues provided by the full description of the situation, and if the situation is not to be repeated, then it seems that parties who attempt to achieve one of the best patterns will have only a fifty–fifty chance of doing so, and the expected return to their joint behaviour will be 3/2 units. Note, however, that if the parties attempt to co-ordinate on the pattern of behaviour which produces consequences valued at 2 units, they can manage to do so, since that pattern is unique. In short, it seems that it would be wisest in this situation, as a practical matter, to shoot for the inferior result valued at 2 units.[5] (This conclusion does not necessarily hold if the situation is to be repeated, since fortuitous achievement of one of the 3-unit patterns in any one repetition would provide cues for co-ordination in later repetitions. The general question of the effect of repetition is one I shall ignore.)

The current example suggests the second basic technique for dealing in practice with multiple best patterns of behaviour—preferring salient inferior patterns when there are no cues which will allow co-ordination on one of the best patterns. Once again, I can provide no general theory of when this technique should be used. Whether this technique should be used depends on whether there are adequate cues for co-ordinating on one of the best patterns, and, as we have seen, we cannot give a general answer to that question. Still, would-be co-operators who keep this technique in mind should be able to identify a variety of cases in which attempting to co-ordinate on an inferior pattern promises the best realistically achievable results.

For example, the technique of preferring a salient inferior pattern might be useful in the situation previously discussed in a different context, represented by the array:

$$
\begin{array}{cc}
3 & 4 \\
4 & 0.
\end{array}
$$

If there are no cues which allow the parties to co-ordinate on one of the 4-unit patterns, and if the situation is *not* to be repeated, then attempts to behave differently would presumably produce the same results as if both parties chose at random between their available strategies with equal probabilities. The expected return to this joint behaviour would be 2¾ units. It would be better for the parties to shoot for the inferior pattern which produces results with value 3 units. If the parties attempt to co-ordinate on this pattern they can do so, since it is unique, and this approach is superior, as a practical matter, to attempts to produce four units which have only a fifty–fifty chance of success.

Note that in this case the approach of shooting for a salient inferior pattern produces just the pattern of behaviour which would be dictated by UG. Indeed this sort of case is pre-eminently the sort of case which accounts for the appeal of UG. The parties are symmetrically situated. Best possible results are achieved only if the parties behave differently. But if the parties attempt to behave differently, in the absence of cues, they will do less well than if it were generally understood that they should behave the same in symmetric situations. This, combined with the appeal of the notion of 'universalizability', suggests the view that symmetrically situated parties ought to behave the same—in short, UG. I shall say more presently about the relation of UG to CU in the context of the grass-walking case, which in important respects is just the current example writ large.

So far I have ignored the possibility of conscious randomization, or the choice of 'mixed strategies', by the parties. If this possibility is taken into account, the current example becomes even more interesting. If we consider mixed strategies, then there is a pattern of behaviour which is salient in the same way the 3-unit pattern is salient among patterns involving only pure strategies, but which is better than the 3-unit pattern. The new pattern is the pattern in which each agent randomizes between his 3–4 strategy and his 4–0 strategy in proportions $\frac{4}{5}$ to $\frac{1}{5}$. The expected return to this joint behaviour is 3 $\frac{1}{5}$ units. This is the unique best pattern in which both agents behave the same (where adoption of the same mixed strategy counts as behaving the same, even if the results of randomization direct different ultimate acts for the parties).[6] This pattern of behaviour is still an inferior pattern, as compared to either pattern in which one party chooses his 3–4 strategy and the other his 4–0 strategy; but it is a salient inferior pattern. It is the best pattern the parties can expect to achieve, in practice, in the absence of cues which allow them to behave differently. This is the third technique for dealing with multiple best patterns of behaviour—the use of randomization in the manner just illustrated. In a sense, of course, the third technique is merely a refinement of the second. We have merely expanded the class of eligible patterns of behaviour from which a salient inferior pattern may be selected. Still, the step from pure to mixed strategies is a significant one, and it seems appropriate to regard the use of randomization as a new technique.[7]

The adoption by each agent of the mixed strategy it would be best for everyone to adopt, our third technique, has also been suggested by J. J. C. Smart as the appropriate *act*-utilitarian approach to cases like our current example.[8] Unfortunately, Smart does not discuss the suggestion in sufficient detail to establish whether it is really appropriate to regard it as act-utilitarian.

For one thing, Smart does not consider whether, if all parties follow this approach, they will in fact all be satisfying AU. It turns out that they will. If both parties in our current example randomize between the 3–4 and 4–0 strategies in proportions $\frac{4}{5}$ to $\frac{1}{5}$, then each will be behaving in such a way as to produce expected results which are as good as possible given the behaviour of the other. Each will be satisfying AU.[9] It is also true, however, that if one party randomizes in the specified proportions, then the other party satisfies AU *whatever he does*. Furthermore, one party satisfies AU by randomizing in the specified proportions *only if* the other party randomizes in those proportions as well. In sum, Smart's recommendation is consistent with AU from the point of view of one agent only if the other agent adopts it; and if the other agent adopts it, then the first agent is in a situation in which any behaviour at all on his part would satisfy AU, and not just the behaviour Smart recommends. (These claims are proved in a note, where they are also generalized, with minor qualifications, to cover all cases involving agents symmetrically situated.[10]) It turns out that Smart's recommendation is an act-utilitarian recommendation only under special circumstances and then only in a limited sense, since any other behaviour would satisfy AU as well.[11]

To be sure, Smart says his recommendation applies only to an act-utilitarian who can expect most of the other agents concerned to reason as he himself does. He considers the objection that this makes AU reduce to some form of rule-utilitarianism, and he concludes that it does not, appealing to the notion of an act-utilitarian 'convention', and citing Lewis and Schelling.[12] But the objections of the previous paragraph are not met by talk of act-utilitarian conventions. As we saw in Chapter 2, a convention may be consistent with AU and yet not be required by AU itself. In fact, Smart's 'conventions' are even less happily viewed as act-utilitarian conventions than the conventions discussed in Chapter 2. In Chapter 2 it was at least the case that *if* there was a general practice of agreement-keeping (for example) then each individual agent was required by AU to keep agreements. But in the situations Smart discusses, if the convention is generally adopted, then AU does not require any individual to follow it.[13] What Smart is really suggesting, in a hazy fashion and in a specific sort of case, is CU.

I have now introduced, in the context of simple examples, three techniques which may be available to would-be co-operators for dealing with practical problems involving multiple best patterns of behaviour. They are: (1) reliance on specific cues to co-ordination, (2) shooting for salient inferior patterns of behaviour, and (3) adoption of randomized strategies. Let us turn to the consideration of a somewhat more realistic problem, which will illustrate the possible uses of these techniques and which will also provide a vehicle for a comparison of CU and UG.

Suppose there is a patch of grass in a public place, which in good condition constitutes a significant public amenity. The grass is so situated that in the course of a year there are 1,000 occasions on which some agent or other is faced with the choice whether to walk on the grass or not and in which his walking on it would secure a net benefit, all things considered *excepting* any damage to the grass. (We ignore any occasions on which there is not even this presumptive reason for walking on the grass.) I assume that the net benefit (exclusive of damage to the grass) is the same for each individual instance of grass-crossing and does not depend on the number or identity of the grass-crossers. I assume also that the total damage to the grass caused by walking on it is solely a function (specifically, a non-linear function) of how many times the grass is crossed. Finally, suppose that the optimum number of crossings of the grass is 100. (The reader will remember from Chapter 3 that an essential feature of the traditional grass-walking problem is that the optimum number of crossings is something greater than zero and less than all the crossings possible.[14] In assuming that the optimum number of crossings is 100, I am assuming, roughly, that the grass can stand a few crossings, but not very many compared to the total number of attractive opportunities.)

In the case just described, there are 1,000 decisions to be made by agents who are in all respects symmetrically situated. Yet best possible results are achieved only if the 1,000 agents can divide themselves into two subclasses, the members of which behave differently. Ideally, we would like to see everyone choose in such a way that 100 agents cross the grass and 900 go around. We have, in short, a magnified version of the example represented by the array

$$\begin{array}{cc} 3 & 4 \\ 4 & 0. \end{array}$$

(It is worth remembering also that the grass case, if realistically described, is a case in which AU is indeterminate, as I pointed out in Chapter 3.[15] The grass case therefore combines in a single complex structure the separate difficulties involved in our two most-discussed examples, the one represented by the array immediately above, and the original Whiff and Poof example. This is true of most of the standard many-agent problems utilitarians have fought over.)

Because the grass case is a magnified version of the example represented by the array above, we would expect the utilitarian generalizer to recommend that everyone avoid the grass, as he does. This is analogous to the recommendation that both agents elect their 3-4 strategy. Note that when I speak of the utilitarian generalizer, I mean the traditional utilitarian generalizer, not a proponent of any of the Lyons-inspired theories discussed and rejected in Chapter 6. Note also that the traditional utilitarian generalizer would probably qualify his direction to stay off the grass by adding 'unless not crossing the grass would have extremely serious consequences', or something to that effect. I shall ignore this qualification, on the assumption that it simply does not come into play in our example. It is difficult to know just what the utilitarian generalizer means by 'extremely serious consequences', but it seems clear that he regards them as occurring infrequently.

What does the follower of CU recommend in the grass case, *assuming, as we have assumed thus far,* that all the agents involved are would-be co-operators? It is possible that the follower of CU would also recommend that everyone stay off the grass, applying our second technique of shooting for a salient pattern of behaviour. Even though the pattern of general avoidance of the grass is not one of the best possible patterns of behaviour, it might be the best that can be achieved in practice. Before we accept this conclusion, however, we should consider whether the other techniques suggested for use by followers of CU might not be helpful in this case.

What about the possibility of relying on cues to co-ordination? In the case as I have described it, there are no cues. But the description is very unrealistic in that respect. In any real-world situation there will almost certainly be some cues built into the problem. On the one hand, the damage from crossing the grass will be less for some agents than others. It will be less for children and persons going barefoot than for heavy adults and persons wearing cleated shoes on the way to a base-ball practice. On the other hand, and probably even more important, the benefits from crossing the grass will vary from instance to instance.

It may seem that the facts just mentioned are not so much cues to co-ordination in a symmetric situation as features which make the situation asymmetric and which in fact reduce significantly the number of genuinely optimal patterns of behaviour. It is true that the facts in question make the situation asymmetric in detail, but there is still a point to the suggestion that the same facts provide cues to co-ordination. The traditional utilitarian generalizer ignores the asymmetries. He regards all the agents as essentially similarly situated and as choosing among essentially the same possible acts.[16] He would presumably defend the decision to regard the situation as essentially symmetric on the ground that the possible gains from precise co-ordination on a best pattern of behaviour do not justify the risk of very bad results which might occur if the agents attempt to achieve a best possible pattern by behaving differently from one another. What the utilitarian generalizer overlooks is that the asymmetries do not merely affect the identity of the best patterns of behaviour. By providing cues, they also make the task of co-ordination, at least to the extent of achieving a pattern of behaviour in the neighbourhood of the best patterns, much simpler. They greatly reduce the risk of the extremely bad consequences which the utilitarian generalizer fears. In short, even if we regard the situation as essentially symmetric, we should not, in evaluating the prospects for co-ordination in the 'symmetric' problem, ignore the assistance the asymmetries may provide when regarded merely as cues making certain of the better patterns in the 'symmetric' problem salient.

I do not suggest that the cues in the real world are enough to allow even willing and intelligent co-operators to achieve the very best possible pattern of behaviour. Even if the costs and benefits of individual acts of grass-crossing are such as to determine a unique optimal pattern of behaviour, it would be unreasonable to expect to achieve this precise pattern in practice. What I do suggest is that a group of 1,000 willing co-operators faced with the patch of grass could do better than they would do by following the utilitarian generalizer's recommendation. If each co-operator does his best to estimate the optimum number of crossings, and also does his best to decide how many other agents there are whose crossing the grass would produce greater net benefits than his crossing, and then crosses only if the second number (of agents) is less than the first (of crossings), then it seems that the co-operators would be very likely to improve on the utilitarian generalizer's solution.

The utilitarian generalizer's unwillingness to exploit cues which permit different behaviour is one weakness in his treatment of the grass case. Another weakness is that he overlooks the possibility of randomized strategies. If every agent in our example randomizes between his choices, assigning a probability of 1/10 to crossing the grass and 9/10 to walking around, there is a high probability that the total number of crossings will be in the neighbourhood of 100, the optimal number. Since we have not specified precisely the function relating the number of crossings and the damage, we cannot assert definitely that the suggested proportions for randomizing are the best possible, or even that everyone's randomizing in these proportions would be better than no one's crossing. However, it is plausible to assume that the damage function is such that these things are true. If they are true, and if we ignore cues to co-ordination, then should not co-operators randomize in these proportions?

The utilitarian generalizer might respond that randomization in these proportions would be more trouble than it is worth, and he might be right. Randomization in these proportions is not easy. If one happens to have a coin in one's pocket, one can flip it three times and thereby have a random event (three heads for example) with a probability of 1/8. But the difference between 1/8 and 1/10 might be just enough to do serious harm to the grass. Still, even if randomizing with the required probabilities is more trouble than it is worth in the present case, there will be other cases in which the ideal proportions are simple enough, or close enough to simple proportions, or in which the gains from co-ordination are sufficient, so that the randomization is worth carrying out.

Furthermore, carrying out the actual randomization may not be necessary at all. Up to this point, I have treated the grass case as if the 1,000 choices between crossing the grass and walking around are made by 1,000 different agents. In a realistic example these 1,000 choices are likely to be made by a much smaller number of agents, or at least by a much smaller number of what we normally think of as agents, namely agents-continuing-over-time. Whoever has one opportunity to cross the grass is likely to have a number. Suppose there are in fact 100 time-extended agents, each of whom is faced with the grass-crossing decision ten times. Now we can get the effect of randomizing in the desired proportions with ease. All that is necessary is that each agent should cross the grass exactly once. I have selected the numbers to make the 'pseudo-randomization', as I shall call this process of each time-extended agent's systematically varying his own behaviour, exceptionally neat. (Indeed, with the numbers I have selected, pseudo-randomization works out better than randomization, since pseudo-randomization guarantees exactly 100 crossings, while randomization does not.) The point remains even if the numbers do not work out quite so conveniently. We can sometimes achieve the effect of randomization, or a similar effect, without actually performing any experiments to guide us. Where the special ability of separate time-slices of the same time-extended agent to co-ordinate with each other can be exploited, there is nothing in CU that forbids us to exploit it.

To sum up, there is good reason to think that, by reliance on cues or randomization or pseudo-randomization, would-be co-operators can do better in a real grass case than they would do if everyone simply avoided the grass entirely.

Although I have contrasted the responses to the grass case of the co-operative utilitarian and the utilitarian generalizer, I would suggest that an enlightened utilitarian generalizer could adopt and integrate into his own approach both the use of cues to co-ordination and the use of randomization or pseudo-randomization. Consistently with his basic premiss that agents similarly situated ought to behave the same, the proponent of UG could allow the use of any cues to different behaviour which were available, on the ground that agents who could find such cues in their situation would be differently situated in a relevant respect. It is obvious that agents who can find cues to different behaviour must be differently situated in *some* respect. The novel part of the suggestion is that the enlightened utilitarian generalizer should be willing to regard as relevant any difference which can actually be exploited as a cue. The utilitarian generalizer could also countenance the use of randomization or pseudo-randomization, on the ground that agents who engage in either of these techniques (all agents in the same proportions, of course) are behaving the same as one another in the sense that matters, even if the randomization leads them to different ultimate acts some of the time.

There is nothing about these techniques for generating different behaviour on the part of similarly situated agents which is inconsistent with the requirement, emphasized by utilitarian generalizers, that moral prescriptions be universalizable. The point of talk about universalizability is to emphasize that moral theories and principles are not agent-specific. Whatever principles give rise to or describe Jones's obligations must give rise to or describe Smith's as well. Plainly there is nothing in the idea that symmetrically situated co-operators should sometimes behave differently if they can manage it which is inconsistent with this fundamental truth about morality.

Before concluding this chapter, I should perhaps pause to emphasize that I have *not* shown CU is equivalent to UG, not even to an 'enlightened' UG. What I have shown is that CU and an enlightened UG may resemble each other closely in the sort of case I have been discussing *when all the agents involved are co-operators.* But this last proviso reminds us of a crucial difference between CU and even an enlightened UG. The adherent of UG in effect assumes that all similarly situated agents involved in any choice problem are co-operators. The adherent of CU does not. The first thing the follower of CU must do in any situation is to figure out which other agents are co-operators. This is a step UG omits entirely. The resemblance between CU and UG which surfaces in this chapter hinges on the fact that this chapter focuses on how CU works (in practice) *after* that initial stage has been passed. Unlike UG, CU does not involve any assumptions about the co-operativeness of other agents, assumptions which, when made in the process of applying UG, may well turn out to be counterfactual. In eschewing potentially counterfactual assumptions about the identity of the co-operators, CU resembles not UG, but AU.

By way of illustration of the points just made, consider the grass case, slightly revised. Suppose that self-interest directs each agent to cross the grass, and suppose that there are 500 agents who are so selfish that they will cross the grass regardless of what the others do. Suppose also, quite consistently with our other assumptions, that 500 crossings exhaust the possible damage to the grass. In this situation, AU requires each of the 500 *unselfish* agents to cross the grass. The behaviour of the selfish agents, by doing all the damage to the grass which can be done, eliminates any possible reason for staying off the grass. CU also requires that the unselfish agents all cross the grass, since that is the (unique) best pattern for them given the behaviour of the selfish agents.[17] UG, however, will direct all or most of the unselfish agents to stay off the grass. As far as UG is concerned, the selfish and unselfish agents are all similarly situated. An unenlightened UG will direct everyone, and therefore all of the unselfish agents, to stay off the grass. An enlightened UG, relying on cues or randomization, may direct some agents to cross. But even an enlightened UG starts from the assumption that everyone is a co-operator, and will therefore produce recommendations designed to bring about approximately 100 crossings by all agents, which can be expected to yield about fifty crossings by the 500 unselfish agents. In the revised grass case, the recommendations of even an enlightened UG are seriously defective.

It might appear that a still more enlightened UG would find some way to take the behaviour of the 500 selfish agents into account. But how is this to be done? The utilitarian generalizer cannot say that every agent's circumstances include the behaviour of every other without involving himself in the tangles discussed in Chapter 6. Some defenders of UG have suggested that others' behaviour is relevant in certain circumstances, even though it is not relevant as a general matter.[18] However, the arguments made in support of such suggestions are *ad hoc* and unconvincing.[19] The reason for the difficulty is that any attempt to take other agents' actual behaviour into account represents a retreat from the fundamental idea of UG.

In one respect, of course, I agree with those who have attempted to make UG more flexible by allowing it to take account of some behaviour of other agents. I agree that some behaviour of other agents is to be taken into account and some is not. But there are right ways and wrong ways of deciding which other behaviour to take into account. The adherent of CU takes as part of the circumstances in which he and the other co-operators act the behaviour of those agents who for one reason or another are not co-operators. The insight underlying CU is simply this: Whether we are dealing with a Whiff and Poof example, or a grass case, or a genuinely important problem like taxpaying or voting or resource conservation, the proper question about which behaviour of other agents to take into account is not 'When?', as the defenders of a flexible UG variously suggest. The proper question is 'Whose?'.

THE COMMUNITY OF CO-OPERATORS

I suggested at the end of Chapter 8 that CU is an intuitively appealing theory quite apart from any claim to adaptability. In this final chapter I shall expand on that suggestion.

As I said in Chapter 8, one of the basic facts about the world is that there is a multiplicity of moral agents. I am a moral agent, and I have moral decisions to make, but I am not alone. I share that condition, both liberating and burdensome, with many other persons. The existence of a multiplicity of moral agents suggests that the business of behaving morally ought to be viewable as a community enterprise. If we believe in consequentialism, then we ought to view the business of producing good consequences as a community enterprise. CU brings this feature of the moral life much more clearly to the fore than any other consequentialist theory.

To put the same point another way, a central problem with which any consequentialist theory must deal is the problem of how each agent is to view the behaviour of other agents. Act-utilitarianism tells each agent in effect to take the behaviour of all others as given. Rule-utilitarianism and utilitarian generalization, in their pure forms, tell each agent in effect to ignore others' behaviour entirely. Only CU embodies an approach to others' behaviour which emphasizes constantly that, whoever the agents are who are willing to try to produce the best consequences possible, they are engaged in a common project.

Let us consider a bit more closely just why the various traditional theories are unsatisfactory in their treatment of others' behaviour. Act-utilitarianism requires of each individual that he do the best thing available to him, given what everyone else is doing. So far as act-utilitarianism is concerned, others' behaviour (or dispositions to behave) affects obligations in precisely the same way as brute natural phenomena. Of course, in deciding what consequences to promote, the act-utilitarian takes others' interests into account. But we are not concerned at this point with how the act-utilitarian regards others' interests. We are concerned with how he regards their behaviour.

There is no reference in the act-utilitarian principle itself to the need for co-operation or to the fact that producing good consequences is a task which many moral agents share. To be sure, act-utilitarianism requires each agent to engage, when he has the opportunity, in behaviour which will improve others' behaviour or which will increase the likelihood of desirable co-ordination. Each agent should try to influence others to better behaviour, to enter into useful agreements, and so on. But there is still a fundamental dichotomy between the agent's own behaviour and everyone else's. The point of view embodied in the act-utilitarian's ultimate criterion of right behaviour is the point of view of one agent alone. It is not the point of view of an agent who is participating in a joint effort.

Rule-utilitarianism slights the communal nature of the moral enterprise in a different way. If rules are justified as a means of co-ordination, then obviously there is explicit reference within the rule-utilitarian's theory to the fact that producing good consequences is a shared task. But the rules are not usually regarded as merely instrumental, as useful tools in the joint enterprise which should be set aside when more effective tools come to hand. Instead, the rules take on an importance of their own. They become the only criterion for the rightness of individual acts. In the final analysis, the rule-utilitarian is directed by his theory to ignore other agents' actual behaviour. He must consider how other agents *might* behave in formulating the best overall pattern of behaviour; but he need not pay any attention to how others behave in fact. The rules take on all the burden of producing co-ordination, and the agent is separated by the rules from other agents who are part of the common enterprise. The agent is encouraged to indulge in a sort of Pontius Pilatism, taking the view that as long as he keeps his own hands clean, the other agents as well as the overall consequences can take care of themselves.[1]

Of course, the preceding paragraph is really directed at

COP. The rule-utilitarian who relies on conditional rules must worry about how others behave in fact. But in doing so he opens himself to the criticism levelled against the act-utilitarian, that he treats others' behaviour as part of his own circumstances, not as part of a joint effort. As we have already seen in a different context, theories on the model of COP–C do not resolve the basic difficulties with the rule-utilitarian approach.

There is an analogy which may illuminate the sense in which a system of rules tends to come between agents who are endeavouring to behave morally. Most persons have, at some point in their lives, played on an athletic team, or danced in an ensemble, or played in an orchestra, or sung in a chorus. The point I have in mind could be made in connection with any of these, but since I am a singer, I consider the chorus. A chorus can make a fairly decent sound, and even sing moderately expressively, if the individual singers are adequate, if each individual knows his part, and if each hews to his part to the best of his ability, more or less ignoring everyone else. But unless the individual singers have achieved only a low level of competence, the chorus will not do its best this way, nor will the experience be very satisfying to the individuals who make up the chorus. If the chorus is really to work as a chorus, it is necessary for each individual to listen to all the others, to tune to them, to breathe with them, to swell and diminish with them, and so on. The unity that is required for really successful choral work cannot be guaranteed even by everyone's paying attention to a conductor, although that helps. Everybody just has to listen to everybody else and feel himself part of a community. 'Rules', in the form of individual parts, are not enough, and preoccupation with the rules interferes both with the achievement of the joint goal and with the individual satisfaction from taking part.

It may be that many rule-utilitarians do not notice or are not bothered by the tendency of rules to come between moral agents because the rule-utilitarians in question are only half-hearted consequentialists. The insistence of rule-utilitarians on rules which are more than rules of thumb suggests a lingering allegiance to a conception of morality quite different from the consequentialist conception. According to this competing conception, individual moral agents are like little kingdoms, and the function of moral rules is to set the boundaries of these kingdoms, the limits beyond which one kingdom may not go in pursuing its goals at the expense of the others. On this view competition and conflict among agents is fundamental, and the point of morality is to set the rules for the game. This is not an implausible view. It may even be correct. But it is distinctly non-consequentialist. The consequentialist recognizes that individuals have different goals at some level. But moral action, for the consequentialist, is action designed to further an overarching common goal constructed out of these individual goals. There is no place in a consequentialist theory for rules designed to tell the agent how far he has a right to pursue his own interests without taking any account of others' interests, and when he must stop because he has entered an area where others' interests are absolutely paramount to his own.[2]

Of the traditional consequentialist theories, the one which most resembles CU in reflecting the communal nature of the moral enterprise is utilitarian generalization. Unlike act-utilitarianism, utilitarian generalization stresses that the individual is a member of a group of moral agents, directing each agent to do what it would be best for him and all others similarly situated to do. Unlike rule-utilitarianism, utilitarian generalization allows the relevant group of moral agents to aim directly at good consequences, without the interposition of a system of rules. Both of these features of utilitarian generalization, the emphasis on group membership and the direct appeal to consequences, are shared with CU.

Despite the similarities to CU, utilitarian generalization differs from CU in significant ways, making it less apt than CU as an embodiment of the idea that co-operation is central to the moral enterprise. On the one hand, utilitarian generalization takes too narrow a view of the potential co-operators. Each agent is directed to consider only how his choice interacts with the choices of other agents similarly situated. No attention is given to the desirability of co-operation between agents whose choices interact but who are not similarly situated. On the other hand, utilitarian generalization takes too broad a view of who the actual co-operators are. Each agent is required to assume in effect that every other agent who is similarly situated will co-operate. This will often not be the case, and it is in no way inconsistent with the co-operative spirit for each agent to consider just which other agents really are prepared to do their parts.

This survey of the traditional versions of consequentialism confirms the claim that only CU reveals the true nature of the moral enterprise as a communal one. CU shows how it is possible for each agent to view his own behaviour and the behaviour of other agents of good will as being on the same plane. The follower of CU neither ignores other co-operators' behaviour nor treats it as merely part of the circumstances in which he acts. Instead, he identifies his fellow co-operators and then self-consciously joins in a shared effort to produce the best possible consequences. It is widely recognized that part of what it means to take others seriously as persons is that one must regard one's own interests and others' interests as equally important. I suggest that another aspect of taking others seriously as persons may be viewing one's own behaviour and other co-operators' behaviour as equally contributions to a common undertaking. If we are a kingdom of ends, we are also a kingdom of agents. Our moral theory should reflect this fact.

To sum up, CU is based on the idea that an agent making a moral decision should first identify other agents who are available to be co-operated with and should then do his part in a co-operative effort. This idea has two distinct advantages. First, it provides the key to a successful combination of the two basic consequentialist intuitions identified in the Preface and Chapter 1. Various other theories—COP–C, RU, UG', UG''—are understandable as attempts to combine these intuitions, but they all go about it in the wrong way. Only CU combines the intuitions in the right way and achieves adaptability. Second, this same idea emphasizes the equality and interdependence of moral persons when they act to produce consequences, and not merely when they suffer them. Among consequentialist theories, only CU is a theory for the community of moral agents.

APPENDIX

This Appendix contains a full discussion of the procedure P set out in Chapter 9. I remind the reader that the comments on the interpretation of FS#1 (pp. 148-50) apply to the interpretation of P as well. The reader may want to review those comments.

There are three further points specifically about the interpretation of P which should be mentioned before we proceed to a discussion of possible circularities in P and to the proof that whatever group of agents satisfy P produce the best possible consequences as a group:

First, as to the meaning of the phrase 'fails to proceed' in various clauses of step 1, an agent fails to proceed from one step to the appropriate next step if she *either* attempts some other step instead of the appropriate one *or* simply abandons the procedure, either without going on to any other step or in the middle of the next step.

Second, since all references to other agents' beliefs or behaviour are to be construed as tenseless, the phrase 'previous step' in step 5 cannot have a temporal meaning. We must specify just what a 'previous step' of another agent is. Imagine that the agent who is applying P keeps a list of the steps she goes through in the order in which she goes through them, attaching primes to the numbers of steps she applies more than once so that each step in her record has a unique index. Thus, one agent's list might go: 0, 1, 2, 3, 4, 5, 2′, 3′, 4′, 5′, 6, 2″, 3″, 4″, 5″, 2‴, 3‴, 4‴, 5‴, 6′, 7. It should be clear enough what sort of thought process would produce this list as a record, though it would take many words to describe it in detail.

Now, for any agent at any point in the process, a 'previous step' of her own is just a step whose index appears earlier on the list. When an agent, let us call her Jones, is asked to decide whether another agent has made a mistake at a previous step or has failed to attempt a previous step, she is in effect asked to consider that other agent's thought process and index it in the same manner. If the other agent's list of indices is the same as Jones's list, up to and including Jones's last previous step, then there is no difficulty about what is meant by a 'previous step' of the other agent. It is a step which corresponds to one of Jones's previous steps. If the other agent's list is not the same as Jones's up to and including Jones's last previous step, then Jones is to view that other agent as having 'failed to attempt a previous step' at the point where the other agent's list of indices diverges from her own.

This all sounds a good deal more complicated than it is. The point is that each agent keeps checking to see that other agents are (tenselessly) progressing towards a decision in the same way she is, and eliminates from her C anyone whose decision process diverges. When we refer to a step of Smith's as a 'previous step' from the point of view of Jones at some stage in Jones's thinking, there is no temporal significance.

At the risk of belabouring the obvious, let me add this comment about the 'tenselessness' of the references in P to other agents' decision processes: It obviously *is* required by P that each agent move through a particular series of steps in a particular order. Furthermore, one of the things each agent considers at step 5 is whether other agents attempt the proper steps in the proper order. Thus each agent is concerned both with the *internal* temporal organization of her own decision process and with the *internal* temporal organization of other agents' decision processes. What is *not* relevant, and what the agent is not required to consider, is the temporal relation between one agent's decision process and some other agent's decision process. Thus, Jones must consider whether Smith goes through the right steps in the right order. But it is of no (theoretical) significance to Jones, or Smith, or anyone, whether Smith's decision-making takes place entirely before Jones's, or entirely after, or whether they overlap.

Third, I note that 'again' in step 6 is interpreted in very much the same way as 'previous step' in step 5. From the point of view of Jones at any application of step 6, another agent is said to attempt step 2 'again' if and only if that agent attempts step 2 at least once more often (overall) than Jones has passed through step 2 up to that point. There is no temporal significance.

Before proving that P is adaptable, I shall consider whether there is any circularity in P of the sort that caused us to reject the proposed step 4* at the end of the discussion of the FS's. Recall that step 4* required each agent to determine *inter alia* whether any other agent made an error *at step 4* itself*. This meant that the correct decision for Whiff at 4* depended on what was the correct decision for Poof at 4* (since only when it is known what Poof ought to do can it be determined whether Poof makes an error). The correct decision for Poof at 4* depended in turn on what was the correct decision for Whiff at that step. As a result, what Whiff was required to do at 4* could not be determined without knowing already what Whiff was required to do at 4*.

P certainly does not involve any circularity as gross and obvious as the circularity in step 4*. There is no step of P at which the agent is required to consider whether other agents make errors at that same step. Still, there are some points at which it might seem that less obvious circularities could creep in.

First of all, it might appear that step 1 could give rise to some circularity. Note that the principal error-catching step in P (that is, the principal step at which each agent checks over the work of other agents) is step 5. We shall look closely at step 5 a bit further on, but the main reason why step 5 presents no serious problem of circularity is that it is purely backward-looking (in an obvious non-temporal sense). Each agent checks over the work of other agents at *previous* steps (which may of course include previous applications of steps 5 and 6). Step 1, on the other hand, is forward-looking. We must therefore consider whether the agent might not be required at step 1 to look forward and determine how some other agent ought to decide at some later step, where the correct decision for the other agent at the later step depends on what the first agent ought to do at step 1. If this situation could occur, we would have essentially the same sort of circle that step 4* gave rise to.

Fortunately, this situation cannot occur. As I have emphasized by the italicization of some key words and phrases in the statement of P, the agent is not required by step 1 to check anything but the *formal* correctness of certain aspects of other agents' decision processes. The agent applying step 1 is required to check that other agents go from step 4 to step 5, and to check that they go from step 5 to whatever other step their *own perceptions* about other agents' behaviour require, and so on. But the agent applying step 1 is not required to determine the correctness of the other agents' perceptions. She is therefore not required to make any determination which could depend on what she does or ought to do at step 1.

Another step which might seem to create problems is step 6. At step 6, the agent is required to ascertain whether any member of her C attempts step 2 'again'. As I have explained, a member of C attempts step 2 'again' (from the point of view of the agent applying step 6) if and only if he (the member of C) attempts step 2 at least once more often overall than the agent applying step 6 has passed through step 2 up to that point. Step 6 therefore has a forward-looking aspect, just as step 1 does. The agent applying step 6 may have to look ahead to determine how many times in all various other agents attempt step 2. Still, this forward-looking aspect does not create any circularity. How often other agents actually attempt step 2 can be determined without any reference to how often they ought to attempt it. It can therefore be determined without first determining anything about what the agent applying step 6 does or ought to do.

Step 5 raises some slightly different problems. As I have already observed, step 5 is essentially backward-looking, and that is why it does not introduce any obvious circularity. But among the steps at which the agent applying step 5 must consider whether other agents have made errors are the forward-looking steps 1 and 6. What happens when one agent, let us call her Jones, arrives at step 5 and inquires into the correctness of a decision made by another agent, let us call him Smith, at step 1 or at a previous pass through step 6? Might not the correct decision for Smith at the step under review by Jones depend on some aspect of Jones's own behaviour, even on some aspect of Jones's own behaviour at the application of step 5 in which Jones is engaged?

The first thing to note is that the difficulty here, if there is one, is not of just the same sort as the difficulty raised by step 4*. What Jones ought to decide at step 5 about whether Smith has made an error at step 1 or some previous step 6 depends on what Smith ought to have done at step 1 or the previous step 6. But what Smith ought to have done at those points does not depend on what Jones ought to decide at step 5. Step 6 does not require Smith to consider at all what Jones does at any step 5. Step 1, as we have seen, requires Smith to consider only certain formal aspects of Jones's decision process. It does not require Smith to ascertain the correctness of any determination made by Jones at any step 5. Of course, to say that there is no difficulty of just the sort raised by step 4* is not to say that there is no difficulty at all. In fact, as we shall see, there is no genuine difficulty with Jones's review of Smith's decision at a previous pass through step 6. There is a difficulty with Jones's review of Smith's decision at step 1, but the difficulty is one for which there is a simple remedy.

With regard to Jones's review at step 5 of Smith's decision at some previous step 6, what we have to worry about is this: At step 6, Smith had to determine whether any member of his C attempted step 2 again. He (Smith) had to determine whether any member of his C attempted step 2 at least once more often overall than he (Smith) had attempted it up to that point. But if Jones was in Smith's C, then Smith had to consider how many times in all Jones attempts step 2. And it would seem that Smith may have been required to take into account attempts by Jones at step 2 which occur *after* the application of step 5 at which Jones is reviewing Smith's decision. In other words, it would seem that in order to decide whether Smith did the right thing at the pass through step 6 under review, Jones might have to know how often she (Jones) would attempt step 2 *thereafter*. Since Jones is still going through the procedure which will determine how often she applies step 2 thereafter, to require her to know the result at this point is decidedly odd, if not downright unacceptable.

Fortunately, the difficulty just described is illusory. *If Jones has made no error* up to her current application of step 5, and if she finds it necessary to review Smith's behaviour at some prior pass through step 6, then it must be the case that Jones's and Smith's decision processes had followed parallel courses up to the application of step 6 in question, else Smith would have been excluded earlier for failure to attempt a previous step. That means that Jones and Smith had passed through step 2 the same number of times up to the application of step 6 in question. But Jones, since she has made no error, has passed through step 2 at least once since then, on the way to her current application of step 5. Therefore Jones *does* attempt step 2 again from the point of view of Smith at the application of step 6 under review. In sum, Jones is able to determine what Smith should have decided about whether she (Jones) attempts step 2 again, without needing to know what she herself does after her current application of step 5. The argument just given depends on the assumption that Jones has made no other error before the current step 5, but that assumption is unobjectionable. All we are attempting to show about P, and all we need to show, is that it involves no circularity or similar impropriety *if correctly applied.*

With regard to Jones's review at step 5 of Smith's decision at step 1, there is a genuine difficulty, of the sort which we have just shown does not exist in connection with Jones's review of Smith's decision at step 6. At step 1, Smith was required to review certain formal aspects of the behaviour of all other agents, including Jones. Some of the steps by Jones which Smith was required to review *must* take place *after* the current application of step 5 by Jones. These steps include at least one application of step 6 and one application of step 7 (assuming Jones applies P correctly all the way through). Therefore if Jones is to review Smith's determination, it seems that Jones must know some facts about how her own decision process is going to unfold after the point she has so far arrived at. This is disturbing.

The solution is simple enough. We can modify P slightly in a way which will remove any suggestion of impropriety without affecting either the identity of the satisfiers of P or the essentials of their decision processes. P should be taken to instruct Jones to *assume* that if Smith excluded her from his C at step 1, then he made a mistake at that point. In effect, Jones is to assume in applying step 5 that she never makes any formal error of the sort which would justify her being excluded by Smith at step 1. It is clear that this modification avoids the necessity for Jones's knowing how her own decision process will unfold. But provided Jones makes no error in any aspect of P not affected by the modification, the result of her following the modified P will be exactly the same as if she followed the unmodified P and relied on correct information about her own later decision process. If Jones makes no error of the sort which would justify Smith in excluding her at step 1, then in treating Smith as having made a mistake if he excluded her at step 1, Jones does just what would be required of her by the unmodified P if she appealed to it directly with full knowledge of her complete decision process. If Jones does make some error which justifies Smith in excluding her at step 1, then following the modified P will cause her to make a further error (by the standard of the unmodified P) when she excludes Smith from her C, since Smith will not have made the error she attributes to him. However, this multiplication of errors by Jones is irrelevant. One mistake is enough to prevent Jones from satisfying P, and it does not matter what other errors she makes once it is assumed that she makes one. (Out of an abundance of caution, I note that no new circularity has just crept in. The hypothesized error by Jones which justifies Smith in excluding Jones from his C at step 1 could not be the same error (by the standard of the unmodified P) which Jones makes by following the modified P when she excludes Smith from her C at step 5, since Smith is not directed at step 1 to check for such errors as improper exclusion of agents from Jones's C.) In sum, the modification of P eliminates the need for an agent to look ahead at her own later decisions, but an agent who satisfies the modified P goes through exactly the same sequence of steps and makes exactly the same decisions at each step as she would if she were correctly following the unmodified P. (If the reader wonders why this modification was not written into the original statement of P, the answer is that it would have made the original statement just that much more complicated; it would have introduced an asymmetry which might make it harder to see intuitively what happens when P is applied; and it would not have allowed us to omit the discussion of the last two paragraphs, since the same discussion would have been necessary to explain why the asymmetry was there.)

Before I leave the subject of possible circularities in P, there are three further observations to be made:

First, although I have discussed what happens when Jones reviews at step 5 prior determinations regarding Jones made by Smith at steps 1 and 6, I have said nothing about what happens when Jones reviews at step 5 prior determinations regarding Jones made by Smith at previous passes through step 5. The reason is that review by Jones of Smith's prior decisions at step 5 involves no genuine difficulty. Smith is required to check at step 5 the substantive correctness (and not merely the formal propriety) of earlier decisions by Jones. But in order to decide at any pass through step 5 whether Smith correctly evaluated at some previous step 5 her (Jones's) decisions before that point, Jones obviously needs only to check over her own previous work. Whatever she did once without circularity, she can do again. No new circularity is introduced.

Second, while I have dealt with problems which arise from Jones's need to review, at step 5, earlier decisions about Jones made by Smith at steps 1, 5, or 6, I have said nothing about the fact that Jones may also be required to review at step 5 earlier assessments by Smith at step 5 of still earlier decisions about Jones made by *other* agents at steps 1, 5, and 6. Once again, there is no genuine difficulty. If Jones at some point finds herself reviewing an earlier decision by Smith about the correctness of some still earlier decision by Brown concerning some feature of Jones's decision-process, then, assuming Jones has made no error thus far, the decision by Brown in question is one which Jones has already reviewed directly, at the step of her own decision process corresponding to the step of Smith's now under review. (If this is not the case, then Smith has no business reviewing that decision by Brown at that point, and can be excluded from C on that ground.) But whatever conclusion Jones reached about the correctness of Brown's decision on her direct review of it she can obviously now rely on in reviewing Smith's assessment of it. The seeming new complication is illusory.

Third, I note that if Jones applies P correctly, she can never find herself in the embarrassing position of being required to review at step 5 a determination by Smith at step 3 about how she (Jones) will ultimately act. Smith is required to ascertain at step 3 only the behaviour of members of –C (as Smith sees it). If Jones is *not* in Smith's –C at the relevant point but Smith inquires into Jones's behaviour nevertheless, then Smith can be excluded from Jones's C on the basis of that misapplication of step 3 without reference to the correctness of Smith's determination of Jones's behaviour. On the other hand, if Jones *is* in Smith's –C at the relevant point, then Smith must have excluded Jones from his C at some earlier stage, and Jones, if she has made no error, will already have excluded Smith from her C when she reviewed Smith's decision at that earlier point. (Although I have not previously stated this conclusion generally, it follows straightforwardly from the discussion of the last few pages that Jones, if she makes no error, will immediately eliminate from her C any other agent who she discovers has eliminated her from his C.) If Jones does not apply P correctly, she may at some point find herself apparently required by P to review Smith's determination concerning her own ultimate behaviour, but then the fault is not in P but in her. Our concern, as I have said before, is only to show that P encounters no such difficulties when it is followed correctly.

I turn now to the proof that P is adaptable, that is, that the class of agents who satisfy P produce the best consequences possible as a group given the behaviour of the non-satisfiers. The proof proceeds in the same manner as the heuristic argument for the adaptability of CU in Chapter 8. We shall simply follow the agents who satisfy P through the process, step by step. We shall see that they all trace identical paths through the loops of P, always eliminating the same agents from their

C's and never eliminating each other, and that eventually they all stop together and act on the same best plan of behaviour (CBP) for the class they all view as C+. It takes only a little more argument to establish that when they do this, they produce best consequences possible as a group. The proof now begins:

Consider the class of agents who satisfy P. Call this class 'S' (for 'satisfiers'). If S is empty, then it is trivially true that the members of S produce best possible consequences as a group. We assume therefore that S is not empty. At step 0, each member of S identifies as the class he calls 'C' the class consisting of all agents in the universe other than himself. At step 1, each member of S eliminates from his C all other agents whose decision processes are formally improper in any of the ways specified by step 1. Observe that since the members of S satisfy P, it is not the case that the decision process of any member of S is improper in any of these ways. Therefore no member of S can be *correctly* eliminated from any other agent's C. Therefore no member of S eliminates any other member of S from his C. The members of S all eliminate from their C's precisely the same set of non-members of S. This means that after step 2 the members of S, although they perceive different C's (because no agent is in his own C), will perceive the same C+ and the same –C. We shall see that this continues to be true. For convenience, therefore, I shall hereafter refer to 'each agent's C' (or use similar phrases), but I shall refer simply to 'C+' and '–C', with the understanding that I mean C+ and –C as perceived by all members of S.

At step 3, the members of S all correctly ascertain the behaviour of the members of –C. At step 4, the members of S all correctly ascertain the best pattern of behaviour (the CBP) for the members of the current C+ in view of the behaviour of the members of the current –C. Since they all perceive the same C+ and –C, the members of S all identify the same CBP.

At step 5, the members of S will identify exactly the same class of error-makers (or non-attempters of previous steps). They inspect the decision processes to date of slightly different classes of agents, because their C's are different, but this does not matter. All error-makers or non-attempters of previous steps are non-members of S, and those who have not been eliminated already are therefore in the intersection of the C's of all the members of S. (I remind the reader that to the extent each member of S must check over prior decisions by other agents at step 1 about his *own* decision process, he applies the modified P previously discussed. As we have seen, the effect is the same as if each member of S correctly applied the unmodified P, so all the members of S will agree about who has made errors, even with respect to errors in the assessment of the decision processes of members of S.)

If an error-maker or non-attempter is found at step 5, then the members of S will all eliminate the same agents from their C's and return to step 2. The members of S will continue to perceive the same C+ and –C. They will obviously continue to proceed through P in parallel fashion, with the same C+, –C, and CBP, for as long as they keep getting thrown back from step 5 to step 2.

Note that S is always included in C+, since no member of S will ever eliminate another member of S from his C. Note also that the members of S cannot get permanently stuck in the 2–5–2 loop because every return from step 5 to step 2 is accompanied by the elimination of at least one agent from C+, and the number of agents is assumed to be finite. The next question, therefore, is what happens when the members of S go on from step 5 to step 6?

There are four states of affairs which apparently might obtain when the members of S arrive at step 6 (whether for the first time or on any later pass): (1) at least two persons in the current C+ attempt step 2 again (where 'again' may now be taken to mean 'at least once more often than the members of S have applied step 2 up to this point', since the members of S have all applied step 2 the same number of times); (2) exactly one person in the current C+ attempts step 2 again, and this person is *not* in S; (3) exactly one person in the current C+ attempts step 2 again, and this person *is* in S; and (4) no one in the current C+ attempts step 2 again. As we shall see, these four states somewhat more than exhaust the possibilities, since two of them will be shown to be impossible.

But that is something we need to prove. That these four states cover all the possibilities (without regard to whether they also cover some impossibilities) is clear on the face of things.

Now, if state (1) obtains—if at least two members of the current C+ attempt step 2 again—then every member of S will see at least one agent in his C who is attempting step 2 again. Every member of S will therefore be directed by step 6 to return to step 2 and will do so. Before doing so, every member of S will eliminate from his C all agents who do not attempt step 2 again, which obviously does not include any member of S. Each member of S will therefore continue to perceive the same C+ and –C as all the other members of S.

Suppose state (2) obtains—exactly one person in the current C+ attempts step 2 again, and this person is *not* in S. This is in fact not possible. Recall that we have been assuming since the first few sentences of the proof that S is non-empty. Consider an agent, Samuel, in S. Samuel sees as his C the current C+ less himself. Therefore Samuel sees in his C the one person in C+ who attempts step 2 again (who cannot be Samuel, since the one person in question is not a member of S). But then Samuel is directed by step 6 to attempt step 2 again, which by hypothesis he does not do. Samuel does not satisfy P, and he is not a member of S after all. This is a contradiction. We conclude that state (2) cannot occur.

Suppose state (3) obtains—exactly one person in the current C+ attempts step 2 again, and that person *is* in S. This also is impossible. If the lone repeater of step 2 is in S, he sees as his C the current C+ less himself. Since he is the lone repeater of step 2 in the current C+, there is no one who repeats step 2 in his C. Therefore he himself is directed by step 6 not to repeat step 2. His repeating step 2 is an error, and he is not a member of S after all. State (3) cannot occur.

Finally, suppose state (4) obtains—no one in the current C+ attempts step 2 again. If this is the situation, every member of S will proceed to step 7 and act on the CBP, as P directs. What is more, every member of the current C+ will proceed to step 7 and act on the CBP as well. This claim about the behaviour of everyone in C+ is important, and the argument is as follows: Every member of the current C+ has gone through just the same sequence of steps as the members of S up to and including the last previous application of step 4. (This is just what the members of S checked for and what they must have discovered at the last previous application of step 5, else they would have returned to step 2 instead of proceeding to step 6.) Therefore every member of C+ shared the same perception of the CBP as the members of S as of the last previous application of step 4. From that application of step 4, all the members of C+ proceeded to step 5, along with the members of S. (We know this is true, because anyone who was not going to do that would have been eliminated from C+ at step 1, under clause (i).) From step 5, all the members of C+ must have proceeded either to step 2 or to step 6, else they would have been eliminated at step 1, under clause (ii). But no member of C+ attempts step 2 more often than the members of S (from the description of state (4)); therefore every member of C+ proceeded from step 5 to step 6. Exactly the same reasoning, combining reference to clause (iii) of step 1 and the description of state (4), allows us to conclude that the members of C+ all proceed from step 6 to step 7. Finally, we can conclude by reference to clause (iv) of step 1 that every member of C+ acts on the CBP as he saw it at his last pass through step 4, which is to say, on the CBP of the members of S. So in state (4), all members of C+ proceed to step 7 and act on the CBP.

To sum up: State (3) is impossible. State (2) is impossible if S is non-empty. (Strictly speaking, state (2) is impossible, period. I have shown already that state (2) is impossible on the assumption S is non-empty. But if S is empty, then the description of state (2) is vacuous, since the description of state (2) makes reference to 'C+' which I have been using to mean the C+ *perceived by members of S*. This is a wrinkle we need not worry about. It is neither important nor intuitively enlightening in the way the arguments already made about the impossibility of states (2) and (3) are.) The only states which really interest us are (1) and (4). If state (1) occurs, the members of S all return to step 2 in the perfect unanimity which reigns among them throughout the procedure. Finally, in state (4) and *only* in state (4) the members of S proceed to step 7 and act on the CBP along with all the other members (if any) of C+.

One question remains about what happens at step 6. Can we be certain that the members of S will at some point be directed to proceed to step 7? The answer is that we can. No individual agent can go through more than a finite number of steps. If no agent can go through more than a finite number of steps, then no agent can find himself required by P to go through more than a finite number of steps, since P directs any agent to stop (exiting from the procedure via step 7, of course) at most about ten steps after the last other agent has stopped.

It may seem that this 'other-agents'-running-out-of-gas' argument for the proposition that P must eventually require agents to stop is disturbingly *ad hoc* and perhaps inappropriately 'practical' given my insistence that practical considerations are irrelevant to arguments about P. These objections are misguided. The reader will remember that we abandoned the attempt to produce a satisfactory procedure by spelling out the FS's on the ground that an infinite number of steps would be required and that no agent could go through an infinite number of steps. I take it the objection at that point was based on the logical impossibility of an agent's going through an infinite number of steps. It was only that logical impossibility which closed off one route to a satisfactory procedure. It is therefore perfectly appropriate to appeal to the same logical impossibility now as part of an argument supporting a different procedure. (The reader may wonder whether we could not have used the 'other-agents'-running-out-of-gas' argument to establish that an appropriately modified infinitely extended FS would not *in fact* have required an infinite number of steps of any agent, and whether we could not have constructed by that route a satisfactory procedure without bothering with P. The answer is that we could have. However, for reasons I shall not go into, it would have been more difficult than this simple question suggests to construct a procedure with *all* the properties we want in P (of which not requiring an infinite number of steps is only one). In fact, this approach would have led eventually to a rather less elegant version of P, if the reader will believe that possible.)

It is important to understand that my appeal to the 'other-agents'-running-out-of-gas' argument to explain why P must eventually require an agent to stop does *not* mean that an agent, in order to satisfy P, must always go through more steps than all other agents. That is not true. P can be satisfied by any number of agents all going through the same number of steps. (Consider the discussion above of what happens when the members of S arrive at step 6 and state (4) obtains.) It is not even the case that P encourages each agent to try to out-last the others. It can be just as much an error to go on too long as to stop too soon. (Consider the discussion above of the impossibility of state (3).) All I have said is that no agent is required by P to go on more than a few steps after everyone else has stopped, so no agent can be required by P to go on indefinitely. The somewhat paradoxical nature of what happens when the members of S stop is further discussed in the text of Chapter 9 (pp. 160–2).

Returning from this digression to the proof in process: We have established that the members of S must stop sometime. We have established in the discussion of states (1)–(4) that the members of S stop only when state (4) obtains upon their arrival at step 6. We have established that when state (4) obtains and the members of S stop, all the members of the current C+ also stop and act on the same CBP as the members of S. If all the members of C+ act on the CBP, which is the best pattern of behaviour for the members of C+ given the behaviour of members of –C, then the members of C+ produce best possible consequences as a group. As we have noted, S is a subgroup of C+, and therefore the members of S produce the best consequences possible as a group (by the corollary to the proof of the 'consistency claim' at the beginning of Chapter 3, p. 56). P is adaptable. QED.

I remind the reader that I have assumed throughout this proof that whenever the members of S are required to identify the CBP, there is a unique CBP. I shall not produce a revised P which would allow us to dispense with this assumption. The necessary revisions are sketched in the text (p. 162).

Up to this point we have spoken of S as a subgroup of the

final C+, and we have not concerned ourselves with whether it is a proper subgroup. But recall that one of the properties I claimed P would have was that each agent who followed P successfully would identify as the class of agents he was 'co-operating' with just the class of other agents who followed P successfully. Since each member of S ultimately regards himself as 'co-operating' with everyone else in the final C+, I am committed to showing that S and the final C+ are identical. I prove that claim as follows:

We know the members of the final C+ make no errors up to and including the last pass (which is the same for everyone in C+) through step 4. That is what the members of S discover at the last pass through step 5. Does any member of the final C+ make an error thereafter at step 5? No. We can show that the correct thing for each member of the final C+ to do at step 5 is to go on to step 6. After all, the members of the final C+, since they make no error up to and including the last pass through step 4, arrive at the last application of step 5 with the same C+ as the members of S. But we know that the members of S go on from there to step 6. If that is the correct thing for the members of S to do, it must be the correct thing for everyone to do, since the only persons in the C's perceived by non-members of S who are not in the C's of all the members of S are the members of S themselves, who of course make no errors. Therefore no member of the final C+ will see at the last pass through step 5 anyone who has made an error, and all the members of the final C+ should go on to step 6. But, as we saw in the course of the proof that P is adaptable, that is just what the members of C+ all do. They all go on to step 6. Furthermore, because all the members of C+ have long since passed the formality check at step 1 (ii), we know that each member of C+ proceeds from step 5 to step 6 if and only if that is what is called for by P *on the basis of his own belief* about the proposition he is required to form a belief about at step 5. We can therefore conclude that each agent in C+ not only proceeds to step 6 but also forms a correct belief at step 5. In sum, the members of the final C+ negotiate the last pass through step 5 perfectly. Essentially the same argument, relying now on step 1 (iii), shows that each agent in the final C+ forms a correct belief at step 6 before proceeding correctly on to step 7, as we have already shown they will do. Finally, each agent in C+ acts on the CBP, as we have already shown, which is just what is required at step 7. In sum, no member of the final C+ makes any error up to and including the last pass through step 4, and no member of the final C+ makes any error thereafter. In other words, no member of the final C+ makes any error at all. The final C+ is therefore included in S. Since we already know S is included in the final C+, we have shown that the final C+ and S are identical. QED.

The last stages of the argument that P is adaptable and also the argument just given for the identity of S and the final C+ are rather convoluted. They may seem circular at first reading. They are not. Everything we have shown about what happens at these last few steps actually follows from a single assumption, which is that the members of S are winding up their application of P (as, at some point, they must). Knowing what the members of S are doing tells us what the members of S are required by P to do, since the members of S follow P perfectly. Knowing what the members of S are required by P to do tells us what the members of the final C+ are doing, even before we have established that the members of the final C+ and the members of S are the same. Once we know what the members of the final C+ are doing, we can show that they are all doing just what they ought to do, in other words, that they all satisfy P.

NOTES

PREFACE

1 R. F. Harrod, 'Utilitarianism Revised', *Mind*, 45 (1963), 151.

2 'Utilitarianism, Universalisation, And Our Duty To Be Just', *Proceedings of the Aristotelian Society*, 53 (1952-3), 126, reprinted in *Contemporary Utilitarianism*, ed. Michael D. Bayles (Garden City, N.Y.: Doubleday & Co., 1968), pp. 25-57.

CHAPTER 1

1 I think the intuition that a theory should have PropCOP is almost the only basis on which rule-utilitarianism or utilitarian generalization should have any appeal for a consequentialist interested in the consequences of satisfaction of theories (that is, for someone who adopts the basic viewpoint of this essay). Among other sources of the appeal of rule-utilitarianism and utilitarian generalization are: (1) covert dissatisfaction with consequentialism in general (see pp. 209-10); (2) a belief that stating moral obligations in terms of rules or general principles may enhance the resolve to be moral, or may facilitate moral teaching or moral criticism (which I take to be part of views emphasizing the consequences of *acceptance* of theories); (3) a desire, by stating obligations in terms of general rules or principles, to avoid stultifying preoccupation with relatively trivial consequences at every moment (this also I dismiss for present purposes as pertaining to issues about acceptance, without meaning to depreciate the seriousness of the problem raised); (4) in the case of utilitarian generalization, an inappropriate inference from the importance of 'universalizability' to the conclusion that similarly situated agents must behave the same (see pp. 203-4). Of course, both rule-utilitarianism and utilitarian generalization can be seen as incorporating useful insights concerning the practical problems of applying a correct consequentialist theory (see, with regard to utilitarian generalization, pp. 195-6). And utilitarian generalization comes as close as any existing consequentialist theory to embodying a satisfactory outlook on the behaviour of 'other agents' (see pp. 210-11).

2 It may occur to the reader that there is an ambiguity in the phrase 'the agents who satisfy T' in the definition of adaptability. Does this phrase refer only to the *entire* class of agents who satisfy T, or does it

refer to *every* class of agents who satisfy T, that is, to the entire class of agents who satisfy T and all of its subclasses? Actually, it does not matter. I shall prove in Chapter 7 that the 'two' definitions of adaptability which are produced by the two choices about how to resolve this ambiguity are equivalent. For what it is worth, I think of the definition of adaptability as stated in terms of the *entire* class of satisfiers of T, and I shall write Chapter 7 as if that were the natural interpretation of the definition as given, but, as I say, it really makes no difference. The reader who has read this note should think in terms of whichever interpretation seems most natural, or better still, forget about the ambiguity. The reason I do not deal with the ambiguity until Chapter 7 is that I shall have very little to say about adaptability until Chapter 7. Until then, I shall discuss whether various theories have PropAU and PropCOP. Along the way I shall prove a proposition which is necessary to the proof that the 'two' definitions of adaptability are in fact one.

3 In the text I assume implicitly that we can separate the consequences of the act or acts chosen by the decision procedure from the other consequences, if any, of the application of the procedure. Strictly speaking, this may not always be possible. There can be cases in which the consequences of the act depend on how it is chosen, or in which the 'other' consequences of the application of the decision procedure vary with the act that is chosen by the procedure. We could deal explicitly with this complication without affecting the basic conclusions of the essay at any point. But the cost in terms of the complexity of the exposition would be significant. Accordingly, I shall continue to speak in this essay as if the consequences of the act chosen and the 'other' consequences of the application of any required decision procedure were always distinct. The reader will see when we return to this topic in Chapter 10 that this is a natural and appropriate way to view the situation in general.

4 See Ch. 7, pp. 110-13, and Ch. 10, n. 12.

CHAPTER 2

1 Although I think we may have a choice about whether to state an objective AU in terms of the facts or in terms of objective probabilities so far as the physical world is concerned, I am not sure we have the same choice about whether an agent should respond to the actual behaviour and dispositions to behave or to objective probabilities concerning the behaviour and dispositions to behave of other agents. See n. 17, below.

2 Singer, 'Is Act-Utilitarianism Self-Defeating?', *Philosophical Review*, 81 (1972), 94-104, at 103.

3 Ibid.

4 See p. 39.

5 See pp. 54-5 and Ch. 3, n. 1.

6 It might be thought that even though the contributory consequences approach has little to recommend it when we focus on satisfaction of an objective AU, it is none the less the best way to interpret AU when we consider the *subjective* obligations to which AU gives rise. The idea is that an agent trying to follow AU with the *marginal* consequences approach could ordinarily reason that the likelihood of his act making a difference to the achievement of a participatory benefit, in a case where there are many agents, is so small that he ought (subjectively) not to participate when there is an obvious act-utilitarian reason for not participating. If all agents reason thus and act on their reasoning, participatory benefits will rarely be achieved.

A full discussion of subjective obligation is outside the limits I have set for this essay, but I think the argument just sketched depends on a misunderstanding of act-utilitarian subjective obligation. An act-utilitarian's subjective obligation is not to do the act which has the greatest subjective likelihood of turning out to be the best act in view of others' eventual behaviour. Rather, his subjective obligation is to do the act which has best expected consequences given the subjective probabilities about others' behaviour. These two formulations are quite different, and if the second is indeed the correct one, then the argument suggested above against the marginal consequences approach to subjective obligation collapses.

Recall our Case 1, from the text, in which the participation of 60 out of 100 agents is required to produce a benefit worth 110 units. Let us analyse this case from the marginalist point of view, but comparing the subjective-likelihood and subjective-expected-return approaches to subjective obligation. Suppose that as far as each agent's subjective expectations are concerned, there is a 1/100 chance that no other agent will participate, a 1/100 chance that exactly one other agent will participate, a 1/100 chance that exactly two other agents will participate, and so on. (These subjective probabilities may not be particularly realistic, but they are convenient, and they will suffice to make my point. More realistic assumptions would only strengthen the case for the proposition that the subjective-expected-return approach avoids the pitfall subjective AU is supposed to fall into.) Now, the subjective likelihood from any agent's point of view that the best act for him, given others' actual behaviour, is to participate, is 1/100. Participation is the best act if and only if exactly 59 others participate. On the other hand, the one time in a hundred when participation *is* the best act, it produces, to the marginalist's way of thinking, a benefit of 110 units. Therefore the subjective expected return to participating is 110/100 units, while the expected (indeed certain) return to not participating is one unit. According to the marginalist act-utilitarian who adopts the subjective-expected-return approach to subjective obligation, each agent's subjective obligation is to participate. Participating is the act with best subjective expected consequences, even though the subjective likelihood that participation will turn out to be the best act given others' behaviour is very small.

The argument of the preceding paragraph is intended *only* to illustrate the importance of having a correct conception of act-utilitarian subjective obligation. I am aware of the large number of objections that could be levelled against it if it were offered as a general argument to prove that an act-utilitarian's subjective obligation is always to attempt to participate in desirable general practices (a proposition which is clearly false). As I have said, the general problem of subjective obligation is beyond the scope of this essay. But the most common argument that marginalist act-utilitarian subjective obligation leads away from desirable group behaviour (the argument sketched in the first paragraph of this note) is, as I hope I have managed to suggest, misconceived. (The interested reader will find in Ch. 11, n. 1 an example in which I assert that an agent's subjective obligation under AU is to do an act which is *known* not to be the best possible act given others' actual behaviour, an act which has both a subjective likelihood and indeed a known objective likelihood of zero of being the best act given others' actual behaviour.)

7 Allan Gibbard uses an essentially identical example to make the same point in a slightly different context. Gibbard, 'Rule-Utilitarianism: Merely an Illusory Alternative?' *Australasian Journal of Philosophy*, 43 (1965), 211-20.

8 The point that universal satisfaction of AU does not guarantee the best possible consequences, for essentially the reason illustrated by my example, is noted in Jordan Howard Sobel, 'Rule-Utilitarianism', *Australasian Journal of Philosophy*, 46 (1968), 165 and in Gerald Barnes, 'Utilitarianisms', *Ethics*, 82 (1971), 61. Neither Sobel nor Barnes notes explicitly that the fundamental problem is AU's indeterminacy. Gibbard (n. 7 above) does in effect note the indeterminacy of AU.

9 'The Disutility of Act-Utilitarianism', *Philosophical Quarterly*, 23 (1973), 291.

10 See pp. 62-3.

11 For example, Jan Narveson, 'Utilitarianism, Group Actions, and Co-ordination', *Nous*, 10 (1976), 173-94, relies on the obviousness argument (since he offers no other) at the point where he asserts that four act-utilitarians named Taylor, White, Green, and Narveson would manage to co-ordinate on the optimal pattern of behaviour with respect to a patch of grass when that pattern calls for Taylor and White to cross and Green and Narveson not to (pp. 188-9). He ignores the question of how these agents are led by their act-utilitarianism to avoid the pattern in which all four cross, which is on Narveson's assumptions a suboptimal pattern of universal satisfaction of AU. (I shall discuss another aspect of Narveson's position at some length in the latter part of this chapter.)

12 For a suggestion that AU might be 'generalized' so as to prescribe for groups, see B. C. Postow, 'Generalized Act Utilitarianism', *Analysis*, 37 (1977), 49-52. Postow's suggestion is one of a number that I regard as tentative moves by act-utilitarians in the direction of co-operative utilitarianism.

13 It might be observed at this point that if Whiff and Poof do choose differently, they will not in fact be symmetrically situated, since Whiff's circumstances, which include Poof's behaviour, will be different from Poof's circumstances, which include Whiff's behaviour. This observation is correct on its own terms. In effect, it duplicates our initial criticism of the argument from symmetry, which was that it overlooks the fact that AU prescribes only for individuals and not for groups. Still, the observation is irrelevant to our present point, which is that even if we look to AU for a prescription for the group, taking it to prescribe any best pattern in which the group universally satisfies AU, it will not always prescribe patterns of behaviour in which agents who are symmetrically placed in terms of the situation confronting the group as a whole behave the same. The issues raised by an approach like the argument from symmetry are discussed in greater detail in Chapter 6, on utilitarian generalization.

14 J. J. C. Smart and Bernard Williams, *Utilitarianism For and Against* (London: Cambridge Univ. Press, 1973), pp. 57-62.

15 See pp. 197-8.

16 'Utilitarianism, Group Actions, and Coordination', *Nous*, 10 (1976), 189.

17 In this lengthy note I shall consider another probability-based argument designed to show AU has PropCOP. The new argument is quite different from the argument considered in the text, but it raises issues which bear on that argument. The reader should be warned that the actual new argument designed to show AU has PropCOP does not appear in this paragraph, nor in the next, nor yet in the next after that. There is a good bit of groundwork to be laid first. To be candid, I am using the new argument designed to show AU has PropCOP as an excuse for a brief divagation into some issues concerning AU which have been too long neglected.

Consider again the latest example introduced in the text, in which the consequences of Whiff's pushing and Poof's not-pushing have a value of five units. If it is assumed that the objective probabilities are that each agent is equally likely to push or not to push, and if it is assumed that AU requires each agent to maximize the expected return to his act in view of these objective probabilities, then, as we have noted, AU requires Poof to not-push. *Even if Whiff pushes,* Poof is required to not-push. Now this is peculiar. Recall that we are at all times discussing *objective* versions of AU. AU requires Poof to do whatever has best consequences. We would naturally think that if Whiff pushes, then the act for Poof which has best consequences would be pushing. But on the present interpretation AU requires Poof to not-push. This can only be explained on the ground that for purposes of AU on the present interpretation what Whiff really does is to 'push with probability one-half and not-push with probability one-half', nothing else. To be sure, when Whiff does this mixed act (as we shall call the act described in terms of probabilities) he must end up either pushing or not-pushing. The mixed act must be realized as one of its components. But if AU requires Poof to respond to the mixed act, regardless of how it is realized, then the mixed act is the only act by Whiff which Poof is to regard as relevantly possible. Similarly, Poof's mixed act must be the only act of Poof that Whiff is to regard as relevantly possible.

If AU directs Poof to regard the mixed act as the only possible act for Whiff, then there is something rather strange about AU's none the less requiring of Whiff the pure act of pushing. Similarly, if AU directs Whiff to regard the mixed act as the only possible act for Poof, then there is something rather strange about AU's none the less requiring of Poof the pure act of not-pushing. There is no logical contradiction. Keeping in mind the relentlessly individualistic approach of AU, we could just say that how AU directs Poof to regard Whiff's act is totally irrelevant to what AU should require of Whiff, and vice versa. Still, the whole situation is rather peculiar. (I shall suggest in the second half of this essay that a moral theory ought to allow each agent to view his own behaviour and others' behaviour in the same light. AU, construed to require each agent to respond with a pure act to the mixed acts of others, certainly does not achieve this.)

One way to avoid the inconsistency in approach would be to say that if there are objective probabilities governing Whiff's behaviour, then Whiff is regarded by AU for *all* purposes as having only the mixed act available to him. This would mean not only that Poof was required by AU to respond to Whiff's mixed act, but that Whiff would be required by AU only to do the mixed act, since AU could not require Whiff to do an act which was not open to him (a pure act, or even any other mixed act) without running afoul of the postulate that ought implies can. The same goes for Poof, if his act also is governed by objective probabilities.

If we take the view that both Whiff and Poof have only the mixed acts available to them, then there is only one possible pattern of behaviour in our example. Since AU requires of each agent the only available act, the unique possible pattern of behaviour is also the unique pattern in which AU is universally satisfied. Universal satisfaction of AU 'guarantees' the achievement of the best consequences possible. Furthermore, if we are prepared to countenance the existence in this case of objective probabilities governing what we would usually think of as chosen human behaviour, then it seems plausible to suppose that all human behaviour is governed by objective probabilities. If that is so, then on our current approach to AU, there is a unique possible pattern of behaviour, which is also the unique pattern of universal satisfaction of AU, in every situation. If we go this far, then the basic claim of this chapter, that AU does not have PropCOP, dissolves. But then so do all problems of ethics, or at least all problems about the rightness of acts, since no agent ever has a real choice. I think few readers would take seriously this argument against my basic claim.

A second way to avoid the inconsistency in AU's approach to the deciding agent's behaviour and to others' behaviour would be to deny that AU requires each agent to respond to objective probabilities concerning other agents' chosen behaviour. One way to reach this position would be simply to claim that there is some human behaviour which cannot be meaningfully described in terms of objective probabilities. I do not wish to defend this claim here—I am not certain of my view about it—but it certainly is not established that all human behaviour is describable in terms of objective probabilities. Even if we are unwilling to claim that some behaviour is not describable in terms of objective probabilities, we can still claim that as to some behaviour at least AU does not require objective probabilities to be taken into account. We can claim that if AU requires a pure act of Whiff in certain choice situations, then it must direct Whiff to respond to the pure acts of other agents who are making choices of the same sort. The preceding discussion gives some reason for taking this position.

The question of whether AU ought to require one agent to consider objective probabilities (if they exist) governing the behaviour of other agents is an interesting question that has been widely neglected. I shall not discuss it further, although I have by no means exhausted the possibilities for discussion. It should be noted that it is only objective probabilities which could be relevant to what is required by *objective* AU, with which we are concerned. I have cast no doubt on the appropriateness of taking subjective probabilities into account in formulating subjective obligations generated by AU. Nor, incidentally, have I cast doubt on the appropriateness either of an agent's responding to objective probabilities concerning the physical world, or of an agent's intentionally randomizing his own behaviour or responding to the intentionally randomized behaviour of another agent in a case where randomization by one or more agents might seem desirable.

18 It might seem that we can avoid the paradox of one agent's act both determining and being determined by the other's, by the simple expedient of supposing that both acts are determined by some third event. This may not seem an unacceptable supposition in our Whiff and Poof example. But if we wanted to deal in this way with the paradoxes inherent in a complex world of perfect act-utilitarians, we would in effect be assuming that all behaviour was determined by outside causes. This may be true, but it is not obviously true, and I doubt we should commit ourselves to this proposition as the price of being able to talk about a world of perfect act-utilitarians. The price seems too great.

Furthermore, I doubt whether positing a common cause of Whiff's choice and Poof's even in our simple example really does what we want. It is not clear to me that if both Whiff's act and Poof's are determined by some third event, then it is true that 'Poof (Whiff) will satisfy AU whatever Whiff (Poof) does'. If Poof's act and Whiff's are both determined by a common antecedent, I have difficulty understanding the nature of the 'whatever' in the sentence just given in quotes without assuming some sort of 'backward causation'. The problem here is closely related to the problem discussed by Robert Nozick, 'Newcomb's Problem and Two Principles of Choice', in *Essays in Honor of Carl G. Hempel,* ed. Nicholas Rescher (Dordrecht: D. Reidel, 1969). To discuss this problem would take us far afield. Worse, it would raise issues I have no idea what to say about.

19 At this point the defender of AU might say: 'It doesn't matter if the parties can't or shouldn't meet and discuss the matter, because we don't require an explicit agreement. Implicit agreement is all we need.' It is important to note that the defender of AU cannot rely merely on the *possibility* of implicit agreement. The central claim of this chapter is that universal satisfaction of AU does not *guarantee* best possible results. If the defender of AU wishes to refute this claim, he must show that if all agents satisfy AU, then an implicit agreement *must* arise. Having said that, I have nothing else to say about the 'implicit agreement' argument. The notion of an 'implicit agreement' is fuzzy at best, and I simply cannot see any way of spelling out this defence of AU which does not turn it into some argument I consider elsewhere, either the obviousness argument (pp. 21-3), the snowball argument (pp. 43-52), or the suggestion that AU can be supplemented with other principles (p. 42).

20 The question might arise whether the proper alternative to keeping the agreement is violating the agreement, as I seem to assume in the text, or whether it is simply ignoring the agreement. We shall see in n. 32 below that in some contexts at least the alternative to keeping the agreement which must be considered is simply ignoring the agreement. That does not affect the argument here. The point of the text here is just that, at least on the face of things, the existence of the agreement does not alter the fact that if neither pushes, both satisfy AU.

21 One response to this argument in defence of AU is suggested by the discussion of n. 17 above. It is by no means certain that human behaviour can be described in terms of objective probabilities, and even if it can, there are reasons for *not* saying that AU requires each agent to respond to the objective probabilities regarding the behaviour of others. A different response is considered in the text.

22 Singer (n. 2 above), pp. 97-100. Note that we are not here concerned with another argument Singer makes, which brings in considerations relevant to a practice of agreement-keeping, and which we shall discuss later on.

23 Mackie (n. 9 above), pp. 293-8.

24 *Consequences of Utilitarianism: A Study in Normative Ethics and Legal Theory* (Oxford: Clarendon Press, 1967).

25 Singer (n. 2 above), p. 98.

26 Singer, p. 99.

27 Singer , p. 100.

28 Mackie (n. 9 above), p. 293.

29 Note that in one situation Mackie might make a vocal noise to communicate, even in the absence of a practice of verbal communication. That is the situation where I am daydreaming and his vocalization

makes me aware of the danger of collision. But neither that noise nor any further noise Mackie might make would help with the co-ordination problem (concerning which way each of us should go) which would remain.

30 Though we now part company with Singer and Mackie in the text, there are two more points which deserve a note.

Instead of arguing that act-utilitarians would do what was necessary to see that verbal communication became established, Mackie might suggest (and he does at one point seem to suggest) that linguistic conventions are different from moral rules, and that we ought to concede the existence in a world of act-utilitarians of useful linguistic conventions. This will not do. One of the central features of utilitarianism is that it makes every question about what to do a moral question, at least in principle. If the foundation of morality is an obligation, of one sort or another, to produce good consequences, then there is no way we can subdivide human behaviour into behaviour that raises moral questions and behaviour that does not. If linguistic conventions are useful, then a completely adequate utilitarian theory ought to *require* that linguistic conventions be established. It ought not to presuppose them, even if, as Mackie and I would agree, it permits them.

Aside from all this, there is another reason why agreements may be less helpful to act-utilitarians than the Singer–Mackie argument suggests. Singer and Mackie in effect consider cases where the parties start off poised in an unstable equilibrium between two possible patterns of behaviour each of which would universally satisfy AU. They argue that any slight push in the right direction will unsettle the equilibrium and bring about the desired result. But what of cases where the parties do not begin in such an equilibrium?

Suppose that Whiff and Poof are confronted with our standard button-pushing example exactly twice. The first time they do *not* have an opportunity to make an agreement, and for some unspecified reason, they both end up not-pushing. Now, when the situation arises for the second time, each agent may have some reason to expect the other not to push. Not-pushing was successful behaviour (in the sense of behaviour which satisfied AU) for each agent the first time around, and it is natural to expect people to repeat behaviour which has been successful. Hodgson might object that there is no reason to expect repetition of successful behaviour from act-utilitarians, since the act-utilitarian principle is purely forward-looking and the success of particular behaviour in the past is logically irrelevant to its consequences in the future. But I am certain that neither Singer nor Mackie would follow Hodgson in this suggestion; nor do I. (My reasons are discussed in Chapter 4.) Now suppose an agreement is made, between the first and second repetitions, to push the second time around. What will be the effect of this agreement? The answer is that we do not know. Even if we concede (for the moment) that the agreement will provide each agent with some reason to expect the other to push, it does not follow that this reason will outweigh the independent reason to expect the other not to push which is provided by experience (that is, by what happened the first time around). Nor does it help to appeal to the spiral of expectations. Whatever the spiral does to amplify one reason, it will do the same to amplify the other. We have no ground whatever for saying that the force of the agreement must overcome the force of precedent which points in the other direction.

Singer and Mackie wish to argue that any impetus from the agreement, however slight, will suffice. This may be true when the parties start out perfectly poised between different patterns of universal satisfaction of AU. But it is not true if before the agreement the parties are leaning in the direction of an inferior pattern of universal satisfaction of AU.

31 David Lewis, 'Utilitarianism and Truthfulness', *Australasian J. Phil.* 50 (1972), 17-19; David Gauthier, 'Coordination', *Dialogue*, 14 (1975), 195-221.

32 At this point it is important that the alternative we are considering to the existence of a practice of agreement-keeping is the non-existence of a practice of agreement-keeping, which we might also call a practice of ignoring agreements, but *not* a practice of (consistently) violating agreements. A practice of consistently violating agreements could serve just the same function in co-ordinating behaviour as a practice of consistently keeping agreements. (Compare David Lewis's suggestion that 'systematic untruthfulness in English is the same thing as systematic truthfulness in a different language *anti-English*, exactly like English in syntax but exactly opposite in truth conditions.' Lewis, n. 31 above, p. 18.) This might even lead us to question whether one can make sense of the notion of a practice of consistently violating agreements, but we shall not worry about that. As I have said, the alternative to a practice of agreement-keeping which we consider is just the absence of any such practice. (I speak in the text of Whiff violating the agreement, or Poof violating it, but that can be regarded in each case as just another way of saying Whiff or Poof not-pushes.)

33 Singer (n. 2 above), pp. 102-3 (actually discussing a practice of punishment).

34 The defender of the contributory consequences approach might object that the absence of a practice of agreement-keeping should be viewed as a consequence of large negative value, so that if there is no practice, then every agent whose non-participation contributes to the absence of the practice gets credit for a negative share. This might lead to the conclusion that individual agents violate AU when there is no practice, but it does not really help. If we view the absence of the practice as a 'negative' consequence, then we are viewing the existence of the practice as the zero-point from which the values of consequences are figured. That means that if the practice does exist, then each participating agent gets credit for his share of consequences of value zero, which is to say that each agent gets zero credit on account of the existence of the practice. But then each participating agent who has some

act-utilitarian reason for not participating violates AU by his participation. This conclusion the defender of contributory consequences plainly cannot tolerate.

I should note in connection with the argument in the text that I am again uncertain just what Singer means to prove, as I was with the 'spiral of expectations' argument. Since he is arguing against Hodgson, it may be that all he intends to prove is that universal satisfaction of AU is *consistent* with the existence of a practice of agreement-keeping. This conclusion I agree with, but we do not have to adopt the contributory consequences approach to establish it. The marginal consequences approach will do quite as well. The reasons are essentially those developed by Lewis, Gauthier, and Mackie in their answers to Hodgson (and by Singer himself in that part of his answer which focuses on an individual case abstracted from a practice), supplemented by some of the arguments I develop in Chapter 4.

35 'Is Act-Utilitarian Truth-Telling Self-Defeating?', *Mind*, 82 (1973), 413–16.

36 See p. 6.

37 Fuller discussions of the time-slice issue will be found in Holly S. Goldman, 'Dated Rightness and Moral Imperfection', *Philosophical Review*, 85 (1976), 449–87; and Jordan Howard Sobel, 'Utilitarianism and Past and Future Mistakes', *Nous*, 10 (1976), 195–219. While I am generally sympathetic to the arguments and conclusions of these pieces, I shall not discuss them in detail. Both authors isolate for consideration the problem of co-ordination between time-slices of the same time-extended agent. My own view, as the text suggests, is that once we have a correct theory of co-ordination between different agents, then the problem of co-ordination between time-slices can be adequately dealt with in theory (and therefore should be dealt with in theory) as a special case of the general problem of inter-agent co-ordination.

38 Although I admit (or perhaps, from some people's point of view, claim) that act-utilitarians *may* have a practice of agreement-keeping or promise-keeping, I have not described in detail how such a practice would work; nor shall I do this in later chapters. The definitive discussion of act-utilitarian promising remains to be written (so far as I know), but the essential points are made by Singer, Mackie, Lewis, and Gauthier in their answers to Hodgson, provided we keep in mind that what these authors say must be construed as relating to how act-utilitarian promising works *if* the practice exists at all. The essential points are two: (1) The function of act-utilitarian promising is not to 'bind' any party to particular behaviour. The functions are to exchange information in shorthand conventional forms, and to make certain patterns of universal satisfaction of AU salient. (2) Promises can serve the functions just mentioned even though no party is expected to keep a promise when violating it would have best consequences, all things (including expectations generated by the promise) considered.

39 See Gauthier (n. 31 above), pp. 205–6.

40 See Preface, n. 1.

41 See Preface, n. 2.

42 My principal example of a snowball theorist, whose position I shall discuss at length, is Jan Narveson, in his 'Utilitarianism, Group Actions, and Coordination', *Nous*, 10 (1976), 173–94. Similar suggestions may be found, I believe, in Jonathan Glover, 'It Makes No Difference Whether Or Not I Do It', *Aristotelian Society*, Supp. Vol. 49 (1975), 177–81, and in a tentative form in Rolf Sartorius, *Individual Conduct and Social Norms* (Encino, Calif.: Dickenson, 1975), p. 76.

43 'Utilitarianisms', *Ethics*, 82 (1971), 61.

44 Narveson (n. 42 above).

45 Narveson, p. 192.

46 Compare the discussion at pp. 29–31.

47 Narveson makes the assumption of general act-utilitarian motivation explicit at a number of points (pp. 179, 182, 188, 191), although I should say he makes it rather casually. For the most part he does not make explicit the further assumptions which I shall show in the text that he needs. At one point (p. 184) he appears to eschew them: '[T]o say that a society is a pure act-utilitarian society . . . is still only to say something about its motivation, not about its information-level or its intelligence, etc.' It might seem that in declining to assume any particular information-level, and so on, Narveson is merely admitting that act-utilitarians can make mistakes, which should be blamed on their human fallibility, not on their moral theory. We shall see in the text that follows, however, that what we assume about the general information-level is relevant to what the moral theory requires. We shall see that unless we make certain assumptions about the general possession of certain information, even universal satisfaction of AU—that is, even group behaviour which does *not* involve any mistakes according to AU—may not lead to the achievement of the best possible consequences.

48 It may seem that in the text I rely on arguments about subjective obligation instead of objective obligation. This is not true. I am discussing the *objective* obligation of any individual would-be instigator. My point is that even if a lone would-be instigator—call him Paul—dashed through the streets, no one would respond. It is true that those who failed to respond would fail because of the beliefs I have attributed to them. But that is beside the point. The argument about why Paul would be sacrificing himself in vain, and why he would therefore violate AU, does not depend on any belief *of Paul's*. It is an argument about Paul's objective obligation. It is also true that the explanation of why someone else, say Patrick, should not dash through the streets depends in part on the beliefs I have attributed to Paul. But again, that is beside the point. That does not make it any less Patrick's objective obligation I am talking about. (The general point of this note applies not only to the paragraph of text to which it is appended, but to the next paragraph in the text as well.)

49 I should point out that Narveson does not absolutely need to

make the whole infinite list of assumptions I have shown how to generate. He could stop making assumptions from this list at any point *provided* he then added a blanket assumption to the effect that no agent would be deterred from taking part in an insurrection by considerations relevant to the omitted assumptions further down the list. This would still leave us with the question of whether the new package of assumptions, including the *ad hoc* blanket assumption, ought to be conceded to the defender of AU. My own doubts would not be assuaged. (I insert here a comment which connects this note and the next argument to be considered in the text: Even the new package of assumptions would be no more adequate than the original infinite list to carry Narveson's *affirmative* point that an insurrection would occur.)

50 Observe that I say 'the opposite' instead of 'the negation'. I have not made Narveson's answering assumptions precisely the negations of Barnes's assumptions, although I could reconstruct the whole argument so that they were. For convenience, I have not been precise about the location of the boundary between situations which support Barnes's view and those which lend support to Narveson. I have stated both Barnes's assumptions and Narveson's answering assumptions somewhat more strongly than necessary.

51 Compare the brief discussion of Narveson in n. 11, above.

52 I ignore the possibility that the well-motivated and well-informed individual might fail to do the right thing because of a last-minute convulsion or temporary insane delusion, or some such.

53 It might be suggested that the whole point of the latest version of the snowball argument is to show that we can, by a complex chain of reasoning, deduce what AU requires of any individual without reference to the actual behaviour of the others. This suggestion would be both mistaken and irrelevant. It would be mistaken because, even if the argument is good, it proves only that the first up to the 500th acts of insurrection are required by AU. But the (unnecessary) 501st act is forbidden (assuming there is some small cost to the 501st participant). Therefore whether anyone is required to take part depends on whether at least 500 others are taking part. What AU requires of any individual still depends on the behaviour of the others. Even if it were not mistaken the suggestion would be irrelevant. We can hardly appeal to the conclusion of the argument to supply a required premiss.

54 The proponent of the argument under discussion might respond that we can number the 500 acts any way we please. But this will not do. To admit that the numbering is arbitrary is to admit that no real explanation has been given of why *any* of the 500 acts is required by AU, since the logic of the argument makes the explanation of why any particular act is required by AU vary with that act's place in the numbering scheme.

CHAPTER 3

1 Suppose there are 100 agents. There is one participatory benefit with a value of 100 units which can be achieved by the participation of at least sixty agents. A second participatory benefit worth 50 units can be achieved by the participation of at least forty agents. No agent can participate in the production of both benefits. Any agent who does not participate in producing either benefit can produce benefits worth one unit by himself. It is clear that the best pattern of behaviour is the pattern in which sixty agents participate in the production of the first benefit and the remaining forty participate in the production of the other. (Actually, this 'pattern' represents a very large number of possible patterns of individual behaviour, but that does not affect the argument.) It is also clear that this best pattern of behaviour is one in which AU with the marginal consequences approach is universally satisfied. None the less, this is not a pattern of universal satisfaction of AU under the contributory consequences approach. Consider an agent named Penelope who is participating in the production of the 50-unit benefit. She gets credit for $\frac{1}{40}$ of 50 units, or 1¼ units of benefit. If she altered her behaviour so that she was participating in the production of the 100-unit benefit, she would get credit for $\frac{1}{61}$ of 100 units, or just under $1\frac{2}{3}$ units. Therefore, Penelope is not satisfying AU under the contributory consequences approach.

This example is more complicated than necessary to prove the assertion in the text that the best pattern of behaviour may be a pattern in which AU with the contributory consequences approach is not universally satisified. It should be obvious that the second (lesser) participatory benefit plays no essential role in the argument for that assertion. The important point is simply that in the best pattern of behaviour many fewer agents participate in producing the first (larger) benefit than would be required to do so by the contributory consequences approach. This would remain true even if the only alternative to participating in the production of the larger benefit were producing whatever benefits can be produced by each agent individually.

I describe the complicated example because it establishes in addition an even more surprising claim—that in some cases universal satisfaction of AU with the contributory consequences approach does not allow the production of all desirable participatory benefits. In the example described, there is no pattern of behaviour in which AU with the contributory consequences approach is universally satisfied and in which both participatory benefits are achieved. (We have already proved this, since both benefits are achieved only if sixty agents produce the first benefit and the other forty produce the second, in which case AU with the contributory consequences approach is not universally satisfied.) The difficulty which this example illustrates does not arise only in cases in which the numbers of agents required to produce the two benefits add up to exactly the total number of agents, but that circumstance makes it easier to see that the difficulty in fact exists.

2 Obviously there is always at least one best pattern of behaviour for the group so long as the total number of possible patterns is finite. If we consider an infinite number of possible patterns, then the possibility arises that the set of values of consequences of possible patterns might be unbounded, or, more plausibly, that this set, though bounded, might not contain its least upper bound. It is the question what plausible assumptions would guarantee that a bounded infinite set of values of consequences of possible patterns contained its least upper bound that I do not propose to discuss.

3 After I had written the text, I discovered that John Harsanyi has suggested that universal satisfaction of AU is sometimes impossible (without resort to randomization), even in situations where there is at least one best pattern of behaviour for the group. 'Rule Utilitarianism and Decision Theory', *Erkenntnis*, 11 (1977), 46. Harsanyi offers no argument for this claim. The context suggests to me that he was misled on a point he did not regard as important by a specious analogy to zero-sum games, where there may be no equilibrium position if the parties are restricted to pure strategies. As I shall have occasion to demonstrate in the text that follows, analogies from game theory, where the parties have different maximands, must be handled with care.

4 The nature of the misunderstanding is indicated briefly in Ch. 2, no. 6, above.

5 I am not entirely happy with this treatment of imperceptible differences. It commits us to the existence of objective probabilities concerning perception-reactions. Although I suggested early in Chapter 2 that we can state an objective AU in terms of objective probabilities if they exist, I would prefer to leave all issues about the existence of objective probabilities open. Unfortunately, I do not see any more satisfactory way to account for imperceptible differences' adding up to perceptible differences. I shall argue a bit further on in the text that consequentialists are committed to the notion that the marginal consequences must 'add up' to the total consequences, *provided* this 'adding up' is correctly understood.

Since I pointed out in Ch. 2, n. 17 some reasons for *not* construing AU to require one agent to respond to objective probabilities concerning the behaviour of others, I should mention that those reasons do not extend to behaviour such as perception-reactions. The reasons extend only to behaviour which we ordinarily regard as a matter of choice. Perception-reactions are not behaviour of this sort. Of course, I can choose to look at the grass or not, and I can choose how carefully to inspect it if I do look, but the probabilities which are relevant to the argument in the text are probabilities about what my perception-reaction will be *given* whatever choice I make about how much attention I shall pay. These probabilities concern features of my behaviour which I do not choose (at least at the time they occur, though past choices on my part may have affected my powers of visual or aesthetic discrimination). For present purposes, then, perception-reactions are like physical phenomena, not like agents' chosen behaviour.

6 The reader who has never encountered the prisoner's dilemma will find an introductory discussion in R. Duncan Luce and Howard Raiffa, *Games and Decision: Introduction and Critical Survey* (New York: John Wiley & Sons, 1957), pp. 94-7.

7 Two further comments on the proof in the text: First, while I have spoken as if an agent's dominant strategy must be unique, that need not be the case. An agent might have more than one strategy which satisfied AU whatever the other agents' behaviour. This possibility has no important effect on the proof. Second, the existence of causal connections between the agents' acts cannot upset the thought-experiment described. The only worry is that changing some agent's choice so that he chooses his dominant strategy might upset the change we have already made with regard to some previous agent. This cannot happen. The previously considered agent is now choosing his dominant strategy, and if this is a strategy which satisfies AU regardless of the others' behaviour, it must be one which the agent in question can choose regardless of the others' behaviour. So no later change in any other agent's behaviour can upset the choice.

8 This is *not* an entirely typical grass case, since AU is not indeterminate in this case. (There are two patterns in which AU is universally satisfied, but the two patterns produce consequences of the same value.) The typical grass case has three features which cannot all be present in a case involving only two agents and two choices for each. These are (1) that the consequences of universal avoidance of the grass are better than the consequences of universal crossing; (2) that the consequences of exactly one person's crossing are better than the consequences of universal avoidance; and (3) that the consequences of all but one person's crossing are inferior to the consequences of universal crossing. (The third feature, which produces the usual indeterminacy, is the one we noted it was plausible to assume in our discussion of the two fallacies in the original Prisoners' Dilemma argument.) These three features are compatible in general, but they are incompatible in the two-person, two-choice case, where 'exactly one person's crossing' and 'all but one person's crossing' refer to the same patterns of behaviour.

9 Suppose that in our Charlotte and Emily example, either agent's crossing the grass would somehow cause the other to do so as well. This would make two of the patterns of behaviour in our original example causally impossible, which we might represent by bracketing the relevant entries in the array, thus:

	Charlotte	
	Not-Cross	Cross
Not-Cross	10	[11]
Emily Cross	[11]	8

It would now seem inappropriate to move along a path of changes involving an impossible pattern. We must simply recognize that a change of behaviour by either agent in fact changes the behaviour of both and moves us in one jump, as it were, from the pattern of general avoidance to the pattern of general crossing. Obviously, the claim that the marginal changes (of which there is just one) add up to the total change remains true.

If we suppose that Charlotte's crossing would cause Emily to cross but that Emily's crossing would leave Charlotte's behaviour an open question, our array would look like this:

$$10 \quad [11]$$
$$11 \quad \ \ 8$$

We can now move from the upper-left corner to the lower-right in either of two ways. We can imagine changing Charlotte's behaviour, in which case Emily's changes at the same time and we move in one jump; or we can imagine changing first Emily's behaviour alone and then Charlotte's, in which case the path consists of two jumps. In either case, the claim about the relation of marginal changes to total change is preserved.

Incidentally, this technique of representing causal connections between the agents' acts by bracketing causally impossible patterns and treating them as not really appearing in the array may be helpful to some readers in seeing that causal interconnections do not upset our other claims about AU, such as the claim that the best pattern of behaviour is always one in which AU is universally satisfied.

10 There is another possible argument against the consistency claim of this chapter, unrelated to anything discussed in the text. Recall an example from Chapter 2:

		Poof	
		Push	Not-push
	Push	10	5
Whiff			
	Not-push	0	6

If we assume (1) that each of Whiff and Poof is objectively equally likely to push or not, and (2) that AU requires each agent to maximize expected utility in view of the objective probabilities governing the other's behaviour, then, as we have already seen, AU requires Whiff to push and Poof not to push. The consequences produced if both satisfy AU have a value of 5 units, notably less than the best possible. Observe that on our present assumptions, the pattern in which Whiff pushes and Poof does not is the *only* pattern in which AU is universally satisfied, and yet it produces inferior results. The best possible pattern is that in which both agents push, but in that pattern Poof violates AU. Apparently, we have a counterexample to the consistency claim. We shall have to take a closer look.

In discussing this same example in Ch. 2, n. 17, I suggested that perhaps AU should not be construed to require one agent to respond to objective probabilities concerning the chosen behaviour of another. In other words, I suggested that perhaps assumption (2) in the preceding paragraph should be rejected. We do not need to go so far as to reject (2) in order to rescue the consistency claim, but it is the earlier discussion of this matter that suggests the way out.

The argument that the current example is a counterexample to the consistency claim depends on the proposition that the pattern of behaviour in which both parties push is the best possible pattern of behaviour, and therefore on the proposition that that pattern is a possible pattern of behaviour. If the pattern in which both push is a possible pattern, then 'pushing' ought to be a possible act of Whiff, since it is the act Whiff does in that pattern. Yet we saw in Ch. 2, n. 17 that if we adopt assumption (2) we are in effect saying that 'pushing' is not among the possible acts of Whiff, at least from Poof's point of view. We saw that the unequivocal command to Poof to not-push makes sense only if Whiff is regarded as 'pushing with probability one-half and not-pushing with probability one-half', however this mixed act is realized. The current argument against the consistency claim therefore depends on characterizing Whiff's behaviour in different ways for different purposes. It characterizes Whiff's behaviour as the mixed act for purposes of ascertaining the consequences of Poof's act and deciding what AU requires Poof to do; but it characterizes Whiff as having the choice between two pure acts for purposes of identifying the best pattern of behaviour for the pair.

The proof of the consistency claim at the beginning of this chapter assumed implicitly that the alternatives open to each agent were characterized the same way when we inquired into the best pattern for the group as when we inquired into the act required by AU of each individual. Surely this assumption of uniform characterization is a reasonable one. But if we insist on uniform characterization in the case before us, the counterexample to the consistency claim evaporates. If we say that Whiff has a choice between two acts, then the best pattern of behaviour is the pattern of behaviour in which both push, and it is clear that in this pattern Poof satisfies AU, since he does the best act available to him given Whiff's behaviour (characterized as 'pushing'). If we say that Whiff has only the mixed act available to him, then AU, with assumption (2), requires Poof to not-push, but the best possible pattern of behaviour is the pattern in which Whiff does the mixed act and Poof not-pushes, so it is still true that Poof satisfies AU in the best pattern of behaviour. Even if, in view of the full strength of assumption (1) above, we say that both agents have only the mixed act available to them, the consistency claim is unimpaired. If there is only one possible pattern of behaviour, then that pattern is both the best possible pattern and a pattern of universal satisfaction of AU. The consistency claim holds good however we characterize the agents' behaviour, provided we are consistent about it.

CHAPTER 4

1 See John C. Harsanyi, 'Rule Utilitarianism and Decision Theory', *Erkenntnis*, 11 (1977), 25-53.

2 See p. 54.

3 D. H. Hodgson, *Consequences of Utilitarianism: A Study in Normative Ethics and Legal Theory* (Oxford: Clarendon Press, 1967), pp. 85-7.

4 Hodgson, pp. 87, 94-5.

5 Hodgson, pp. 87-90, 91-4. In particular, my rendition of Hodgson's argument is intended to capture what I take to be the point of his discussions of rebuttable presumptions. Peter Singer (Ch. 2, n. 2, above) interprets Hodgson's argument about punishment much as I do. (Singer's response is based on the contributory consequences approach to AU, which I rejected in Chapter 2.)

6 See pp. 39-41.

7 It is perhaps worth noting that the dubious inference occurs twice. It occurs explicitly at the beginning, and it occurs implicitly at the end, when it is asserted that 'Rex should not punish at O_1' contradicts 'Rex should punish at $O_1, O_2 \ldots$' The assertion that there is a contradiction here depends on the assumption that we can detach 'Rex should punish at O_1' from the proposition 'Rex should punish at $O_1, O_2 \ldots$'

8 'On a Supposed Antinomy', in *The Ways of Paradox* (New York: Random House, 1966), pp. 21-3 (reprinted with changes in terminology from *Mind*, 62 (1953)).

9 See pp. 29-30.

10 The argument in the text does not take account of certain logical possibilities, such as that Rex's behaviour at some point in time may cause beliefs to arise which are unalterable thereafter; or that potential offenders know Rex's views by telepathy; or that Rex can affect potential offenders' beliefs about him by what he says even though those beliefs are totally impervious to any influence from his other behaviour. Each of these possibilities would raise some interesting questions. None is worth discussing here.

11 We are still ignoring the possibility that AU is indeterminate in the punishment case. If Rex took account of that, he would alter his statement in two ways: (1) He would point out that even if potential offenders unalterably believed he would satisfy AU, they could not logically deduce that he would never punish, since the earlier argument that AU requires non-punishment depended on the existence of unalterable expectations of a specific pattern of punishment. (There are some possible complications here we do not consider.) (2) He could not say that he was going to punish because AU required it. He would have to say he was going to punish because that was the pattern with the best consequences among the patterns AU allowed.

12 Hodgson, pp. 46-7, 87-8, 99.

13 See p. 59.

14 Hodgson, pp. 89, 94.

CHAPTER 5

1 It might be objected that we cannot always state agents' obligations unconditionally without running afoul of the postulate that 'ought implies can', since logical and causal connections between agents' acts may bring it about that what Jones can do depends on what Smith does. The problem raised by logical connections I think we could deal with by allowing only sufficiently 'basic' descriptions of acts. The problem raised by causal connections is harder to deal with. Even this problem could be dealt with adequately, but at the cost of considerable complication. Since I do not propose to defend either COP or any other theory discussed in this chapter, it seems reasonable to ignore this problem entirely. The example discussed throughout this chapter is one in which there are no causal connections between the agents' acts.

2 Consider the following theory, which I shall not state with quite the precision I have used in stating COP.

(COP–M) If there is a unique best UPA, do what it prescribes. If there is not a unique best UPA, act in such a way as to maximize the number of agents (including yourself) who satisfy the most widely satisfied equal-best UPA.

If there is a unique best UPA, COP–M obviously reduces to COP. If there is not a unique best UPA, what COP–M requires an agent to do is to identify the various equal-best UPA's, to ascertain how many *other* agents are satisfying each of the equal-best UPA's, and then to satisfy some equal-best UPA which is satisfied by at least as many other agents as any other equal-best UPA. (There must be some equal-best UPA which is satisfied by at least as many other agents as any other equal-best UPA, provided the total number of agents is finite, which I now explicitly assume.) In this way, the agent in question will maximize the number of agents (including himself) who satisfy the most widely satisfied equal-best UPA, which is what COP–M requires.

It is not difficult to show that COP–M has PropCOP, which is to say that universal satisfaction of COP–M guarantees that best possible consequences are produced. Actually, I shall show the converse. I shall show that if best possible consequences are *not* produced, then some agent must fail to satisfy COP–M. Suppose that in some situation the group of agents concerned behave in such a way that best possible consequences are not produced. Now, if best possible consequences are not produced, then *no* equal-best UPA is universally satisfied. (If some equal-best UPA were universally satisfied, then best possible consequences would be produced.) There is, however, some equal-best UPA which is satisfied by as many agents as any other equal-best UPA. (Note that there may be no unique equal-best UPA which is more widely satisfied than any other; and note also that the the most widely satisfied equal-best UPA's may be satisfied by no agent at all. The argument which follows is unaffected by these possibilities.) If we consider any equal-best UPA which is as widely satisfied as any other (call it UPA*), and any agent who does not satisfy UPA* (call him Jones), it is clear that Jones does not satisfy COP-M. If Jones satisfied UPA*, instead of doing whatever he actually does, then the number of agents satisfying UPA* would be one greater than it actually is, and the number of agents satisfying the most widely satisfied equal-best UPA would be one greater than it actually is also, since UPA* represents the current maximum. Therefore, whatever Jones is doing, he is not acting in such a way as to maximize the number of agents satisfying the most widely satisfied equal-best UPA. In sum, so long as best possible results are not produced, there must be some agent, such as Jones, who does not satisfy COP-M. Conversely, if every agent satisfies COP-M, best possible results must be produced. COP-M has PropCOP.

Two other points about COP-M: (1) COP-M is not entirely in the spirit of COP. It is true that it employs only *unconditional* UPA's. On the other hand, it directs each agent to consider the other agents' behaviour in deciding which UPA to follow. (2) COP-M does not have PropAU. In our standard Whiff and Poof example, where there is a unique best pattern of behaviour, COP-M directs Whiff to push even if Poof does not. If Whiff pushes while Poof does not, he does not produce the best results possible in the circumstances.

3 'Utilitarianisms', *Ethics*, 82 (1971), 57.

4 For the reader who remembers note 2, observe that the device by which COP-M copes with multiple best patterns of behaviour cannot be used to save RU from its difficulty concerning multiple best UPA-C's. Consider the following theory, which bears roughly the same relation to RU that COP-M bears to COP:

(RU-M)   If there is a unique best UPA-C, do what it prescribes. If there is not a unique best UPA-C, act in such a way as to maximize the number of agents (including yourself) who satisfy the most widely satisfied equal-best UPA-C.

Note first of all that applying RU-M is not quite so straightforward as applying COP-M. In applying COP-M, the agent was required to count up the other agents satisfying each equal-best UPA, which it was possible to do without knowing how he himself behaved. But UPA-C's (unlike UPA's) may condition the behaviour required of others on the behaviour of the agent who is attempting to apply RU-M. Therefore the agent applying RU-M cannot decide how many other agents satisfy each UPA-C except on hypothetical assumptions about his own behaviour. Still, this is not a serious problem. Given any particular behaviour by the agent applying RU-M, the class of other agents who are then satisfying each UPA-C is well defined, so the instruction to each agent to act in such a way as to maximize the number of agents (including himself) who satisfy the most widely satisfied equal-best UPA-C is perfectly coherent. It is just a bit more complicated than at first appears.

Unfortunately, the method of proof by which we established in note 2 that universal satisfaction of COP–M would guarantee universal satisfaction of some equal-best UPA can *not* be used to show that universal satisfaction of RU–M would guarantee universal satisfaction of some equal-best UPA–C. In the course of the proof in note 2, we picked out some maximally-satisfied equal-best UPA, which we called UPA*. We considered an agent, Jones, who was not satisfying UPA*, and we observed that Jones could not be satisfying COP–M. The reason was that if Jones satisfied UPA* the number of agents satisfying the most widely satisfied equal-best UPA would be higher by one than it was given Jones's actual behaviour. This argument will not work with RU–M. Suppose we select some maximally satisfied equal-best UPA–C, which we call UPA–C*, and suppose we consider some agent Smith who is not satisfying UPA–C*. We cannot show that Smith is not satisfying RU–M, because we cannot be certain that if Smith satisfied UPA–C*, instead of doing whatever he actually does, the number of agents satisfying UPA–C* would increase by one. It is true that by altering his behaviour Smith could add himself to the list of agents who satisfy UPA–C*. But the alteration in his behaviour might knock some other agent *off* the list of satisfiers of UPA–C*, since UPA–C* is a *conditional* prescription, and whether any particular other agent satisfies it may depend on how Smith behaves. Strange as it sounds, an agent may perfectly well find himself in a position where he maximizes the number of agents who satisfy UPA–C* (or any other UPA–C) by *not* satisfying it himself. It is remarkable how the conditionality of the UPA–C's keeps getting in the way.

What I have just said does not of course constitute a proof that universal satisfaction of RU–M does not guarantee universal satisfaction of some equal-best UPA–C. It is merely an explanation of why the argument that may have occurred to the reader on behalf of RU–M does not work. In fact, even RU–M is universally satisfied in our standard Whiff and Poof example when both not-push. (I leave the demonstration to the reader.) It turns out that RU–M is no improvement at all over RU.

5 Richard Brandt, 'Toward a Credible Form of Utilitarianism', in *Morality and the Language of Conduct*, ed. Hector-Neri Castañeda and George Nakhnikian (Detroit: Wayne State Univ. Press, 1963), pp. 119–23. The linguistic peculiarity is that Brandt instructs each agent in effect to satisfy 'that' UPA–C, universal satisfaction of which would produce 'at least as much intrinsic good' as universal satisfaction of any other. There is an obvious ambivalence on the question of whether the best UPA–C is unique.

6 David Lyons, *Forms and Limits of Utilitarianism* (Oxford: Clarendon Press, 1965), pp. 121–35.

7 Other writers have made many of the points I make in this chapter against various formulations of rule-utilitarianism: e.g. Lyons, pp. 137–9; Sobel (Ch. 2, n. 8 above), pp. 153–5, 165; Holly S. Goldman, 'David Lyons on Utilitarian Generalization', *Philosophical Studies*, 26 (1974), n. 17; Sartorius (Ch. 2, n. 42 above), p. 17. I am not aware of any

source in which these points are collected and organized, and I do not believe anyone has previously shown just how intractable the difficulties are that are created by the admission of conditional rules.

8 The concept of exclusive act-orientation, introduced at pp. 10-11, is further discussed at pp. 109-15, where it is also argued that all consequentialist theories in the traditional mould are exclusively act-oriented.

CHAPTER 6

1 UG sometimes has a problem similar to the problem of COP in the face of multiple best patterns of behaviour. Consider the following example:

		Poof	
		Push	Not-push
	Push	10	0
Whiff			
	Not-push	0	10

In this situation, either pushing or not-pushing by Whiff is an act which has at least as good consequences as any other act if performed by Whiff and all other agents similarly situated (namely, Poof). UG does not help with the real co-ordination problem. This point is made by Sartorius (Ch. 2, n. 42, above), p. 17.

We cannot simply exclude from consideration in this chapter cases involving multiple best patterns of behaviour. Most of the cases utilitarian generalization was invented to deal with involve multiple best patterns of behaviour. However, the difficulty Sartorius points to does not arise in every case where there are multiple best patterns. It arises only if there is no unique best pattern *among the patterns in which everyone behaves the same*. We shall consider in this chapter only cases in which there is a unique best pattern among the patterns in which everyone behaves the same, cases in which Sartorius' problem does not arise.

2 For discussions of this question, see, e.g., Goldman (Ch. 5, n. 7 above); Gregory S. Kavka, 'Extensional Equivalence and Utilitarian Generalization', *Theoria*, 41 (1975), 125-47; Harry S. Silverstein, 'Goldman's 'Level-2' Act Descriptions and Utilitarian Generalization', *Philosophical Studies*, 30 (1976), 45-55.

3 As Holly Goldman has shown (Goldman, Ch. 5, n. 7 above), it is essential to the plausibility of UG that the class of other agents to whom each agent assimilates himself should all face the same alternatives.

Note that I do not claim that the notion of 'similarly situated' employed in traditional utilitarian generalization, which UG represents, is perfectly clear in all respects. For example, there is a question about whether two agents who have opportunities to cross the same patch of grass, thereby doing exactly the same damage, but who suffer somewhat different degrees of inconvenience from not crossing are similarly situated. I think the traditional utilitarian generalizer would say these two are similarly situated if the difference in inconvenience from not crossing is small, but that they may not be similarly situated if the difference is sufficiently large. This does not affect the claim that agents similarly situated face the same alternatives. If the difference in inconvenience is small enough so that UG regards the agents as similarly situated, then it also regards the two potential acts of not-crossing as essentially equivalent, and each agent does face the same alternatives. It seems clear that traditional utilitarian generalization presupposes that the class of agents whose acts are hypothetically varied are a class who all face either precisely the same alternatives, or sets of alternatives regarded as equivalent. In any event, the vagueness in the notion of 'similarly situated' commented on in this note will not be present in any example discussed in this chapter.

4 If randomized strategies are allowed, then UG requires each agent to choose the best pure or randomized strategy for both to adopt, which turns out to be a strategy assigning a probability of 4/5 to pushing and 1/5 to not-pushing. (The proof that this is the best strategy for both to adopt is simple, but it is postponed to Chapter 11, where the role of randomization is discussed in more detail.) If both agents adopt this strategy, the expected return to their joint behaviour is $3\frac{1}{5}$ units. This is less than the best possible return (4 units), so UG still fails to have PropCOP. It happens that if both parties adopt this strategy, each does produce the best (expected) consequences possible in the circumstances. This does not mean, however, that UG has PropAU. UG requires Whiff to opt for this particular randomized strategy regardless of what Poof does. If Poof, instead of adopting the strategy required by UG, simply pushes, then Whiff's choosing the randomized strategy required by UG does not produce the best possible results in the circumstances. It would be better for Whiff to simply not-push. Therefore, UG does not have PropAU.

5 Lyons considers the following formulation, which he calls 'GU': 'If, and only if, the consequences of everyone's doing a certain sort of thing would be worse than those of some alternative, then it would be wrong for anyone to do such a thing.' Lyons (Ch. 5, n. 6 above), p. 54.

6 The point that Lyons's approach to the agent's circumstances makes the identity of the class of agents similarly situated with Whiff depend on Whiff's behaviour has also been noted in effect by Holly Goldman (Ch. 5, n. 7 above). I say 'in effect' because Goldman does not speak in terms of who is 'similarly situated', but rather in terms of how many other agents are in a position to do the same fully described act as the agent upon whose decision we are focusing. Goldman regards the dependence in question as posing a difficulty for utilitarian generalization, but she neither considers the possibilities for reading a Lyons-like notion of 'similarly situated' into UG (as I do in the text that follows) nor concludes that Lyons misconstrues the traditional theory.

In response to Goldman, Harry Silverstein (n. 2 above) argues that the number of agents who can do any particular fully described act does *not* depend on how Whiff behaves. This claim, *as Silverstein intends it to be understood,* is true. What Silverstein is pointing out is that *in one sense,* the number of agents who can 'push while exactly one other agent is pushing' is two, regardless of how anyone actually behaves. And so on. But note that on Silverstein's view, the number of agents who can perform the various acts open to Whiff varies from act to act, even though it does not vary with how Whiff behaves. Thus even on Silverstein's view it turns out that the number of agents who can perform *the same act as Whiff* depends on how Whiff behaves. Silverstein does not regard this as posing a problem for utilitarian generalization. He suggests that each agent should do that act which has best consequences when performed by himself and as many other agents as can perform the act in question concurrently with himself. This theory is effectively the same as the theory I call UG″, discussed in the text below and shown to be equivalent, in an important range of cases, to AU. Silverstein does not discuss the relationship between his theory and AU. The equivalence of Silverstein's theory and UG″ is explained in n. 11 below, after UG″ has been introduced in the text.

7 Note that this choice of the notion of 'similarly situated' involving complete descriptions is necessary to the proof below that UG″ is extensionally equivalent to AU. It is *not* necessary to my basic criticisms of UG′ and UG″, which can both be shown to be defective in simple two person cases where there is no difference between threshold-related and complete descriptions .

8 Allowing randomized acts would undermine this particular criticism of UG′, for reasons not worth discussing. It would not affect the much more serious criticism of UG′ which follows in the text, as I show in the next note.

9 The argument of the text is unaffected by the possibility of randomized acts. Suppose Poof does not push. If Whiff does any act, pure or randomized, other than not-pushing, then the class of 'Whiff and all agents similarly situated' turns out to be Whiff alone. But the (expected) consequences of Whiff's doing any act (pure or randomized) other than not-pushing are inferior to the consequences of his not-pushing. Therefore, no act by Whiff other than not-pushing is right according to UG′. If Whiff does not push, then the class of 'Whiff and all agents similarly situated' turns out to be Whiff and Poof. The consequences of the members of this class not-pushing are inferior to the consequences of their pushing. Therefore, Whiff's not-pushing is not right according to UG′. We conclude that no act by Whiff, pure or randomized, is right according to UG′.

10 The argument in the text is rather simplistic. If we wanted it to be good in all contexts, we would need to spell it out in more detail and to qualify the conclusion in some significant ways. However, the argument and conclusion are perfectly adequate as they stand for the context we have been considering. As long as we are dealing with symmetric cases in which all the agents' acts interact, it is true that any pair of agents

are similarly situated (in our current Lyons-inspired sense) if and only if they behave the same. Note that the class of 'symmetric cases in which all the agents' acts interact' includes most of the standard schematically described cases which are traditionally associated with the debate about utilitarian generalization. In such cases the argument and the conclusion in the text are perfectly correct. It should also be noted that the argument in the text is completely unaffected by the possibility of randomized acts.

11 As I have already mentioned in n. 6 above, UG'' is effectively the same, in the range of cases we are dealing with (see n. 10 above), as Silverstein's theory that each agent should do the fully described act which has best consequences when done by himself and as many other agents as can perform the act in question concurrently with himself. The reason is that 'as many other agents as *can*' perform the same fully described act concurrently with the agent is precisely however many other agents *do* perform the same act. Suppose Alice's circumstances are such that an act of pushing by her would be fully described as 'pushing while exactly n other persons push'. Plainly, the number of other persons who can do this fully described act concurrently with Alice is n. If exactly $n + 1$ persons push, then each of them is doing the act of 'pushing while exactly n others push'. If more or fewer than $n + 1$ push, then no one is doing that act. Not only is n the number of others who *can* do this concurrently with Alice, it is also the number of others who *do* do the act concurrently with Alice, if Alice does it. In effect, Silverstein's theory, like UG'', directs Alice to consider the consequences of the performance of each act by herself and a certain class of others, and the class of others turns out to be just the class who actually perform the act in question, if Alice does. So Silverstein's theory, like UG'', really directs Alice just to consider the consequences of her own act. Both theories reduce to AU.

The argument just given assumes that Silverstein relies on complete descriptions (and not just threshold-related descriptions) of each agent's act. That seems to be what Silverstein has in mind.

12 By way of comparison, note that UG does involve the hypothetical variation of a class of acts; and UG' has the problem not of doing too little hypothetical varying, but of doing too much. UG' hypothetically varies the behaviour of a different class of agents for each possible act of the deciding agent, and the directions gleaned from these multiple varyings tend to conflict.

13 It would be unrewarding for me to explain just what I don't like about each of the myriad responses to Lyons. I will say that the most nearly satisfactory, to my mind, are Harry S. Silverstein, 'Simple and General Utilitarianism', *Philosophical Review*, 83 (1974), 339–63, and Paul Horwich, 'On Calculating the Utility of Acts', *Philosophical Studies*, 25 (1974), 21–31. The trouble with Silverstein is that he makes matters so complicated. I am not certain one would learn what was wrong with Lyons by reading Silverstein, if one did not already know. Horwich, in

contrast, is crisp and lucid. But Horwich's piece has a mystifying surprise ending. After explaining very clearly why Lyons's argument does not work, Horwich claims at the end of his piece to rehabilitate Lyons's conclusion. But if I understand him, the rehabilitation is accomplished by excluding from consideration all the cases involving causal interaction that the debate has been about. I find it hard to believe that Horwich is unaware of what he is doing, but he does not comment on the point-lessness of his final manoeuvre.

14 Note that the argument in the text casts no shadow on the claim in Chapter 3 (pp. 63–5) that the marginal differences as we move in a thought-experiment from one pattern of behaviour to another always add up to the total difference. While there is a sense in which our thought-experiments allow us to attribute the consequences of a class of acts to a series of individual fully described acts, the *class* of acts in question is not a class of fully described acts. It is not the class of fully described acts which we move through in the thought-experiment, since each of those acts takes place against a different background, and no two of them could possibly co-occur. Nor is it the class of fully described acts which make up the final pattern of behaviour, since only one of the series of fully described acts (the last one changed) occurs in that final pattern of behaviour.

CHAPTER 7

1 Strictly speaking, we must exclude from this claim COP–C and UG'. Even COP–C and UG' are in the general mould of exclusively act-oriented theories. But their logical flaws make them fail the test for exclusive act-orientation I shall eventually formulate. See n. 9 below.

2 The reader may wish to remind himself of what I mean by 'dispositions to behave' by consulting p. 4.

3 See p. 56.

4 See Ch. 10, n. 17.

5 See p. 90.

6 I am content to implicitly define the 'trying to satisfy . . .' version of rule-utilitarianism as a non-traditional theory. I think it is. Note that if the set of rules it would be best for everyone to try to satisfy requires only acts like 'pushing', then a version of rule-utilitarianism which required each agent to *satisfy* the set of rules it would best for everyone to try to satisfy would still be a traditional theory.

7 See pp. 177–85.

8 This point is discussed at length in R. Eugene Bales, 'Act-Utilitarianism: Account of Right-Making Characteristics or Decision-Making Procedure?', *American Philosophical Quarterly*, 8 (1971), 257–65.

I should perhaps observe that one might, consistently with what I take to be the spirit of traditional theories, regard randomized acts as eligible to be required. This concedes that traditional theories may, even in standard cases, impose requirements of a certain sort on the agent's decision processes. It remains true that traditional theories are in general indifferent to how an agent decides to perform a randomized act in the first place. If a randomized act is required by a traditional theory, then the agent satisfies the theory if and only if he does that randomized act, regardless of how he decides to do so. I shall ignore randomized acts for the remainder of the chapter. The eligibility of randomized acts would make no real difference to the proof (below) that an exclusively act-oriented theory cannot be adaptable, though it would complicate it slightly.

9 COP and UG" also satisfy the partial definition. Note that COP–C and UG' do not satisfy the partial definition. That is because COP–C turns out to be logically unsound (involving a non-referring description) and because UG' in some circumstances identifies the empty subset. Both COP–C and UG' set out to be traditional theories, but they fail for reasons any traditionalist would recognize as disqualifying them. This suggests that the claim in the next sentence of the text should be understood to mean that any logically sound traditional theory which always specifies at least one right act for each agent will satisfy the partial definition.

10 In the text further on, I shall refer to the possibility of formulating partial definitions of exclusive act-orientation which are analogous to the partial definition currently under dir cussion, but which are tailored to other cases besides our Whiff and Poof example. It should be noted that in cases in which causal connections between the agents' acts are not excluded by hypothesis, the appropriate partial definitions would have, in place of the phrase 'on any assumption about Poof's (Whiff's) behaviour,' the phrase 'on any assumption about [the other agents'] behaviour or *dispositions to behave*'.

11 Consider the following example:

		Poof	
		Push	Not-push
	Push	10	6
Whiff			
	Not-push	6	6

Strange as it sounds, AU is indeterminate in this example. AU is universally satisfied if both agents push. It is also universally satisfied if both agents not-push. It is clear, however, that an exclusively act-oriented theory which directs each agent to push, regardless of the other's behaviour, is 'adaptable' in the context of this case. Any agent who pushes produces best possible results, and if both agents push best results overall are achieved. The oddity of the case is, of course, that while each agent has a 'dominant' act-utilitarian choice, he is not always and unequivocally required by AU to make that choice. Of course, he is always permitted to. That is why we cannot focus on the inferior pattern of universal satisfaction of AU (in which neither makes his dominant choice) and claim that each agent does in that pattern just what any theory with PropAU would have to require of him in the circumstances.

Note that this demonstration that AU may be indeterminate even in a case where every agent has a dominant act-utilitarian strategy is not inconsistent with the proof in Chapter 3 (pp. 62–3) that a pattern in which every agent *chooses* a dominant act-utilitarian strategy cannot be an inferior pattern.

12 The claim that an exclusively act-oriented theory cannot have both PropCOP and PropAU is stronger than the claim that such a theory cannot be adaptable just because the conjunction of PropCOP and PropAU is weaker than adaptability. Of course, the conjunction of PropCOP and PropAU is equivalent to adaptability *in the context of two-agent cases* such as the standard Whiff and Poof example. But the paraphrase of the proof makes clear that the proof is applicable to appropriately selected cases involving any number of agents, as the text goes on to show.

13 I would remind the reader that, as I pointed out in n. 8 above, allowing traditional theories to require randomized acts would not affect the present discussion in any significant way.

14 As I have previously noted, this last requirement is stronger than necessary. I have not attempted to formulate the weakest adequate requirement of this sort.

15 I do not want to make any definite claim about Kant's ethical views, but the theory that an agent should 'act on a universalizable maxim' might well be construed as an objective non-exclusively-act-oriented theory. The theory is non-exclusively-act-oriented if acting on a maxim involves having the maxim in mind. The theory is objective if 'universalizability' really is a property of maxims and not of the agent's attitude to them.

16 A further observation about how the proof works which supplements the observation in the text will be found at the end of n. 18 below.

17 I have refuted two of these 'self-defeat' arguments in Chapters 3 and 4.

18 It may seem that the argument in the text depends on an unjustified implicit assumption, specifically the assumption that what T requires of each agent varies only with what the others do, and not with how they decide what to do. It may seem that only this assumption can justify my speaking of a pattern of behaviour such that if that pattern is realized T is satisfied, and my then going on to assume that the same pattern of behaviour would constitute universal satisfaction of T even if the agents all followed D(T) and satisfied T*. This objection can be answered, but it requires some discussion.

First, the objector is right about one thing. A theory can be exclusively act-oriented and still make what one agent should do depend on how *other* agents decide what to do. All that our partial definitions of exclusive act-orientation forbid is requirements on the agent's *own* decision processes. (The partial definition for the Whiff and Poof case said that an exclusively act-oriented theory must 'on any assumption about Poof's behaviour' identify some act for Whiff. This reference to Poof's behaviour can be taken to mean his decision-process-plus-ultimate-act, even though at other points in this essay I use 'behaviour' to mean 'ultimate act'.)

Of course, so long as we consider only exclusively act-oriented theories which do *not* vary what is required of one agent with the decision processes of the others, the argument in the text is perfectly adequate. We can focus on some pattern of behaviour in which T manifests its non-adaptability, and we can say that the same ultimate acts would satisfy T even if all the relevant agents had followed D(T), from which it follows that T* is not adaptable. (Observe that all exclusively act-oriented theories which have been extensively discussed in the literature—AU, RU, UG, and so on—are theories which do not vary what is required of one agent with the decision processes of the others, at least in standard cases. Therefore even the reader who is not persuaded by the remainder of this note that *no* exclusively act-oriented theory can be made adaptable by the addition of a perfect decision procedure should recognize that no 'established' exclusively act-oriented theory could be converted to an adaptable theory by this means.)

But suppose we consider a theory which *does* make what one agent should do depend on the others' decision processes. What then? What the objector must have in mind is something like the following. Let us simplify by returning to the context of our standard Whiff and Poof case, and let us consider a theory T which tells Whiff under most circumstances just to satisfy AU, but which says that if Poof follows any perfect decision procedure for T, then Whiff should push. Analogous directions are given to Poof. Now, T is exclusively act-oriented and is therefore not adaptable. But what about T*? T* requires each agent to follow a perfect decision procedure for T. If Poof follows a perfect decision procedure for T, then Whiff is required by T to push. Similarly if Whiff follows a perfect decision procedure for T, Poof is required by T to push. If both Whiff and Poof follow T*, each follows a perfect decision procedure for T, each is required by T to push, each must in fact push, and best possible consequences are achieved.

If this argument made any sense in the context of the Whiff and Poof example, it could be generalized to deal with all possible cases. But it does not make sense in the Whiff and Poof example. The first step of the argument is to suppose that T makes what Whiff should do depend on whether Poof follows a perfect decision procedure for T. But this is circular. We cannot define T by reference to a perfect decision procedure for T, where the procedure is not otherwise defined. On the other hand, we cannot make the argument for the adaptability of T* unless T requires Whiff (Poof) to respond to Poof's (Whiff's) use of a perfect decision procedure for T.

It might seem that there is still hope. Could not T require Whiff (Poof) to push in response to Poof's (Whiff's) using some decision procedure which is not defined in terms of T, but which turns out to be a perfect decision procedure for T when T is defined in the appropriate way by reference to it? This possibility I do not deny. The attempt to give substance to this possibility might well lead us to co-operative utilitarianism. I will say, however, that once we move to defining T in terms of a decision procedure which is not itself defined in terms of T, we can hardly claim to be making an exclusively act-oriented T adaptable by the addition of a decision procedure *for* T. That is all I claimed we could not do.

This discussion of exclusively act-oriented theories which make what one agent should do depend on the decision processes of others may raise doubts in the reader's mind about the adequacy of the original proof that no exclusively act-oriented theory can be adaptable. The original proof did not explicitly advert to the possibility that the exclusively act-oriented theory under consideration might make varying demands upon Whiff depending on how Poof decided what to do. Did the proof assume implicitly that this was not the case, and does it fall apart if this possibility is explicitly considered? No. (Note that even if the general proof did founder on this possibility, the proof would still be good for all 'established' exclusively act-oriented theories—AU, RU, UG, and so on—since these do not make varying demands on Whiff depending on how Poof decides what to do. But in fact the general proof is unaffected, as I shall now show.) Suppose that, in our Whiff and Poof example, Poof decides whether to push or not by flipping a coin: 'Heads I push, tails I don't.' Now, if Poof flips the coin and it comes down tails and Poof therefore not-pushes, any exclusively act-oriented theory must give Whiff some direction. Furthermore, any exclusively act-oriented theory which purports to be adaptable must direct Whiff to not-push. To be sure, the same theory might direct Whiff differently if Poof adopted a different decision procedure. But on the assumptions just made about Poof's decision procedure, the theory must tell Whiff to not-push. What is more, the theory must be *satisfied* by Whiff's not-pushing in these circumstances regardless of how *Whiff* decides not to push. That is what the partial definition of exclusive act-orientation guarantees, and that is the crucial point. Whiff satisfies the theory even if, for example, he not-pushes because *he* flips a coin just as Poof does. But then by symmetry, if both flip coins and see tails and not-push, both satisfy the theory under consideration. Therefore the theory is not adaptable. The point is this: The original proof may look suspicious, in the context of this note, because it makes a claim about what Whiff must do in response to Poof's not-pushing without saying anything about how Poof decides not to push. But we have only to assume explicitly that Poof decides not to push by some method which could not possibly be exploited as a step to adaptability even by a T which varied Whiff's obligation with Poof's method of decision, and the proof goes through as before.

CHAPTER 8

1 The formulation of COP–M in Ch. 5, n. 2, did not begin this way, but that is because I allowed myself an informal statement of that theory.

2 The reader may wonder whether we have such control over our beliefs that particular beliefs can be *required* by a moral theory without risking running afoul of the postulate that 'ought implies can'. I shall address this point in Chapter 10. Strictly speaking, CU need not require any beliefs, but for reasons which will become clear it is most convenient to speak of it as if it did. I shall therefore speak of it that way, consistently. What CU actually must require, if we are unwilling to allow it to require beliefs, is still enough to make it non-exclusively-act-oriented.

3 An agreement can be useful as evidence of a common understanding of the basic situation, as a feature of the situation which makes certain patterns of behaviour salient, and so on.

4 *Convention: A Philosophical Study* (Cambridge, Mass.: Harvard Univ. Press, 1969).

5 *The Strategy of Conflict* (1960; rpt. New York: Oxford Univ. Press, 1963). Further evidence of my debt to Schelling will be found in the notes to Chapter 11. Lewis acknowledges his reliance on Schelling in *Convention*, p. 3.

6 e.g. Harsanyi (Ch. 4, n. 1 above); Mackie (Ch. 2, n. 9 above); Smart (Ch. 2, n. 14 above); Narveson (Ch. 2, n. 11 above); Gauthier (Ch. 2, n. 31 above); Postow (Ch. 2, n. 12 above).

7 Harsanyi has come closest to discussing these issues, with his distinction between 'rigid' and 'flexible' agents and his suggestion that a rule-utilitarian should adopt the best behaviour for himself and the other flexible agents (pp. 34–5). But Harsanyi's suggestion will not do.

At the end of his piece (p. 43), Harsanyi suggests that a rigid agent is one whose behaviour can be predicted with reasonable certainty. But earlier (pp. 35–8) he has suggested as one of the virtues of rule-utilitarianism, which directs the choices of the flexible agents, that it makes the behaviour of agents who follow it predictable. In sum, if the flexible agents follow the theory designed for flexible agents, they become rigid agents. Something is awry. For further confirmation, consider a concrete case involving a different problem. Suppose that in our standard Whiff and Poof example each knows the other is going to not-push. So long as each knows what the other is going to do, each is directed by Harsanyi's approach to treat the other as a rigid agent. Each regards himself as the only flexible agent, and each, by not-pushing, does his part in the best pattern of behaviour for the class of flexible agents as he sees it. Each therefore does exactly what Harsanyi's approach would have him do. But the pair of agents fail to co-ordinate. The problem, simply put, is that the co-operators and the non-co-operators cannot be distinguished on the basis of their behaviour alone.

I hope it will not seem that I am reading Harsanyi unsympathetically. His suggestions about rigid and flexible agents are sketchy in the extreme.

If he had pursued them, he might well have produced a theory like CU. My point is not so much that he is wrong as that he only scratches the surface of a very complicated problem.

8 Recall our somewhat specialized usage of 'disposed to behave', introduced at pp. p. 4.

9 This sketch of what it means for an individual to co-operate with whoever else is co-operating ignores a problem I shall treat in later chapters, the problem of multiple best patterns of behaviour for the group of co-operators.

10 'What If Everyone Did That?', *Durham University Journal*, 22 (1960), 10.

11 *Mind*, 45 (1936), 151.

12 See pp. 169-72, and Ch. 11 generally.

13 Harrod (n. 11 above), p. 152.

14 Compare n. 7 above.

CHAPTER 9

1 See p. 141.

2 P is not even a decision procedure for CU. It is a model of CU, in a sense to be clarified below (pp. 166-7), but that is not the same thing.

3 Recall our idiosyncratic usage of 'dispositions to behave', introduced at p. 4.

4 Recall earlier discussions of the time-slice view at pp. 40-1 and p. 69.

5 Alterations would also be required in step 1 to take care of new possible ways of making mistakes at the last minute, but the basic idea of step 1 and its interaction with the last few steps of the procedure would remain unchanged. This reference to the interaction of step 1 with the last few steps may be a bit mystifying until the Appendix has been read. The Appendix reveals that step 1 has a specialized and crucial role to play in guaranteeing that everything comes together properly at the point where the satisfiers of P finally stop and act.

6 We could specify some mechanism for choosing at random among the set of best patterns and show that the probability of non-success by the nth step approaches zero as n goes to infinity. We could even, with a little extra fiddling, guarantee that the probability in question approached zero quite rapidly. I do assume that the number of best patterns is finite. If this is not the case, then the agents who are trying to be moral are in a quandary from which no procedure or theory of any sort is likely to extricate them, except in special cases.

CHAPTER 10

1 There is a reason why I say that the right act according to CU is the act which the agent who successfully follows CU is directed to do,

262 NOTES TO PAGES 167-176

instead of saying it is the act which the agent would be directed to do if he successfully followed CU. This latter characterization of the right act would not be unequivocally wrong, but it would be misleading. The statement that the right act is the one that CU *would* direct *if* correctly applied (as opposed to the act that it *does* direct *when* correctly applied) would tend to carry with it the suggestion that all various agents really need to do to get the benefit of following CU is for each to do the act which CU would direct if he correctly applied it. This last suggestion is definitely mistaken, for reasons which are explained in the text at pp. 177-8.

2 See p. 160.

3 See pp. 161-2.

4 I am here using 'similarly situated' in the traditional sense, not the sense introduced by Lyons. See Ch. 6, above.

5 I shall omit a proof of this claim, since there are enough complicated proofs in this essay. The sceptical reader should be able to construct a proof for himself, following the proof of the adaptability of P as a model, with appropriate alterations. The satisfiers of the revised CU would not identify each other as the co-operators, as they do under the original CU, but each satisfier would know how many satisfiers there were from each subclass of the universe of agents, and there would be no other significant difference between the revised CU and CU as we have previously described it.

6 As the text indicates, the simplified procedure captures the core idea of CU, which is that one should first decide which other agents are available to be co-operated with and should then co-operate with them. Even the simplified procedure therefore shares the intuitive appeal of CU, in so far as that appeal is based on CU's distinctive approach to the behaviour of other agents. (See the end of Ch. 8 and the elaboration in Ch. 12.)

There is another point about the practical application of CU which is worth mentioning somewhere, but which does not appertain specifically to any portion of the text of this chapter. In theory, co-operative utilitarians have no need for promises or agreements. In practice, they will find conventions like promising useful. These conventions will work essentially as they do for act-utilitarians who happen to have the conventions in question. They will be practical aids to expeditious information exchange and to the creation of saliency in situations where there are multiple best patterns of behaviour. See Ch. 2, n. 38.

7 I remind the reader that in cases involving many agents, CU can be construed to require only beliefs about the numbers of agents in various subclasses who are willing to co-operate, and so on. Perhaps I should also remind the reader that the satisfier of CU does not have to understand why CU works. He does not have to be able to follow the proof concerning P in the Appendix or the arguments of this chapter.

8 The reader who gives the matter thought may turn up an assortment of puzzles involving causal connections between the agents'

decision processes. In particular, he may come across the question: 'What if one agent's decision-making or behaviour causally influences whether some other agent is a co-operator?' To discuss these puzzles and this question adequately would take a good deal of space. I propose to set them aside, though I think a discussion of them is probably the highest priority item in the theoretical development of CU which is not covered in this essay. I will make two observations:

(1) Even in situations where there are causal connections, I think there are no good objections to the claim that CU is adaptable, that is, to the claim that any agents who actually manage to satisfy CU produce the best consequences possible. The only good objections to CU are of the ought/can variety and are based on analogues of the Whiff and Poof case of perverse responsiveness described in the text.

(2) I said at the end of Chapter 3 that the time had not yet come when we could not improve our understanding of consequentialism without improving consquentialists' metaphysics. I think that the appearance of CU in the ranks of consequentialist theories brings us considerably closer to that time. One of the reasons it is difficult to discuss cases involving causal connections in a reasonable compass is because they force us to confront deep metaphysical issues.

9 See pp. 7-9.

10 In connection with my earlier observation that CU is not a decision procedure *for* some independent criterion of right action (see p. 167, and n. 1, this chapter), note that the present text makes clear that we should not even regard CU as a decision procedure for the exclusively act-oriented analogue of CU. It is CU that has the virtues we want, not any exclusively act-oriented facsimile.

11 This feature of adaptability when applied to co-ordination problems at higher-level decisions is a genuine point in CU's favour, although perhaps not a very important one. It might seem that it does not represent any advantage CU has over other theories, since it is merely a palliative for a problem that CU, by requiring a decision procedure, creates for itself. But we shall see (pp. 183-4) that exclusively act-oriented theories may encounter practical problems like the current problem for CU, even if they avoid the present difficulties in theory.

12 In view of the recent discussion of higher-level decisions in connection with CU, it seems appropriate to add a comment about what I mean when I say that exclusively act-oriented theories do not require any decision procedure. I do *not* mean that exclusively act-oriented theories can not be applied to higher-level decisions. I do mean the following things: (1) If we start off with a problem like our standard Whiff and Poof problem, then if we think about the problem in terms of traditional theories, the issue of a required decision procedure, and of what to do at higher-level decisions, ordinarily does not arise. (2) *Whatever* choice problem we apply an exclusively act-oriented theory to, it does not direct a particular decision procedure for making the precise choice in question. Thus, an agent might apply AU to the second-

level decision about the buttons, where the list of possible choices is '(i) make the first-level decision by applying CU; (ii) make the first-level decision by applying AU . . .' But if he does, it remains the case that he will satisfy AU, as applied to that problem, if and only if he chooses from the list just given the particular decision procedure AU requires him to apply at the first level, regardless of how he chooses that decision procedure. AU, applied to the second-level decision, does not require any particular decision procedure at the second level. CU does.

13 See pp. 44–6.

14 See pp. 47–52.

15 I ignore consequences of following CU other than the consequences of not-pushing, since I have argued that they are usually negligible. My point is not that AU$'$ turns out not to be adaptable because it forbids the application of CU, as it would if we counted the slight cost of applying CU. My point, as the continuation of the text reveals, is that AU$'$ turns out not to be adaptable because it fails to *require* the application of CU even if the slight cost of applying CU is ignored.

16 I now ignore any possible difference between the cost of applying AU and the cost of applying CU. Compare n. 15, above.

17 There is one final matter to dispose of, for which there has been no specially appropriate occasion in the text. In Chapter 7, I said that I would describe a theory which had both PropCOP and PropAU, but which was not adaptable, after we had discussed CU. We can construct a theory which has PropCOP and PropAU, but which is not adaptable, by requiring each agent to embark on CU and to apply it correctly for so long as he does *not* exclude anyone else from the class of putative co-operators, but adding that as soon as the agent (correctly) excludes someone from the class of putative co-operators he may abandon CU and is thereafter required only to satisfy AU. This theory obviously has PropAU, since any agent who satisfies it will satisfy CU if there are no non-satisfiers of CU and will satisfy AU if there are any non-satisfiers of CU. The theory also has PropCOP, since if everyone satisfies it, everyone will satisfy CU. The theory is not adaptable, however. If there are three agents, then as soon as one reveals himself as a non-satisfier of CU the other two are released from any further requirement of following CU and are required only to satisfy AU, which because of the indeterminacy of AU they might both do without producing best possible consequences as a pair given the behaviour of the third agent. There is nothing to recommend the theory I have just described, which is merely an artificially hobbled CU. But it does show that the conjunction of PropCOP and PropAU does not entail adaptability.

CHAPTER 11

1 In case the reader is worried by the fact that my practical suggestions sometimes lead agents to abandon the attempt to produce the best consequences theoretically possible, I note that the same is true of

a sensible practical approach to the application of any consequentialist theory. For example, consider AU, in the context of a new Whiff and Poof hypothetical.

		Poof	
		Push	Not-push
	Push	10	0
Whiff	Not-push	0	10
	Override	9	9

Suppose that from Whiff's point of view the subjective probabilities are that Poof is equally likely to push or to not-push. It is clear that subjective AU requires Whiff to override (producing a subjective expected value, and indeed a certain value, of 9 units) instead of either pushing or not-pushing (each with a subjective expected value of 5 units), even though overriding cannot possibly be the best act in the circumstances, given Poof's actual behaviour. Whatever Poof does, there is some act of Whiff's which is preferable to overriding. Still, a reasonable approach to the practical problem requires Whiff to abandon all hope of producing the best consequences possible.

2 *The Strategy of Conflict* (1960; rpt. New York: Oxford Univ. Press, 1963), 53-118, 162-72, 267-303.

3 For similar observations, see Gauthier (Ch. 2, n. 31 above), pp. 107-13.

4 For a variety of interesting examples, see Schelling (n. 2 above).

5 See Schelling, p. 296.

6 The claim in the text is proved as follows: The problem is to find the strategy, possibly randomized, which, when adopted by both parties, produces best results. The family of possible strategies in this simple case is representable in terms of a single parameter, the probability assigned to the 3-4 strategy, which we will call 'p'. The probability assigned to the 4-0 strategy must be 1-p. The expected value of the results of the adoption by both parties of the mixed strategy assigning a probability of p to the 3-4 strategy is

$$p^2(3) + 2(p)(1-p)(4) + (1-p)^2(0),$$

or, $-5p^2 + 8p$. The derivative of this expression with respect to p is of course $-10p + 8$. Setting this equal to zero, we discover that there is an extremum of the expected value of the outcome when p is equal to $\frac{4}{5}$, and we can verify that this extremum is indeed a maximum and that the expected outcome at this value of p is $3\frac{1}{5}$ units.

7 It is perhaps worth noting that in the example discussed in the text the move to mixed strategies reinstates the possibility that the parties will achieve the best results theoretically possible (that is, the outcome valued at 4 units). But it should also be noted that the mixed strategy which, when chosen by both parties, maximizes the expected return is *not* the mixed strategy which, when chosen by both parties, maximizes the likelihood that the 4-unit outcome will be achieved. So there is a

sense in which the parties are still eschewing the attempt to produce the best results theoretically possible. (Compare n. 1 above, and accompanying text.)

8 J. J. C. Smart and Bernard Williams, *Utilitarianism: For and Against* (London: Cambridge Univ. Press, 1973), pp. 57–62. Smart first advanced this suggestion, in a less developed fashion, in 'Extreme and Restricted Utilitarianism', in *Contemporary Utilitarianism,* ed. Michael D. Bayles (Garden City, N.Y.: Doubleday Anchor Books, 1968), 112–13. (The article in the Bayles anthology is a reprint of an earlier article, but the point we are interested in appears for the first time in the reprinted version.) The same suggestion, in the context of a specific case, and accompanied by even less discussion of its status as an act-utilitarian suggestion, appears in Narveson (Ch. 2, n. 11 above), p. 189.

9 Note that although we here regard AU as requiring each agent to produce best possible expected results given the probabilities concerning the other's behaviour, this is not inconsistent with the strictures against requiring each agent to respond to objective probabilities concerning the other's behaviour in Ch. 2, n. 17. The difference is that here the probabilities which are being responded to are the result of the other agent's conscious choice of a randomized strategy, and the deciding agent is regarded as having a comparable freedom to choose mixed strategies if those produce the best expected results.

10 First, we prove the claims about this particular example. If one party randomizes in the specified proportions ($\frac{4}{5}$ to $\frac{1}{5}$), then the expected value of the other's assigning a probability of q to the 3–4 strategy and a probability of 1–q to the 4–0 strategy is represented by the expression

$$q(4/5)(3) + q(1/5)(4) + (1-q)(4/5)(4) + (1-q)(1/5)(0).$$

This expression reduces to $\frac{16}{5}$. Observe that q drops out. The fact that q drops out means that so long as one party randomizes in the specified proportions, then the other satisfies AU whatever he does (which entails, of course, that he satisfies AU if he also randomizes in the specified proportions). This establishes the first two claims in the text. As to the third claim, that one party can satisfy AU by randomizing in the specified proportions *only if* the other randomizes in those proportions, observe that AU allows randomization (in a non-trivial sense, assigning positive probabilities to both pure strategies) only if the expected payoffs to the pure strategies are the same. If the expected payoffs to the pure strategies are not the same, then AU will require the agent to choose unequivocally (that is, assigning a probability of zero to the other pure strategy) the pure strategy with the greater expected payoff. The question, then, is what behaviour by one party makes the expected payoffs to the pure strategies the same from the other party's point of view. If the first party randomizes between the 3–4 strategy and the 4–0 strategy in proportions p to 1–p, then for the other party the payoff to the 3–4 strategy is p(3) + (1–p) (4), or 4–p, while the payoff to the 4–0 strategy is p(4) + (1–p) (0), or 4p. Setting 4–p = 4p, we discover that the payoffs to the two pure strategies are the same for the second party only if p is $\frac{4}{5}$. Thus it is only if the first party randomizes in the specified proportions that the second party can satisfy AU by a mixed strategy.

We have now proved the particular claims made in the text about the example there discussed. As I have observed, these claims are generalizable, and it is to the generalization that we now turn. I think I should warn the reader that the remainder of this note sketches arguments which presuppose more mathematical background than most philosophers, or even most philosophers specifically interested in utilitarianism, possess. I do not think the arguments could be recast so as to be accessible to all readers of this essay, but the intrinsic interest of the conclusions seems great enough to justify this brief excursion. The reader who does not puzzle out the remainder of this note can take the general lesson to be the following: the particular claims in the text, and the criticisms of Smart's suggestion as not really act-utilitarian which depend on those claims, do *not* just happen to be true in the example discussed in the text. They are fundamental claims and criticisms, not merely accidental ones.

The first general claim for discussion is the claim that in any situation involving arbitrarily many agents choosing among arbitrarily many pure strategies, but all symmetrically situated, if every agent chooses the randomized strategy which is best for all to select concurrently, then every agent will in fact be satisfying AU also. Note that when there are arbitrarily many agents and arbitrarily many pure strategies, the statement that the agents are symmetrically situated means that each agent faces the same selection of pure strategies and that the payoff to any pattern of behaviour involving pure strategies depends only on how many agents choose each pure strategy, and not on who chooses which. It follows from this that the expected payoff to a pattern of behaviour involving mixed strategies depends only on how many agents select each possible mixed strategy and not on who chooses which.

To prove rigorously that everyone's selecting the best randomized strategy for all to select concurrently entails universal satisfaction of AU would be pointlessly tedious. I shall sketch a proof which could be spelled out without difficulty. Let us call the strategy which it would be best for all agents to adopt concurrently P. P is a vector of probabilities, of dimension equal to the number of pure strategies available to each agent. (I speak as if P is unique. It does not matter if P is not unique, except that if there is more than one equally good 'best' strategy for all agents to adopt together, then I must be taken to focus, not merely on situations where every agent chooses some one of the 'best' strategies, but on situations where every agent chooses the *same* one. Hereafter I shall continue to speak as if P were unique.) What we wish to prove is that if all agents choose P, then each agent satisfies AU. We shall assume the contrary, and develop a contradiction.

Suppose that when all agents choose P, there is some agent who is not satisfying AU. Call her Persephone. Now if Persephone is not satisfying AU, there must be some strategy, call it P^*, which would produce a better expected outcome than P if selected by Persephone while everyone else chooses P. Now, given the properties of probability vectors, if P and P^* are both mixed strategies open to Persephone, so is any weighted average $wP + (1-w)P^*$ (where $0 \leqslant w \leqslant 1$). Furthermore, since the expected value of the outcome from any choice by Persephone is just the scalar product of the probability vector she chooses and a vector of constants representing the expected results associated with each of Persephone's pure strategies (given the choices of everyone else), the expected value of the outcome from the strategy $wP + (1-w)P^*$ is just the weighted average of the expected values of the choices P and P^*, with weights $(w, 1-w)$. Since the expected results of P^* are better than the expected results of P, the expected results of any average of P^* and P are better than the expected results of P, so long as $w < 1$. This means we can produce a vector arbitrarily close to P (by selecting w sufficiently close to 1) which has better expected results than P if selected by Persephone. Any incremental change from P in the direction of P^* improves the expected results.

What is true for Persephone is true for every agent. Since the agents are symmetrically situated, and since the situation we are considering incremental changes to is one in which they all behave the same, we can conclude that an incremental change from P in the direction of P^* in the behaviour of *any* individual agent would improve the expected results.

But then there is some incremental change such that if we make it in the behaviour of all agents simultaneously, we can improve the overall expected results without violating the constraint of identical behaviour. (Note that I am now relying on the possibility of 'adding up' the effects of the incremental changes made in the behaviour of all the agents at the same time. This may seem inconsistent with what I said in Chapter 3 about the first fallacy in the initial version of the 'Prisoners' Dilemma' argument (pp. 57–8) or with my criticism of Lyons's talk about the consequences of classes of fully described acts (p. 102). In fact, the present case is different, since we are dealing with *incremental* changes within a strategy set which is made continuous by the admission of mixed strategies. The expected outcome in such a case is a continuous and differentiable function of all the probabilities involved and can therefore be approximated locally by a function with just the additivity property I have assumed.) However, if we can improve the expected results without violating the constraint of identical behaviour, then P is not in fact a 'best' choice for all agents together. This is a contradiction. We conclude that when all agents choose P, every agent satisfies AU. QED.

Observe that this proof works equally well for any subclass of the universe of agents who are symmetrically situated, even when it is not the case that all agents are symmetrically situated. For any symmetric subclass of the universe of agents, if all the members of that subclass choose the strategy which is best for all to choose concurrently (given the behaviour of non-members of the subclass), then each member of the subclass satisfies AU.

The second claim in the text, to the effect that if one agent chooses the strategy which is best for both together then it does not matter what the other does, generalizes with a minor qualification, as follows: If there are arbitrarily many symmetrically situated agents, and if all but one choose the randomized strategy which is best for all, then it does not matter what the remaining agent does *provided* she assigns positive probabilities only to pure strategies assigned positive probabilities in the strategy which is best for all. Consider Persephone. As we observed earlier, the expected outcome, from Persephone's point of view, is just the scalar product of her chosen probability vector with a vector of constants representing the outcomes associated with each of her pure strategies (given everyone else's behaviour). In other words, the expected outcome from her point of view is just a weighted average of the outcomes associated with her pure strategies, weighted by the relevant probabilities. But if a vector of weights maximizes a weighted average of constants (as we have shown P does for Persephone, so long as everyone else chooses P), then all of the constants receiving positive weights must be equal. But if all of the constants receiving positive weights are equal, then any other vector of weights will produce the same average, provided the new vector assigns positive weights only to those constants assigned positive weights by the original vector. QED.

As to the third claim in the text, to the effect that one agent satisfies AU by adopting the randomized strategy which is best for all *only if* the other agent does so as well, this claim does not generalize immediately, like the first claim, nor does it generalize even as neatly as the second claim. I shall therefore not attempt to state precisely the conditions under which an individual agent can expect to satisfy AU by adopting the randomized strategy which is best for all agents. The basic point, however, is as true in the multi-agent case as in the two-agent case of the text. The basic point is that the best strategy for all to adopt concurrently is likely to be mixed and that mixed strategies are 'rarely' acceptable under AU, since AU forbids randomization except where two or more pure strategies produce the same expected outcome.

11 For similar observations, see Harsanyi (Ch. 4, n. 1 above), pp. 40–1.

12 *Utilitarianism: For and Against*, pp. 60–1.

13 In explaining why Smart's conventions are less happily viewed as act-utilitarian conventions than the conventions discussed in Chapter 2, the text may oversimplify a bit. To put the point more accurately for general purposes: In the optimal pattern of behaviour with regard to agreement-keeping (for example), AU will require most agents to do precisely what they do in that optimal pattern. In contrast, if one of Smart's conventions is generally adopted, AU will leave every agent an almost entirely free hand. The 'almost' reflects the fact that the agent can choose any strategy, provided that the strategy he chooses assigns

positive probabilities only to strategies assigned positive probabilities by the 'conventional' strategy. See n. 10, above.

14 See p. 59.

15 See pp. 58–9.

16 See p. 94 and ch. 6, n. 3.

17 The discussion in the text suggests a minor paradox. Given the assumption that self-interest directs each agent to cross the grass, better results may be produced if there are 100 selfish agents than if there are none. If all 1,000 agents are co-operators, then they face a practical problem which the methods we have suggested will be more or less adequate to deal with depending on the details of the situation. However, if there are 100 agents whose selfishness will lead them to cross the grass in any case, then the other nine hundred have only to co-operate among themselves by *all* staying off the grass, which is a simple matter. We see that the presence of some egoists may simplify the co-ordination problem faced by the altruists. Of course, the fact that co-operation is sometimes easier in the presence of non-co-operators provides no significant argument against co-operativeness. *In general*, the consequences of all agents' behaviour will improve as the number of agents willing to co-operate is increased.

18 e.g. Jonathan Harrison, 'Utilitarianism, Universalisation, and Our Duty to Be Just', *Proceedings of the Aristotelian Society*, 53 (1952–3), 126–30 (others' behaviour is relevant if it is *known* how others behave); Marcus G. Singer, *Generalization in Ethics* (New York: Alfred A. Knopf, 1961), pp. 152–61 (others' behaviour is relevant in a 'state of nature').

19 See Lyons's discussion of Singer and Harrison in *Forms and Limits of Utilitarianism*, pp. 102–3, 108–11.

CHAPTER 12

1 The point that reliance on rules may camouflage evasion of the responsibility to do an act which is necessary but repugnant is made by Kai Nielsen, 'Against Moral Conservatism', *Ethics*, 82 (1971–72), 219–31.

2 What I say in the text is not inconsistent with the possibility that some useful rules of thumb would direct the agent to consider whether a proposed act appears to affect primarily his own interests, about which he is likely to be well informed, or others' interests, about which he is less likely to be well informed and which he may tend to slight unless he takes care not to.

Neither is the text inconsistent with the suggestion that a utilitarian might support laws or public rules of organizations which seem to operate like the rules described in the text. See Rolf Sartorius, *Individual Conduct and Social Norms* (Encino, Calif.: Dickenson, 1975), 51–9; Joel Feinberg, 'The Forms and Limits of Utilitarianism', *Philosophical Review*, 76 (1967), 377.

INDEX

Acceptance utility 1-2, 229
Act-utilitarianism
  and agreements 32-43, 236, 239,
    269
  and common sense 22-3, 185
  and 'contributory consequences'
    approach 13-17, 231-2, 238-9,
    242-3
  and conventions 198, 237, 269-70
  and 'co-opting' CU 187-9
  and deception 77-9, 81
  and decision procedures 113, 263-4
  and decision processes of other
    agents 258, 259
  and expectations 99-7, 66-82
  and general information 45-7, 240
  and grass-crossing 56-65, 204-5
  and higher-level decisions 263-4
  and imperceptible differences 60-1
  and 'indeterminacy' 20, 161, 233-5,
    247, 256-7
  and 'marginal consequences' ap-
    proach 13-17, 231-2, 239, 242
  and morality as a community enter-
    prise 207-8
  and motivation 44-5, 240
  and objective obligation 12, 240
  and 'obviousness' argument 21-3,
    48, 232
  and others' behaviour 207-8, 234-5
  and 'perfect act-utilitarians' 26-31,
    49-52
  and power of example 39, 43-52
  and practices (in general) 39
  and the prisoner's dilemma 56-
    63, 257
  and probabilities 12-13, 25-6, 61,
    230, 231-2, 233-5, 236, 266
  and promising 10, 16, 82, 239
  and PropAU 17-18
  and PropCOP 18-19
  and publicity 67-8, 69, 78-9
  and punishment 9, 66-82

and randomization 24-5, 197-8,
  235, 266-9
and rules of thumb 171
and Silverstein's theory 254
and the 'snowball argument' 43-52
and subjective obligation 25-6, 57,
  189, 231-2, 235, 240, 265
and supplementation with further
  principles 42, 236
and symmetry 23-5, 233, 267-9
and 'time-slices' 40-1, 72
and truth-telling 10, 16, 35-7, 82
and utilitarian generalization 95-7
and UG" 254
as not self defeating 9, 54-65, 66-
  82, 120-1
assumptions acceptable in defence
  of 41-2, 46-7, 52, 237
common confusion about ix, 52-3
compared to co-operative utilitarianism xii, 23, 175, 183-4, 185-6,
  189, 204-5, 207-8
'consistency claim' concerning 54
exclusive act-orientation of 110-11,
  115
individualism of 23, 72, 186, 208,
  234
interpretation of 12-17
intuition underlying 3-4
possibility of universal satisfaction
  of 55-6
universal satisfaction of, as necessary
  but not sufficient condition for
  best possible consequences 20-1
universal satisfaction of, consistency
  with best possible consequences
  9, 20, 54-82
universal satisfaction of, meaning of
  29-31, 46-7
universal satisfaction of, not ensur-
  ing best possible consequences
  12-53
AU' 188